Society, Work and Welfare in Euro|

Also by Christine Cousins and from the same publishers

CONTROLLING SOCIAL WELFARE: A Sociology of
State Welfare, Work and Organisation

Society, Work and Welfare in Europe

Christine Cousins

First published in Great Britain 1999 by
MACMILLAN PRESS LTD
Houndmills, Basingstoke, Hampshire RG21 6XS and London
Companies and representatives throughout the world

A catalogue record for this book is available from the British Library.

ISBN 0–333–72994–3 hardcover
ISBN 0–333–72995–1 paperback

 First published in the United States of America 1999 by
ST. MARTIN'S PRESS, INC.,
Scholarly and Reference Division,
175 Fifth Avenue, New York, N.Y. 10010

ISBN 0–312–21889–3

Library of Congress Cataloging-in-Publication Data
Cousins, Christine, 1943–
Society, work and welfare in Europe / Christine Cousins.
p. cm.
Includes bibliographical references and index.
ISBN 0–312–21889–3 (cloth)
1. Welfare recipients—Employment—Europe. 2. Public welfare–
–Europe. 3. Labor market—Europe. 4. Europe—Social policy.
5. Europe—Economic conditions—1945– I. Title.
HV245.C695   1999
362.5'094—dc21   98–35436
                                                        CIP

This book is printed on paper suitable for recycling and made from fully managed and sustained forest sources.

10   9   8   7   6   5   4   3   2   1
08   07   06   05   04   03   02   01   00   99

Printed in Hong Kong

Introduction

The aims of this book are twofold: first, to further our understanding of processes of convergence and divergence in selected
European societies and of explanations for these; and secondly,
to provide an understanding of processes of social change, especially in the spheres of work, employment and welfare. In this
respect the focus of the book is on the changing relationship
between work and welfare, which has become one of the central
academic and policy debates at the end of the twentieth century. One of the principal reasons for interest in this changing
relationship is that the restructuring of the welfare state is directly related to transformations in the economy, increased international competition, and, notably, the erosion of the standard
employment relationship on which social policies were premised
in earlier decades of the post-war period. The current characteristics of European economies with low economic growth and
high structural unemployment increasingly means the exclusion
and marginalization of many groups from participation in the
labour market and therefore from social protection based on
continuous employment. High unemployment also exacerbates
the costs to the welfare state, although, as we discuss in the
following chapters, the European welfare states have responded
in different ways to unemployment. Women's increased participation at work has also undermined the male-breadwinner family
model which underpinned social policies in the early post-war
period and has led to a continuing debate about the relationship of women's paid and unpaid work and their access to welfare. These changes constitute the themes of this book.

The transformations affecting the European economies can be
related to a number of processes which include increasing internationalization of the economies, a shift to neo-liberalism and
European integration, although in practice these three areas are

closely linked. The economic integration or internationalization of the advanced economies has been accelerating throughout the post-war period and is now said to have entered a new and qualitatively different stage of 'globalization'. Falling international transport costs, new technology and the communications revolution, financial deregulation, increased mobility of capital and the restructuring role of the transnational companies are all having an impact on this process. The implications for welfare states are that governments now pursue policies which aim to enhance the competitiveness of their countries; they are less willing to pursue socially redistributive policies, seeking instead to reduce, or avoid increasing, non-labour wage costs, taxes and public expenditure. In the terms of the Regulationist school of writers the present restructuring of the welfare state is therefore understood as part of the search for new forms of accumulation and regulation which require social policies to be subordinated to international competition and labour-market flexibility (for example, Jessop 1994).[1]

The globalization thesis also posits that the nature and autonomy of nation states and their traditional forms of governance have been affected. As firms seek locations in other parts of the world and form strategic alliances with firms from other nations, they establish rules of cooperation separate from the rules of government in their home country. This has weakened the ability of nation states to regulate transnational activities and been damaging to previous nationally specific neo-corporatist arrangements which existed through national associations of capital and labour and which supported domestic welfare provision (Crouch and Menon 1997). At the same time the collectivist institutions of labour are weakened and the power of capital increased, so that political alliances for the defence of welfare are more and more difficult.

The globalization thesis has been vigorously refuted by Hirst and Thompson (1996), especially the version which suggests that national governments and labour organizations are powerless when faced with global economic integration and have no choice but to accept neo-liberal and deregulation strategies. Hirst and Thompson show that the openness of the world economy and mobility of capital is not new, we have only just begun to return to levels of international trade reached in the period 1870–1913, international trade and investment is massively concentrated in the advanced countries and that multinational firms continue to operate from distinctly national bases in terms of the location of their assets and sales. Furthermore, the national level remains the arena in which policies for wages, labour markets and welfare provision are made, even though the rhetoric of policy choices may be in terms of global competitive threats. As we show in the following chapters, although international competition, the operations of multinational companies and the diffusion of new organizational and managerial models constitute similar pressures and directions of change, these are mediated through the social, political and institutional structures within each country and national labour markets and welfare states remain distinctive. One view is that within Europe internationalization is uneven in its impact on different industries and sectors: it has had least effect on national labour markets and welfare systems and most effect in financial markets, mass media, organizational ideologies and 'best practice' in work organization and technology (Rhodes *et al.* 1997).

A neo-liberal shift in all European countries is the second development which we can identify. Neo-liberal policies give primacy to measures which release the free play of market forces and seek to reduce legislation or institutions which are seen to impede the market, for example state ownership, centralized collective bargaining, environmental and health and safety constraints, employment protection and minimum wage levels. While it is possible to discern a neo-liberal shift in all European countries (see Chapters 1 and 2), it is difficult to distinguish the adoption of neo-liberal policies from the internationalization process, since the aim is to encourage the investment of multinational companies in particular locations (Crouch and Menon 1997). However, as we discuss in the following chapters, there have been striking differences between European countries in the extent and timing of shifts to neo-liberalism as well as differences in the respective roles of governments and employers in their enthusiasm for such policies.

The third pressure for change concerns European integration, especially the Single European Act of 1987, the creation of a single market in the 1990s, and preparation to meet the convergence criteria for monetary union in 1999. The European integration process is itself a neo-liberal project in which the policies of the Single European Act aimed to release forces of competition through the free movement of capital, labour, goods and services. The Cecchini Report of 1988 suggested that there would be gains from increased economies of scale, increased efficiency and lower prices, relocation of resources reflecting comparative advantage and an increased rate of technical change. European integration therefore induces further pressures on welfare states: fiscal constraints in preparation for monetary union, policies which enable regions or countries to gain comparative advantage, and concern to avoid burdening business with high taxes and non-labour wage costs. However, recognition that there would be economic dislocation resulting from the completion of the internal market, especially in less-developed regions, was the impetus behind the development of the social policy proposals of the Social Charter and the Social Protocol attached to the Maastricht Treaty. Avoidance of 'social dumping' practices and policies, that is, gaining competitive advantage by lower social costs and employment protection, was a further reason for the development of this social dimension (see Adnett 1995).

However, there is general agreement that the history of European community politics and the economic nature of the original treaties has subordinated a European social policy agenda to the aims of market integration and monetary union (Ross 1995, Streeck 1995, Leibfried and Pierson 1995). There is also agreement that the ability of European Union decision makers to dictate a positive course of action for social policies is limited (Streeck 1995, Leibfried and Pierson 1995). This is due to the existence of a weak central European Union authority for social policy making so that the substantive achievements are few and often oriented to the 'lowest common denominator'. However, Leibfried and Pierson argue that the movement to market integration results in 'spillover' effects, by which they mean that 'the process through which the completion of the internal market (for example, the unhindered mobility of labour and the liberalization of services) produces pressures for the EU to invade the domain of social policy' (1995:44). Market integration is, therefore, being accompanied by the gradual erosion of the autonomy and sovereignty of national welfare states which 'will become more and more enmeshed in a complex, multi-tiered web of social policy' (Leibfried and Pierson 1995:45), including the important rulings of the European Court of Justice.

Member states are also limited by the autonomy of European-level organizations, for instance, the European Commission has developed a capacity for agenda setting (for example, the Social Charter and the Social Chapter of the Maastricht Treaty), direct intervention (for example, the poverty and social exclusion programmes [see Chapter 6 of this book]), the setting of social regulations (for example, protections for women workers [see Chapter 5 of this book] and health and safety standards), as well as 'spillover' effects (see also Spicker 1996 and Greve 1996). However, the existing scope and diversity of national systems of social policy pre-empts many policy initiatives by the European Union and makes a coherent and overarching European welfare state unlikely. Member states too may wish to retain control over national social provision as an important source of political legitimacy and they will, therefore, be resistant to the transfer of authority to the European Union. On the other hand, as Leibfried and Pierson (1995) argue, they may also find that blaming the EU allows for unpopular changes that national governments may otherwise be reluctant to contemplate.

The impact of the process of European integration on national welfare states and their labour markets is, therefore, complex. One further change concerns a shift in social policy emphasis at the European Union level during the 1990s with the recognition that low economic growth and high structural unemployment are the major problems facing Europe. The White Papers 1993 and 1994 and the Luxembourg Jobs Summit 1997 point to a policy agenda concerned less with social regulation at the European level than with labour market deregulation, a reduction in non-wage labour costs and tax reforms (see Chapter 2). While this is in line with the pressures noted above with respect to the search for international competitiveness, the shift to neo-liberalism and the increased strength of capital, this does not necessarily mean that the influence of business over European social policy is absolute. Rather business organizations and actors are internally divided, have different interests across territorial and sectoral lines (for example, between high wage and low wage areas of Europe, firm size, sector and export orientation), and are subject to political competitiveness especially from other interest groups (see the arguments of Streeck 1995 and Leibfried and Pierson 1995). Rhodes (1996), in fact, argues that the recent stance of the European Commission may be seen as a 'minimalist, third path' version of the social dimension between the neo-liberal and social-democratic options.

One of the effects of European integration is that economic development and policy making at the regional level have become more important, although such development is of a highly variable nature. There has been a differential impact on different regions in Europe with increased concentration of economic activity in an expanded European Union core, but a perpetuation of disadvantages for the peripheral regions (Cheshire 1995). As we discuss in Chapter 4, the characteristics of the successful regions in Europe are being emulated by other regions and actively promoted by the European Commission as a means of promoting economic growth. While this has been successful in some regions (for example, see the case of Wales in Cooke *et al.* 1995 and in urban regions based on cities such as Glasgow, Lyon and Bologna [Cheshire 1995]), weaker regions are much more subject to the tendencies of economic concentration and international competition.

In the context of these pressures for change this book examines similarities and differences in employment and welfare state structures of selected European societies. The following chapters demonstrate that these processes of change are accelerating a convergence between European countries, but there remains substantial diversity in national responses reflecting the legacies of past institutional, social and political structures and differences in the role and power of governments, employers, trade unions and social movements. The way in which responses to common problems of change are refracted in each country, in turn, creates new sets of problems and tensions, as we identify in the following chapters.

The focus in the book is on four European countries, namely, Germany, Spain, Sweden and the UK, rather than all 15 member states which currently comprise the European Union. The reason for this is that a more in-depth analysis of fewer countries and their different welfare and labour market structures can be undertaken, although reference is made throughout to other European member states. The four countries selected represent divergent approaches to employment regulation and social protection. The literature on typologies of employment and welfare regimes usually suggests that we can identify three distinct types in Europe: Scandinavian or social democratic regimes, neo-liberal regimes and continental or conservative-corporatist European regimes (for example, Due *et al.* 1991, Esping-Andersen 1990, 1996a).[2] However, it is argued here that Spain can be distinguished as a separate regime with many features in common with other Southern European countries (Leibfried 1993, Ferrera 1996).

The book is divided into three Parts, the themes of which are reflected in the book's title. The first Part examines the distinctive and unique national patterns of development of the selected European societies in the post-war period. Although all European countries have experienced similar trends in their post-war economic histories, Chapter 1 discusses those salient developments in each society which enable us to understand the different social and institutional structures, economic directions and policy orientations. In this first chapter the focus is on what were, and still are, mainly male institutions of the state, employers' associations and trade unions. Underlying these structures, however, were particular assumptions of gender relations and the role of migrant workers.

The second Part of the book focuses on changing patterns of employment and work in Europe. Increasing internationalization has been accompanied by long-term changes in the structure of economies, especially the decline in manufacturing industry and (male) manual manufacturing employment, and increased structural unemployment. Two further developments have particular significance for welfare, that of an increase in 'non-standard' or flexible work and the increased feminization of the labour market in service sectors. The erosion of the 'standard employment' relationship (a full-time, permanent, and socially secured relationship) which underpinned social policies in earlier decades of the post-war period is the theme of Chapter 2. This chapter discusses the reasons for the erosion of standard employment and charts the politics, policies and experiments of flexible labour markets pursued by European governments in the 1980s and 1990s. As increasing proportions of workers have 'non-standard' forms of employment, or 'flexible' work such as part-time or temporary work, so they lose their entitlements to social protection based on continuous, life-long employment.

An increase in the non-standard employment relationship has also coincided with the increased participation of women in the labour market. This has led many to see interconnections between the two phenomena, so that as women have entered the labour market they are increasingly being integrated through the new forms of flexible work (Rubery and Fagan 1994). However, as we discuss in Chapter 2, the form, nature and intensity of women's flexible work differs considerably in the different European countries. These differences have implications not only for the gender contract in each country but also for household coping strategies and opportunities.

One of the most profound changes in work in the past two decades has been the increased participation of women in the labour market. Chapter 3 discusses women's participation in European labour markets and demonstrates that women's employment patterns across Europe show both convergence and cross-national differences. In all countries, however, there is evidence of strong similarities in gender occupational segregation, lower pay levels and in most countries higher levels of unemployment. We cannot yet say that increased participation has led to increased equality and integration of women into paid work.

Chapter 4 draws on the debate around one of the theoretical approaches to post-Fordism, that of the transition from mass production to flexible specialization. Here the renaissance of regional economies as sources of economic growth is considered, as is the reorganization strategies of transnational corporations and the implications for local economies in Spain and the Baden-Württemberg region of Germany. This chapter is less concerned with the changing relationship between work and welfare but rather demonstrates the complexities of economic change, especially changing relations between firms, pressures of international competition and the conditions of regional inequalities in Europe.

The third Part of the book focuses on two salient areas in the changing relationship between work and welfare, namely women and social policies, and poverty and social exclusion. In the first of these, feminist writers have cogently argued a case for

including gender in the comparative study of welfare states and
have provided analyses which take into account the relationship
between paid and unpaid work and social policies. These writers
have been particularly critical of Esping-Andersen's (1990) work
on welfare regimes. They have pointed out that although Esping-
Andersen consider the relationship between paid work and welfare,
he ignores the importance of unpaid work in the family, work
carried out predominantly by women (although see the Conclusion to this book for reference to Esping-Andersen's more recent
work in which he explicitly addresses this issue).
Central to Esping-Andersen's analysis is the concept of
decommodification. This is defined as 'the degree to which individuals or families can uphold a socially acceptable standard of
living independently of market participation' (Esping-Andersen
1990:37). Welfare states differ in their capacity to decommodify,
that is they differ in the degree to which they allow their citizens
to make their living standards independent of pure market forces.[3]
However, while decommodifying social rights gained can counteract
the unequal bargaining power between capital and labour, such
social policies can produce new inequalities which can operate
to exclude women or ethnic minority groups (Ostner 1994a).
Ostner points to the ways in which women's life trajectories are
shaped by the 'normal expectations' of women's roles within each
society and which underpin social policies adopted. Other writers
have suggested that the concept of decommodification should
be replaced or supplemented to take account of gender divisions and the relation between paid and unpaid work and welfare (for example, Lewis 1992, 1993 and Orloff 1993). These
concepts and dimensions are discussed in Chapter 5 and util-
ized with respect to the development of social policies for women
and the underlying assumptions of the 'normal expectations' of
women's roles within each society.
   In the last chapter we explore the relationship between work
and welfare by an examination of the extent to which groups in
different European countries are excluded from, or have difficulty in gaining access to, either employment or social protection. Chapter 6, therefore, considers the nature and extent of
poverty and social exclusion in selected European societies. The
different traditions and theoretical paradigms in conceptualizing
poverty and social exclusion (Room 1995a, Silver 1994) are

discussed and the changing nature of social disadvantage is examined in the context of the social structures of Germany, Spain, Sweden and the UK. This examination of different paradigms of social exclusion also enhances our understanding of the divergent foundations of the welfare states of Europe and the ways in which different groups in each society are included or excluded.

The book is guided by the view that cross-national comparison enables us to question what might otherwise be taken-for-granted phenomena or relationships in one national context. The discussions in the following chapters subscribe to a 'societal' perspective in which differences between countries need to be explained by reference to the interrelationship between political, economic and social factors within each country (Rubery 1988). The book is intended to be complementary to those studies of European Union policy making and the effect of harmonization and integration policies on the individual member states (see, for example, Cressey and Jones 1995, Hantrais 1995, and Leibfried and Pierson 1995).

European labour markets, work organizations and welfare states are subject to rapid economic and political change at the end of the 1990s, undermining the employment conditions and welfare systems developed under different conditions of accumulation and regulation in the earlier post-war period. As we have identified in this Introduction, these pressures for change include increased international competition, the shift to neo-liberalism and the process of European integration. The following chapters discuss a variety of theoretical perspectives and empirical evidence which throw light on the complexities of cross-national similarities and differences in employment and welfare state structures in selected European societies.

PART ONE

Post-War Developments and National Variations

1

National Diversity: Germany, Spain, Sweden and the UK

This chapter concentrates on the unique patterns of development of European countries in the post-Second World War period. The emphasis is on the distinctive socio-economic formations in Germany, Spain, Sweden and the UK and differences between the countries in the role and power of governments, employers and trade unions. However, the debate on convergence or divergence of European societies also stresses that, despite the diversity of experience discussed below, all countries (as advanced capitalist societies) have experienced similar trends in their post-war economic histories. In a stylized way we can divide the post-war period into three phases: first, the period of 1945 to 1950/2 as one of reconstruction after the War; secondly, the early 1950s to the late 1960s/early 1970s as a period of rapid economic growth and prolonged full employment (variously labelled as 'the 25 golden years' of capitalism or the 'Fordist' era); and thirdly, the period from the mid-1970s has been characterized as one of recurrent economic crisis, slower growth, welfare state and public expenditure retrenchment and the adoption of neo-liberal economics. These developments are common to all countries and widespread structural changes have resulted in the erosion or demise of the political arrangements established in the earlier post-war period.

The chapter is divided into two sections. The first discusses developments in each country from the 1950s to the 1970s, including the transition to democracy in Spain. The second section concentrates on the shift to neo-liberalism and the main economic trends and issues in the 1980s and 1990s (the reasons for the widespread adoption of neo-liberal policies are discussed in Chapter 2). The aim of the following discussion is not to provide a detailed account of economic and political developments but rather to focus on those salient developments in each country which enable us to understand the different social and institutional structures, economic directions and policy orientations. However, a chronology of the main key dates for each country is set out in Tables 1.1–5.

The distinctive development of each of the countries discussed in this chapter lies in the different routes to industrial capitalism and modernization processes established in earlier centuries. It is outside the scope of this chapter to trace these different development trajectories and the responses proposed to the problems and contradictions identified in industrial capitalist and democratic processes. In fact, the countries discussed here represent extreme responses to the problems of modernization and capitalism, with Spain and Germany developing into fascist/authoritarian regimes in the 1930s and Britain and Sweden responding with different types of democratic solutions.

1950s to 1970s

Federal Republic of Germany

The political economy of the Federal Republic, founded in 1949, was based on the philosophy of the 'social market economy' (*sozialemarketwirtshaft*), an economy which synthesized a free market economy, a denaturalized federal government and distributive social justice. The German theorists of the social market (the 'ordo-liberals') rejected totalitarian dictatorship, either fascist or communist, and believed that a free market order required regulation to prevent degeneration into the cartel-riddled corporatism of the 1930s. The social market, therefore, embodied the principles of a competitive market economy, liberated from central state planning but with a sense of responsibility to all groups in society (although the expansion of social welfare had to wait until the economic prosperity of the 1960s) and a legally enforced system of industrial democracy and industrial training. A further feature, and one which has been one of the outstanding achievements in the post-war period, is the establishment of an independent central bank (the Bundesbank) which is obliged by law to preserve a stable currency and price stability. The *Ordnungspolitic* tradition stresses that markets should operate within a regulatory framework, set not by passing governments, but by a broad political and social consensus.

Table 1.1 Germany: key dates, 1945 to 1990

1945–9	Occupation by the Allies
1949 May	Basic Law of the Federal Republic of Germany comes into force
1949 Oct.	Constitution of the German Democratic Republic adopted
1949	The 16 trade unions formed the German Trade Union Federation (DGB)
1950	Federation of German Employers' Associations (BDA) founded
1952	Codetermination Act
1950–66	Economic reconstruction and expansion
1966–9	Great Coalition between CDU/CSU and SDP
1969	SDP and FDP win narrow majority in Bundestag election, Brandt elected Chancellor
1969–82	Social-liberal coalition (SDP–FDP) and tripartite concertation
1972	Works Constitution Act
1973 Oct.	First 'oil shock'
1974	Schmidt elected Chancellor
1976	Codetermination Act
1982	Kohl elected as Chancellor CDU/CSU-FDP coalition
1982	Kohl Chancellor CDU/CSU-FDP coalition
1990	Unification of west and east Germany

Box 1.1 The main features of the social market economy in west Germany

1. Strong trade union and employer structures. Union organization was reconstructed in 1949, along new lines to consist of 16 centralized unions representing each industrial sector. Parallel to these are well organized and disciplined central employers' organizations, for example, the German Employers' Association (BDA) and the Federation of German Industrialists (BDI). These associations represent their members as quasi-political bodies and operate as unofficial forums of industrial, social and economic policy making (Lane 1989a). Effectively, as Lane notes, the power of the central state can be curtailed by the existence of these influential interest groups of labour and capital.

2. A highly regulated system of collective bargaining. After the Second World War the principle was re-established that wages and most other conditions of employment were to be determined by collective bargaining between trade unions and employers' organizations without participation by government. Collective bargaining is organized on a regional and sectoral basis and wage contracts set which are essentially minimum basic. The contracts (*Tarifvertrage*) cover working time, holiday entitlements, and dismissal procedures, and are valid for one year. Some 90 per cent of the workforce is covered by such wage contracts, even though only one third of employees are members of unions. In practice actual wages paid are higher than the contracts, a policy which Streeck (1992) argues has made employers more willing to invest in training and retraining as a way of matching workers' productivity to the externally fixed high costs of labour.

3. Industrial democracy or codetermination, which exists at two levels. Since the Works Constitution Acts 1952 and 1972, in firms with more than five employees, works councils are obligatory as the only authoritative representative of employees at the workplace. The union for its part has no standing within workplace collective bargaining; rather this takes place at multi-employer or regional level. The purpose of this dual system was to entrench a 'works constitution' obliging employees' collective representatives to collaborate with management and therefore exclude potentially oppositional unions from the arena of production (Hyman 1989). Since 1952 there has also been codetermination at the level of the enterprise through worker representation on the supervisory board. The supervisory boards have a strategic role within a firm, while the management board has responsibility for day-to-day management. Since the 1952 Act codetermination has been

extended to other industries (Co-determination Act 1976).[1]
4. Regulation of education and training. For apprentices there
is a dual system of vocational training in a company with vocational education in a college. Industrial training is not only
recognized as a highly valuable societal resource, but the skilled
worker's certificate (*Facharbeiterbrief*) gains access to a high
and steady income, responsibility and autonomy at work. The
result is also an excess pool of polyvalent workers and skills
that constitute an important advantage in periods of fast technological change (Streeck 1992, see also Chapter 3).

The main features of the social market economy in west Germany as it emerged in the post-war period are briefly summarized in Box 1.1. Institutional analyses of the social market present
a web of the interlocking features presented in Box 1.1, which
combine to produce an industrial culture often referred to as
'stakeholder' capitalism. This involves an insider system of corporate governance, based on the supervisory boards and works
councils, which sustains a practice of collaboration between
management and employees. Employers are obliged to consult
with their workforce and seek their consent. Having an assured
voice in the management of the firm makes it possible for workers to forego short-term advantages for long-term benefits (Streeck
1992). Banks have also assumed a key role on the supervisory
boards of the larger firms, building up long-term relationships
with the firm. The maximization of profit for shareholders is not
viewed as the prime purpose of the firm, in contrast to Britain;
rather it is the long-term stability of the firm which is sought.
The relationship between the regional, municipal and co-operative
banks and the small and medium-sized firms is particularly ad-
vantageous. The banks have a closer and more intimate knowledge of the firms and can offer a supply of predictable and
reasonably priced capital, enabling them to achieve capital and
labour productivity as well as export and innovation activity. This
accounts for the larger and more competitive medium-sized-firm
sector in Germany than in Britain (Lane 1995).

Firms at the local or regional levels are also embedded in
strong and consensual associational networks, not only trade unions
and employers' associations, but also chambers of trade and

commerce, research institutes, banks and the local and regional state organizations. These dense networks of intermediary institutions support the business activities of firms and have been seen by many writers as the source of those firms' economic success (see the discussion in Chapter 4 and the example of Baden-Württemberg). Finally, a further feature of the German industrial culture is the high level of jurification of the industrial relations systems (in great contrast to the UK) with respect to collective bargaining, working conditions, co-determination, training and, as we discuss in Chapter 2, employment protection.

This account of west German institutions probably over-emphasizes stability, coherence and heterogeneity, for although these institutional features have persisted in comparison with the other three countries discussed in this Chapter, the 1990s have been a period of decisive change. As we discuss below, unification with east Germany, international competition, the changing strategies of banks and employers and new technology are all beginning to force fundamental changes in German institutional structures.

Spain

Giner (1985) and Sapelli (1995) have argued that the countries of southern Europe – Greece, Italy, Portugal and Spain – have, despite striking internal variations, an unmistakable commonality and distinctiveness within the larger framework of European society. They find that these four countries exhibit a number of common traits with respect to historical evolution, modes of political domination, and system of class relations. All four countries have experienced the imposition of a modern 'despotic regime' through authoritarian dictatorships during the twentieth century, all have made the transition to democracy (three in the 1970s) and all have had socialist governments in power for some or a large part of the post-transition period.

Three common features stand out as most salient in their contribution to the distinctiveness of the socio-economic formations of southern European countries. These are, first, the late timing and qualitatively different form of industrialization and modernization processes; secondly, the central role of the Church; and thirdly, the nature of the 'despotic regimes' through which all these societies passed. In the case of Spain it is perhaps the nature of the long rule of Franco's dictatorship and its legacy which has been one of the most important features shaping the contemporary social structure.

The National Syndicalist state of Franco was founded on the principles of 'unity, totality and hierarchy'. Every branch of the economy was organized in vertical syndicates, or unions, membership of which was compulsory for employers, technicians, administrative staff and workers. Although free trade unions were banned, as was the right to strike, in return workers were granted job security virtually for life, and received the 'cumbersome and complex paternalism' of the social security system (Carr and Fusi 1987).

Giner and Sevilla (1984) have argued that Spanish Francoist corporatism was largely a sham. There were a number of fascist corporatist features such as the vertical unions, the rubber stamping parliament of the Cortes, an ideology that class conflict had been overcome and a harmonious pyramid of state, province, municipality and family established. However, the authors argue that it was a corporatism of exclusion, rather than inclusion, and subordination rather than mobilization. Spain had a weak civil society and weakly organized interest groups. Those groups who did not support the regime were made bereft of the means of organization of their interests. 'Paradoxically, Francoist corporatism meant the decorporatism of a large and subordinate part of Spanish society' (Giner and Sevilla 1984:120).

The twenty-year period after the Civil War was characterized by international isolation, extreme poverty, retarded economic development and political repression of subordinate classes. The economy was strongly regulated by the principle of autarchy (that is, economic self-sufficiency). The state sought control over the economy, and attempted to achieve rapid industrialization based on import substitution and the desire for self-sufficiency. Not until 1950 did the index of industrial production rise above the level of 1929 (Salmon 1991). However, the principle of autarchy failed in that it was impossible to construct a totally self-reliant economy and traditional exports of agricultural products were insufficient to finance essential imports. Under pressure from the IMF, OECD and the USA (who wished to make Spain a prime factor in defence against the USSR), a Plan of Stabilization and Liberalization was introduced in 1959. The Plan included a lifting of barriers to external and internal trade. These liberalizing measures were to lead to rapid economic growth and industrialization during the 1960s.

The period of economic development 1960 to 1974 ('*el desarrollo*') was aided by fast-growing domestic demand as the population, who had starved during the hungry years of the 1940s after the Civil War, became consumers of mass-produced goods for the first time. Industrial development was aided by abundant reserves of cheap labour, which in turn was fuelled by a massive dislocation of population from the rural areas of Spain to the industrial cities. Three factors aided rapid economic growth: first, the newly developing tourism; secondly, remittances sent home from those who migrated as guest workers to north European cities; and thirdly, foreign investment which began in this period.

Foreign investment was attracted by the low labour costs, but in turn, domestic firms were protected against foreign competition. This policy of protectionism meant that firms were able to prosper even though they were not specialized, nor used modern technology or machinery to full capacity. The industrial structure was characterized by fragmented, numerous small businesses that lacked innovation, had a low technological level, and lacked skilled labour and management skills. Labour relations during this period 'oscillated between extreme authoritarianism and paternalism' (Jimeno and Toharia 1994:5). From 1958 some firms were permitted collective bargaining, so that a dichotomy emerged between the conditions in these firms and those where workers were unable to organize.

Table 1.2 Key dates during the Franco regime, 1939–75

1939–59	Period of autarchy, international isolation and economic decline
1938	Franco Labour Act
1940	Syndical Organization founded
1953	First international contacts USA, Vatican
1958	Collective Bargaining Act
1959	Stabilization Plan
1960–74	Period of economic growth and rapid industrialization, *el desarrollo*

Table 1.3 The transition and consolidation of democracy in Spain 1975–96 – selected dates

1975	Death of Franco
1976	Law of Political Reform opens the way for legislation of political parties and trade unions
1977	First democratic elections since 1936, won by centre right UDC party
1977	Moncloa Pacts (agreements on prices and incomes policies between government and political parties) also agreed to by trade unions and employers
1978	Constitution introduced *civil rights*, for example the right to equality, to freedom, and religious liberty, *political rights*, for example the right to freedom of expression, assembly, association, participation and strike, *socio-economic rights*, for example, the right to work, to collective bargaining, and to education. Socio-economic *commitments* included protection of the family, of the elderly and of health
1982	PSOE (socialist/social democractic) wins general election and begins programme of economic rationalization
1986	Spain becomes full member of EC
1996	Popular Party (conservative) wins general election

The transition to democracy in Spain. The reforms which accompanied the political transition to democracy in the late 1970s included a number of distinctive features but also a high degree of continuity with the Franco regime. First, new social actors, previously excluded from decision making, were now able to participate in debates about public policy. These new groups included the political parties, the newly legalized trade unions, and the employers' associations. At the same time however, none of these groups had experience of the governing or opposition processes (Perez-Diaz 1987). Decision making took the form of a series of 'social pacts' between these new social actors – state, political parties, the employers' association and trade unions – and until 1986 agreements were reached on economic and social policies, working conditions, union rights and collective bargaining.

Secondly, although the political institutions changed with elections in 1977 and the Constitution of 1978, the bureaucratic inheritance from the past regime has been weighty, and it has remained unwieldy and inefficient. There has been as much continuity as change in the apparatus of the state (Pridham 1989).

The size of the administrative apparatus was already large and this made it difficult for the democratic governments to undertake radical reform. After 1982, the socialist government (PSOE) found it especially difficult to reform the state administration. A form of 'socialist clientelism' was practised in which there was extensive overlap between PSOE membership and employment by the state (Pridham 1989). In Petras's (1993) view, however, the Socialist's electoral regime reproduced the same style of politics as its Francoist predecessor. The same centralization and concentration of legislative and executive power, the same emergence of personal power, and the bureaucratization of civil society. This also included continual efforts to subordinate trade unions to the state (see below).

A third feature concerns the uncoupling of Church and political party in the 1970s (see also Chapter 5 for the influence of the Church during the Franco regime). The Church had largely detached itself from the regime by the early 1970s, and the new political forces which were emerging had to some extent been nurtured or assisted by the Church. No Christian Democrat party achieved widespread support during the transition (De Ussel 1991, Giner and Sevilla 1984). The Constitution of 1978 states there will be no state religion and complete religious freedom. In practice, however, the Church has been influential in issues such as education, divorce and abortion.

The fourth and probably most important feature however, was that the transition process took place during an international economic crisis whose impact was much worse in Spain than other countries. The employment population ratio was already low in the 1970s but fell even lower, so that by 1985 it was 43.8 per cent, the lowest ratio in the OECD area. The process of deindustrialization which was occurring elsewhere occurred at a faster rate in Spain than in any other European country, with the exception of the UK. Industries in which Spain had specialized during the boom years – machinery, textiles, electrical equipment – were the hardest hit. Unemployment increased by more than two million people to 21.7 per cent of the workforce by 1985. This was also a period in which the number of small establishments grew through a dismantling of large firms and an increase in wider networks of subcontracting (see Chapter 4).

Sweden

Sweden in the mid-twentieth century was characterized by strong
neo-corporatist arrangements which were supported by a social
democratic hegemony and a strong and centralized trade union
movement. These arrangements had their origin in the solution
to unemployment at the beginning of the 1930s, the Saltsjobaden
Agreement,[2] and the acceptance by the social democrats of the
labour market model proposed by economists Gosta Rehn and
Rudolf Meidner of the blue-collar trade union confederation
(*Landorganisationen i Sverige* LO). The aims of the Rehn–Meidner
model were full employment, price stability, economic growth
and a fair distribution of wages. The government was seen to be
responsible for full employment and economic stability, whilst
the trade unions and employers' association were seen to be
responsible for the process of wage formation.

Table 1.4 Sweden: key dates, late nineteenth century to 1995

1889	Social Democratic Party (SAP) formed
1899	Trade Union Confederation (LO) founded
1902	Employers' Association (SAF) founded
1918	Suffrage for men and women
1932	Social Democratic Party elected with working agreement with Centre Party
1936–9	Coalition between SAP and Centre Party
1938	The Saltsjobaden Agreement
1945–51	SAP in power alone
1951–7	Coalition between SAP and Centre Party
1957–6	SAP in power alone
Late 1950s and 1960s	Adoption by SAP and LO of the Rehn–Meidner model
1974	Security of Employment Act
1976	Act on Codetermination at Work
1976–82	Coalition of Centre, Liberal and Moderate parties
1982–91	SAP government
1991	Coalition government of Moderate, Liberal, Centre and Christian Democrat parties
1994	SAP government elected
Jan. 1995	Sweden joins European Union

The main characteristics of the Rehn–Meidner model as it was adopted by the Social Democratic governments from the late 1950s can be summarized as follows:

1. *Centralized wage bargaining.* Sweden has had one of the most centralized systems of wage bargaining of any OECD country. The unions supported this process because it facilitated the policy of wage solidarity and employers supported it since they believed it would prevent wage inflation and guarantee industrial peace. During the agreed central wage contract the parties were supposed to respect the peace obligation and not resort to industrial action to settle disputes. In comparison with most other advanced countries Sweden had a fairly harmonious industrial relations system in the decades following the Second World War.

2. *A solidaristic wage policy.* The aim of this policy is that all employees should receive equal pay for equal work regardless of the particular financial position of their employer. Wage-rate differentials should therefore disappear between regions, industries, sexes and age groups. In practice less profitable companies were unable to pay these wages and reduced their work forces or went out of business. More profitable firms paid lower wages than they could afford. However, the model has been seen to accelerate structural adjustment and economic growth. The solidaristic wage policy harmed low-productivity firms and favoured high-productivity firms and therefore speeded up the transfer of employment from old, labour-intensive sectors to modern, technologically advanced sectors.

3. *An active labour market policy.* With centralized wage bargaining and a solidaristic wage policy a special kind of dynamic arose in the economy, that is, a combination of a large demand for, and a large supply of, labour (Delsen and van Veen 1992). Demand stemmed from high-productivity sectors and supply from low-productivity sectors. To ease matching problems between the two an active labour-market policy developed which aimed to enhance the mobility of workers who lost their jobs. Measures that have been developed include relocation grants, training and retraining programmes, temporary public sector schemes and private sector recruitment subsidies.[3]

4. *A restrictive fiscal policy.* The above policies kept unemployment low throughout the post-war period until the late 1980s.

In order to avoid inflation another element of the Swedish model was a restrictive fiscal policy. Personal income tax was, until recently, high.[4] Special measures also enabled private-sector firms to put profits into special investment funds and these were not taxed, thereby channelling company profits into regional investment, new technology or education and training of workers.

The late 1960s was characterized by what has been called 'the industrial labour offensive' – a radicalization of industrial class politics. The industrial unions, Metall in particular, were the main source of ideas and the Social Democratic Party acted as the political vehicle. Three goals were pursued: first, increased equality of income, achieved through taxation policies and wage bargaining; secondly, industrial legislation which brought greater employment protection in the Act of 1974 and an extension of economic democracy in the Codetermination Act of 1976; and thirdly, a transfer of property rights from the corporations to trade-union ownership through 'wage earner' funds. The latter arose as a consequence of the solidaristic wage policy, which enabled large profitable companies to gain extra profits. In 1976 the LO proposed that collective profit sharing would be a means of persuading workers to accept wage restraint in the face of high profits, but also to be able to have a share in those profits. The 'wage earner' funds were eventually introduced in a watered-down form in 1984, but employers strongly resist these funds (see also the discussion below).

Debates in the academic literature on the Swedish model in the 1970s and 1980s centred on the extent to which the characteristics of Swedish social structures – the strong labour movement with high unionization, the long period of rule by the Social Democratic Party, the extensive welfare state and solidaristic wage policies – indicated that Sweden was in transition to socialism. Writers such as Stephens (1979) and Korpi (1983) were optimistic with respect to the radicalization of policies in the 1970s – the 'industrial labour offensive' to which we have referred above. As Korpi (1983) has argued, the 'power resources' of the labour movement sought to use political power within the Social Democratic government to generate greater equality in Swedish society. Policies have led to a much greater redistribution of wages and incomes. The Codetermination Act of 1976 and proposals to transform ownership from private capital to union-controlled investment funds, it was also argued, pushed the Swedish model towards radical reform of capitalist relations of production (Esping-Andersen 1985, Stephens 1979).

However, Fulcher (1987) considers that industrial democracy legislation failed either to increase union power or undermine capitalist relations. Further, the 'wage earner' funds when they were eventually introduced precluded a general union takeover of ownership of private capital. Fulcher argues that the strong labour movement of the 1970s stimulated the formation of a strong employers' association which counterbalanced the labour movement. The Social Democratic governments have also not been prepared to legislate changes that might threaten capitalist relations of production. As we discuss below these developments became much clearer in the 1980s and 1990s.

The UK

1945 to 1973: the post-war 'settlement'. The history of Britain in the first half of the twentieth century can be seen as the gradual development of collectivist ideas but not put into effect until after the Second World War. After the Labour victory in 1945 the ideas of the two liberals, Keynes and Beveridge, formed the settlement between labour and capital and the basis of the internal policy consensus in the early post-war years (see Chapter 5 for a discussion of the Beveridge Report). To the ideas of Keynes and Beveridge, the Labour government also added its own plans for the National Health Service and the nationalization of the major public utilities. The most appropriate description of this settlement would appear to be a 'liberal collectivist' model (Cutler *et al.* 1986, Ginsberg 1992): 'Liberal collectivism requires that a social commitment be made to certain minimal objectives which are seen as a condition of existence for a liberal society' (Cutler *et al.* 1986:1). Poverty and economic insecurity, as had occurred in the 1930s, may ultimately be threatening to capitalist society and require state intervention. However, such intervention should be limited in nature so that the valuable political and economic freedoms are safeguarded.

The period from the end of World War Two to 1974 was one in which Britain participated in a long economic boom, but in which she failed to grow or invest at the same rate as other capitalist economies. The post-war settlement was therefore inherently contradictory with a commitment to a comprehensive welfare state but in a context of the relative weakness and decline of the British economy. Much of the analysis of Britain's economic performance in the post-war period has, therefore, been concerned with Britain's relative economic decline compared with her competitors. Some of the key features of this can be summarized as follows:

(1) The manner of Britain's insertion into the international economy, that is, with a commitment towards imperial markets in Asia and Africa (subject to import penetration from new capitalist economies with much higher levels of labour exploitation) rather than the fast growth and dynamic economies of North America, and western Europe.

(2) Low levels of investments which were often 'add-on', concerned to compensate for deficiencies in existing processes of production rather than to introduce new techniques and processes. British firms also failed to reach the same levels of productivity from similar production processes and machinery as were obtained in other countries.

(3) An industrial relations system characterized by multi-trade-union structures and voluntaristic collective bargaining processes which, especially in the private sector, were 'decentralised, fragmented, informal, ad hoc and disorderly' (Jessop 1988:16).

(4) A structural propensity to compensate for deficiencies in domestic production through the import of mass consumer goods, which was not compensated by the export of capital goods.

(5) A hegemony of financial capital over industrial capital, the importance of the role of the City and the primacy given to the stable value of Sterling. A further consequence of the dominance of finance capital was the export of capital abroad.

(6) Finally, the inability of the state to facilitate, support or direct economic, political or social modernization. While elsewhere states were able to pursue effective strategies, whether through liberal, corporate or dirigiste arrangements, the British state was unable to pursue any such strategy consistently, producing U-turns and leading to a growing sense of a crisis of political legitimacy in the 1970s (Gamble 1991, Hay 1996, and Jessop 1988, 1991a).

Table 1.5   UK: key dates, 1945 to 1997

1945–51	Labour Party in government
1951–64	Conservative Party in government
1964–70	Labour Party in government
1970–4	Conservative Party in government
1973	Britain joins the EEC
1974–9	Labour Party in government
1975	Period of Social Contract
1975	Employment Protection Act
1979–90	Conservative Party with Margaret Thatcher as leader in government
1990	Major becomes Conservative Party prime minister
1992	Conservatives win the general election
1997 May	Labour Party in government, Blair as prime minister

1973 to 1979: economic and political crisis. In comparison with Sweden and Germany, Britain developed weak forms of neo-corporatism in the post-war period. Tripartite bodies were developed at national level, the National Economic Development Council from 1962: the Economic Development Committees from 1963, and in 1974 the Manpower Services Commission and the Health and Safety Commission. Income and price controls were sought from 1966. The most far-reaching attempt was the Social Contract arrangements of the mid to late 1970s under the Labour government. This has been called 'bargained corporatism' by Crouch (1977), in that policy concessions to the unions in return for their cooperation included the setting up of ACAS, the Employment Protection Act (1975), the Health and Safety at Work Act (1976), the Sex Discrimination Act (1976), and the Royal Commissions on industrial democracy and the distribution of income and wealth. As Marsh (1992) has observed, the Social Contract was in effect an incomes policy based at first on the active cooperation and subsequently on the acquiescence of the unions. In the end it collapsed, eventually leading to industrial action in the 'winter of discontent' of 1978–9, as the 'TUC could no longer deliver the support of its member unions and the union leaders could no longer deliver the support of their members' (Marsh 1992:52). Many commentators have argued that trade unions have not been able to play an active role in national level neo-corporatism in Britain because of weak, fragmented and decentralized structures and an ideological commitment to voluntarism. Capital itself was also weak, the formal organization of employers much less developed than either Germany or Sweden, and divided between industrial and financial sectors (Crouch 1995, Jessop 1991a).

The deepening economic crisis after 1973 was characterized by a rise in the price of oil, increasing unemployment, an increase in inflation to almost 25 per cent in 1975, and the 'fiscal crisis' of the state in 1975. The stringent terms of the loan which the Labour government sought from the IMF led to the first attempts at retrenchment of public expenditure from 1975 onwards. In 1978–9 the press scapegoated public-sector union members for taking industrial action against the national interest and holding the country to ransom in the 'winter of discontent'. However, writers have seen this moment as a fully fledged crisis of the British state, a culmination of the unresolved contradictions and tensions of the post-war settlement, and a moment of transition, although 'a crisis that was to become "lived" in the terms provided by the new right' (Hay 1996:17). For Gamble (1994), for example, the crises of the 1970s were exacerbated by the longer-term crisis of Britain's political institutions, its former world role and the relative decline of the British economy. It was in this climate that 'the political project that became Thatcherism was conceived' (1994:33).

1980s and 1990s

Germany

In Germany, although there has been a neo-liberal rhetoric and some legislation, there has not been the radical economic and social transformation achieved in Britain. The commitment of the Kohl coalition government after 1982 was to *Wendepolitik* (a policy of change), a neo-liberal economic strategy combined with a neo-liberal social policy. In a similar way to Thatcher in Britain, Kohl promised a deregulation of the German economy combined with a sustained effort to dismantle an increasingly expensive welfare system. In contrast to Britain, however, the assessment of commentators is that the radical right agenda has been largely confined to the rhetoric of policy. There has been some retrenchment of welfare and public expenditure and de-regulation of labour law (see Chapter 2), but the institutional framework of policy making, the role of the trade unions and constraints imposed by coalition governments have acted as a brake on radical transformations. Similarly, although the corporatist arrangements established in the 1970s have been eroded to some extent in the 1980s and 1990s, the high degree of formalization and legal regulation of industrial relations has probably ensured a greater continuity of consensus among the social partners. Of particular importance is that there has been no collapse of union legitimacy as in Britain, and the trade unions still retain a place in the policy-making community, although largely in a consultative capacity.[5]

The most important event for Germany was the unification of east and west Germany under the German Economic, Monetary and Social Union in 1990. The east has assimilated the industrial, labour market, collective bargaining, and social security institutions and practices, together with price determination and property rights, of the west. Five new Landers were created in the east: Mecklenburg–West Pomerania, Brandenburg, Saxony–Anhalt, Saxony, Thuringia, and a reunited Berlin as a city state, thus making 16 Landers in the reunited Germany. The difficulties of transition to a market economy has, however, resulted in a high loss of jobs. By 1992 more than half of all jobs in manufacturing and two-thirds of those in agriculture had been lost.[6] That is, 37 per cent of the east German workforce were out of work, although short-time working, early retirement, training programmes and commuting to the west were used to cushion the effect of job destruction. Living conditions are widely determined by social security benefits, with up to two-thirds of households depending completely or mainly on them (Clasen 1994). This means that the new Lander working population contribute a low proportion of tax revenues and social insurance contributions. Transfers from the west to the east are therefore still high.

In west Germany in the 1980s the loss of manufacturing jobs was not as sharp as in Britain: manufacturing jobs declined by 7 per cent between 1980 and 1990 in Germany, compared with 25 per cent in the UK during the same period (OECD 1991). West Germany prior to unification had the fourth highest GDP per head in the world compared with Britain's eighteenth place (OECD

1991). However, during the early 1990s recession, industry shed an unprecedented number of jobs and unemployment reached record heights for the post-war period. As we discuss in Chapter 2, although there has been economic growth since 1994, unemployment is still continuing to increase: by August 1997 it was 4.39 million nation-wide with 18.2 per cent in the east and 9.8 per cent in the west. High labour costs and high social expenditure in conjunction with global competition and the recession of the early 1990s stimulated renewed debate on Germany's future competitiveness, especially in relation to Japan and the USA – the *Standort Deutschland* (Location – Germany) debate (see also Chapter 4). International competition, the costs of sustaining growth in the east and the difficulties of meeting the European monetary convergence criteria have contributed to a continual questioning of the traditional form of German corporate governance discussed earlier.

One profound shift has been the emergence of 'Anglo-Saxon' financial investment strategies as German companies have opened up to foreign investment banks with an increase in mergers and take-overs. The long-term perspective and societal responsibilities of German companies are being replaced by the concept of shareholder value. As a result workforces are reduced in order to raise stockmarket quotations (Flecker and Schulten 1997).

Spain

Initially the shift to neo-liberalism in Spain took place under the administrations of the socialist government, in power for four terms of office between 1982 and 1996. The socialist PSOE party came to power in 1982 in inauspicious circumstances, with inexperienced leaders, an economic crisis, a fragile and unconsolidated democracy and a perceived need to modernize Spanish capitalism (Share 1989). It was the latter which was to dominate as the socialist government sought to liberalize, privatize and deregulate the economy and integrate into Europe, rather than promote social democratic policies of redistribution and social justice. The neo-liberal policies increasingly alienated the trade unions and especially the UGT, which had close historical and associational ties with the PSOE party. The unions have been said to be the main oppositional force against the government during the late

1980s (Gillespie 1990) and several general strikes have been concerned with the lack of unemployment cover, the level of pensions and youth employment plans. Some writers consider that the basic purpose of the Socialist's neo-liberal policies has been to shift the balance of power decisively from labour to capital in the post-Franco period (for example, Petras 1993). The breakdown of neo-corporatist arrangements (established in the earlier period 1977–86) has also been seen as a process of labour exclusion from policy reforms (Martinez Lucio and Blyton 1995). However, as we discuss in Chapter 2, more recently there have been central agreements between the employers' association and the trade unions with respect to industrial relations and labour market reform.

Since the end of the recession in 1993 the Spanish economy has been growing. By mid-1997 Spain had become one of the fastest-growing countries of the European Union, with a predicted growth rate in 1997 of above 3 per cent and the achievement of the economic criteria for joining the single European currency in 1999. Nevertheless, unemployment in Spain has been the highest in any OECD country throughout the 1980s and 1990s and still presents a grave economic problem for the country. In 1994 unemployment reached over 25 per cent of the working population, and was still 20.9 per cent in the second quarter of 1997. A growth in employment but a large increase in labour market participation, especially among women (see Chapters 2 and 3) has meant that unemployment of over 2 million people has persisted.

A further problem is the emergence of a polarized and segmented society. In the 1970s and 1980s Spain experienced a 'tertiarization of society': a rapid expansion of the service sector which is now the main source of employment especially for women. For some writers, this means that Spanish society exhibits the characteristics of a post-industrial society with the new elites and the new middle classes based in the high technology, high service or financial institutions (Kurth 1993).[7] Many people are, however, still employed in the low technology or putting-out sectors of the economy, or in the low service or tourist sectors. Whilst these sectors have always been present in Spain and other southern European countries' economies, they expanded in the 1980s. Finally, Spain exhibits an extreme form of fragmentation of the labour market. Economic restructuring and labour market reforms have produced divisions between those who are employed compared to those unemployed, those in secure work compared to those in temporary and insecure work, and those in legal work compared to those working illegally or in the submerged economy (Miguélez Lobo 1990; see also the discussions in Chapters 2 and 3).

Sweden

In Sweden the policies of the Social Democratic government from 1982 were proposed in the light of a 'third way' to take Sweden out of economic difficulties without giving up full employment and a universal welfare state. They were seen as an alternative to the neo-liberalism of Thatcher and Reagan on the one hand, and traditional Keynesian policies on the other. The aim was to reverse the trend of industrial decline by increasing net exports, profitability and investments. Complementing these aims were two other policies, a direct labour market policy and an 'implicit incomes policy' to ensure moderate wage increases. These initiatives were successful in the short-term. Devaluations of the Kroner in 1981 and 1982 led an export recovery until the end of the 1980s. By then a labour shortage had emerged and inflation increased. However, by 1990 Sweden had one of the lowest unemployment levels in Europe at 1.5 per cent.

By the end of the 1980s deeper structural problems in the Swedish economy remained: low rates of productivity growth (at an average annual increase of 1 per cent), and of economic growth (at less than 2 per cent average annual GDP growth) (Ryner 1994).[8] In 1990, facing an inflation rate of almost 10 per cent, a financial crisis and a wave of strikes, the government introduced a wage, price and dividend freeze and temporarily suspended the right to strike. The wage freeze and suspension of the right to strike violated a fundamental principle for those on the political left, and those on the political right reacted against the dividend freeze. 'In a unique moment of unity, Conservatives, Liberals, the Centre Party, Greens and Communists defeated the bill and forced the government to resign' (Ryner 1994:405). The Social Democratic Party was later reappointed and together with the Liberals implemented an austerity package. In September

1991 the social democrats met electoral defeat and a conservative coalition came to power between 1991 and 1994, instituting for the first time a shift to neo-liberalism, although – as we describe in the following chapters – of a far more moderate version than in Britain.

The leading actors in this shift have been Swedish business leaders. Swedish multinational companies have become increasingly international in orientation so that now the majority of production and their workforces operate outside Sweden. As Stephens (1996) has remarked, Swedish businesses have become markedly less interested in a compromise with domestic labour. In the 1980s there was erosion of centralized collective bargaining, termination in 1990, and then in 1991 a withdrawal of the employers' association representatives from all state bodies. Employers wished to prioritize wage flexibility and opposed centralized bargaining and wage solidarity. Stephens (1996) also suggests that a further reason was a desire to see the weakening of the LO, the blue-collar trade union confederation.

The contraction in the Swedish economy between 1990 and 1993 was worse than any OECD country except Finland. The depth and duration of the recession and the extent of unemployment has been likened to that of the 1930s and was certainly the worst since that period.[9] Three sectors were particular effected: manufacturing, construction and retail. Manufacturing and mining were the hardest hit, losing 226 000 jobs between 1990 and 1993 (OECD 1994b). By the mid-1990s, though, public sector jobs were also being lost as public expenditure retrenchment and the privatization of welfare services had their effect. Although the economy began to recover in 1994 unemployment is, as in Germany, continuing to increase. In May 1997 unemployment on the OECD's standardized rate was 10.9 per cent, while the employment rate fell from 84 per cent in 1990 to 73 per cent in 1996 (*Financial Times*, 12 September 1997).

The UK

In the UK the period 1979 to 1990 is seen by many writers as a profound social, political, cultural and economic break with the discourses and practices of the post-war settlement. For some this is a period in which the structures of the state have been fundamentally transformed and, with Thatcherism as a hegemonic project, a vision of new political and social order pursued (for example, Gamble 1994, Hay 1996). The impact of neo-liberal ideologies which have underpinned conservative governments' policies since 1979 are discussed in the following chapters of this book. Here we can note that neo-liberal ideologies have influenced the ending of any commitment to full employment and Keynesian demand management, and an erosion of the role of intermediary institutions in policy making, for example, the professions, trade unions, local government, the NHS, and trade associations. Of particular importance has been the decline of trade unions in policy making, a gradual abolition of all tripartite mechanisms for addressing economic questions, and a dismantling of the institutions of collective bargaining above the level of the company (see, for example, Marsh and Rhodes 1992, Harris 1990, Crouch 1995).

In addition, strategies have included 'authoritarian populism', initial attempts at monetarism, a 'two nation' project, Britain as a principle site for international (mainly foreign) financial institutions, flexible labour markets, social security reforms towards discretionary, means-tested and minimalist benefits and a reorganization of the state system (see Gamble 1994, Jessop *et al.* 1988, Jessop 1991a, 1991b). As Jessop notes, though, these strategies have evolved on a trial-and-error basis with varying degrees of success (see also Marsh and Rhodes 1992). Additionally, policies have been complex and often contradictory, for example sections of the public sector have been deregulated or privatized only to be replaced by new regulatory bodies. Policies have also had unintended consequences, for example, the increase in unemployment has led to large increases in social security payments. Furthermore, as Gamble (1994) has argued in his study of the Thatcher administrations, strong state centralism is required in order to implement a neo-liberal project. The internal structures of the central state have therefore shifted in 'sometimes reactive, sometimes strategic, but generally uncoordinated and constitutionally unreflective movements' towards 'undemocratic centralism' (Jessop 1991a:150).

In conjunction with these policy shifts, there have been profound structural changes in the economy and in the composition of employment. Britain has shown the sharpest decline in manufacturing jobs of the advanced nations, declining by 25 per cent between 1980 and 1990 (Nolan and Walsh 1995). Manufacturing job loss was particularly steep during the first part of the 1980s, with a loss of two million jobs. Trade union membership has also shown 'the longest continuous decline on record', falling from a density of 53.4 per cent in 1979 to 31 per cent in 1993 (43 per cent) (Waddington and Whitson 1995).[10] There are large differences between public and private sectors, though, with 62 per cent union density in the public sector compared with 23 per cent in the private sector (EIRR 261 1995).

Many see advantages in the direction taken by the UK in the past 18 years and claim that the UK has gained competitive advantage with its higher levels of labour-market flexibility, and lower wage and non-wage costs. Others, however, point to the social costs which have been generated. One particularly damaging consequence has been a social polarization of the population, with an increase in income inequality and poverty which, as we discuss in Chapter 6, has been unique in its pace and extent in Europe. As we also discuss in later chapters, in the mid-1990s there has been falling unemployment but the problem of long-term unemployment persists, with an unequal distribution of jobs among households. Lack of public investment in the social infrastructure, lower levels of educational attainment, and community disintegration have also been associated with neo-liberal policies and structural change in Britain.

Conclusion

It is useful to summarize developments in European countries in the first three decades after the Second World War with reference to the forms of neo-corporatist arrangements which emerged in each country. All of the countries discussed in this chapter pursued forms of neo-corporatism although, as we have seen, with significant variations. In west Germany neo-corporatist arrangements were not in place until the late 1960s, and although these arrangement have been eroded to some extent in the 1980s and 1990s the high degree of formalization and legal regulation of industrial relations, as well as the post-war tradition in which employers and unions negotiate independently from state intervention, has probably ensured a greater continuity of consensus among the social partners. Sweden in the mid-twentieth century was characterized by strong neo-corporatist arrangements which were supported by a social democratic hegemony and a strong and centralized trade union movement, although as we have seen this model has been considerably eroded in the past decade. In Britain from the mid-1960s there was nothing comparable to the tripartite bargaining structures of Sweden or the concertation strategy of Germany. The high point of neo-corporatism came in the mid-1970s under a Labour government but this was undermined by weak and fragmented trade unions and employers' peak associations, a more adversarial industrial relations system and the use of neo-corporatism as a strategy to undermine shop-floor militancy and public-sector unionism, and gain the acquiescence of the unions. Neo-corporatism in Britain also differed from the forms in Germany and Sweden in that such arrangements were used as a last-resort crisis management for the unresolved tensions and problems of the post-war settlement which culminated in the 1970s.

Spain presents a very different picture because of the long duration of Franco's rule. Under Franco a form of state corporatism existed although – as we noted – this was corporatism of exclusion and subordination. Neo-corporatist relations were instituted during and after the transition to democracy with tripartite social pacts becoming important instruments of economic and employment policy-making.

Whatever neo-corporatist arrangements were in place, in each country, at the national level, these have broken down or have been eroded since the late 1970s, although with considerable variations, as we discuss in the following chapters. The reasons are to be found in the structural changes which all the advanced countries have experienced since the mid-1970s and also the particular power relations and political strategies of governments and employers in each country in the 1980s and 1990s. Structural changes include the decline of standardized mass production and manufacturing jobs (see Chapter 4), which means that unions are less representative of labour as a whole, and their bargaining power – which depended on a cohesive workforce – is weakened. At the same time, as we discussed in the Introduction, internalization, decentralization and increased sub-contracting of firms mean that the interests of business are more difficult to represent through national business associations. National states too have less capacity to determine economic policies and conditions. Neo-liberal policies also envisage a reduced role for interest organizations as these are regarded as impeding the operation of free markets. Nevertheless, as this chapter has demonstrated, there have been considerable variations in the responses of actors in the different countries.

As we discussed in the Introduction, for all European countries the main problems of the 1990s have become low economic growth and high structural unemployment. Indeed the inability of countries to create new jobs has been seen by the European Commission as the most fundamental challenge facing member states (*Employment in Europe* 1996). In this respect too, however, there has been considerable diversity in responses to unemployment, ranging from neo-liberal strategies (the UK) to active labour market policies (Sweden), and early retirement and a reduction in the working week (Germany). This is clearly seen in the next chapter as we discuss differences in the nature of labour market reforms in selected European countries in the context of the shift to neo-liberalism.

Further reading

For a detailed account of the Germany economy and unification with the east, see Owen Smith 1994. Smith *et al.* 1996 provide an analysis of recent developments in German politics and society. On the institutional structures of west Germany excellent accounts are presented in Streeck 1992 and Lane 1989a and 1995. For social policy developments, see Clasen and Freeman 1994, and Esping-Andersen 1990 and 1996a.

Excellent accounts of the political economy of southern European countries are provided by Giner 1985 and Sapelli 1995. On the Franco regime and the transition to democracy, see Carr and Fusi 1987, and Giner and Sevilla 1984. For recent political developments Heywood 1995 provides a good account, as do Salmon 1991 and Jimeno and Toharia 1994 on the Spanish economy. For a critical analysis of politics since the transition to democracy, see Petras 1993, Pridham 1989 and Share 1989. Cousins 1995, Guillen 1992 and Ayala 1994 present accounts of the development of the Spanish welfare state.

There are many accounts of post-war developments in Sweden, for example, Korpi 1983, Esping Andersen 1985, Fulcher 1987 and 1991, Delsen and van Veen 1992, and Therborn 1991. On developments in

the 1990s, see Stephens 1996 and Pestoff 1993, and on industrial relations Kjellberg 1992. For analysis of the Swedish welfare state, see Esping
Andersen 1990 and 1996a, and Olsson 1990.

Critical analyses of post-war developments in the UK include Cutler
et al. 1986, Jessop 1991a and 1991b, Gamble 1991 and 1994, and Hay
1996. On developments in the 1990s, see Rowntree Foundation 1995a,
Hutton 1996, Barrell 1994, and on industrial relations Edwards 1995.
There is a vast literature on transformations of the welfare state, see
for example, Baldwin and Falkingham 1994 and Hills 1993.

On developments in member states in the 1990s more generally, see
Amin and Tomaney 1995, Rhodes *et al.* 1997, Hyman and Ferner 1994,
Michie and Grieve Smith 1994, and *Employment in Europe* annual.

PART TWO

Changing Patterns of Work and Employment

2

Labour Market Reform and 'Non-Standard' Employment

Policies and legislation which aim to make the labour market more flexible appear to have been pursued to a greater or lesser extent by governments in all European countries from the 1980s onwards. This chapter examines and evaluates the extent and nature of such policies, especially in the four countries of Germany, Spain, Sweden and the UK, and discusses the reasons why labour market reforms have been introduced. The chapter also examines recent trends in flexible employment patterns associated with these policies.

The 'standard employment relationship' is typically characterized as full-time, permanent employment with one employer. Non-standard employment is, therefore, any type of employment which is not full-time or permanent, for example, part-time, temporary, fixed-term contract work or self-employment. Non-standard employment is also often referred to as flexible, or atypical employment. Many labour market reforms have as their aim the promotion of flexible patterns of employment to promote employment growth or a wider distribution of employment. However, as we discuss below, the increase in non-standard employment is often seen as undermining or eroding the principle of standard employment, which in the post-war period has been the basis of entitlement to social security provision in most European countries.

Box 2.1   The regulatory framework of the employment relationship

The regulatory framework includes both rules set by collective bargaining between trade unions and employers, and rules derived from 'law, custom and mutual acceptance which determine the rights and obligations, or rather, powers, of each party' (Rhodes 1989:229).

The regulatory framework differs in each country, reflecting 'divergent state and legal traditions, national character of trade unions and employers' associations and historically determined differences in the balance of industrial power' (Rhodes 1989:229). An important difference between countries is the nature and extent of state intervention in the industrial relations system (see Due *et al.* 1991, Van Ruysseveldt *et al.* 1995). In this respect a contrast is often made between the neo-liberal Anglo-Saxon model and the neo-corporatist 'Rhine' model. In Britain, traditionally, the state has been largely absent from the regulation of industrial relations and labour markets, whilst in Germany collective bargaining and the employment relation are still highly regulated, despite a shift to neo-liberal policies. In addition, other countries such as Spain, Italy, and Greece have in place an even higher degree of employment protection for individual and collective workers. France is also different and is characterized by active and direct state intervention with respect to employment and working conditions (see Box 2.5).

Box 2.2   The employment relationship

The employment relationship here refers to an exchange relationship between employer and employee with asymmetrical power structures. The conditions under which an employer decides to hire labour and under which the employee decides to sell his or her labour to the employer are the result of continuous exchange (individual or collective bargaining). These conditions are related to the different aspects of the deployment of labour, for example wages, working hours, job security and other employment terms (Ruysseveldt *et al.* 1995).

Writers have explained differences in non-standard work in Europe in terms of the nature of the regulatory framework of the employment relation (see Box 2.1 and Box 2.2) in each country, sectoral composition and size of firms, employer policies and competitive strategies, labour market flows, especially between unemployment and employment, tax and social security systems, labour supply characteristics and policies, and provisions for combining paid work and family life (for example, Hakim 1990, Rubery and Fagan 1994, Gregory and O'Reilly 1996). Space prevents an in-depth analysis of all these variables and the main emphasis of this chapter is on the policies and politics associated with the particular regulatory framework of the employment relationship and how these may shape the nature and extent of non-standard work in each country. In Chapter 3, though, labour-supply characteristics are considered, especially those affecting differences in women's labour-market participation. As we shall see, the increase in non-standard employment during the 1980s and 1990s has coincided with the increased participation of women in the labour market in many European countries.

The chapter is divided into five sections. The first considers the period of full employment from the 1950s to early 1970s, a period which had been described as one of 'socially controlled welfare capitalism' by Sengenberger (1984) and others, and a period in which standard employment became the norm. The second section discusses the shift in labour market policies from the mid-1970s to a period of 'free market capitalism' associated with an increase in non-standard employment. Section three examines differences in the nature and extent of non-standard employment in Germany, Spain, Sweden and the UK. Section four considers labour market reforms in the four case-study countries, and there is also reference to France, as a country with different labour-market policies to many other European countries, and to the Netherlands as the country with the highest levels of part-time working in Europe. Finally, section five evaluates the consequences of these reforms for individual workers and households.

1950s to early 1970s

The achievement of full employment in the advanced countries in the 1950s and 1960s was historically unprecedented, at least for such a prolonged period (Bernabe 1988). One consequence was a strengthening of the bargaining power of workers which allowed them to increase their relative share of income and improve the institutional conditions of regulating the labour market, including job security. The political environment was relatively favourable to social reforms as the attainment of full employment coincided in many countries with the coming to power of social democratic parties or coalitions of the left. At first the reforms involved a gradual extension of the welfare state and only later were public policies directed at labour markets and improving the job security of workers. Lane (1989a) following Sengenberger (1984) has referred to this period as one of 'socially controlled welfare capitalism'. 'In this model state intervention serves to curtail the free workings of the market in order to moderate or cancel out its more adverse affects on labour' (Lane 1989a: 586). Lane compares Britain, France and Germany with respect to employment and welfare policies during this period. In all three countries policies on these issues were devised with the interests of labour in mind. Labour attained a higher standard of living and a reduction in individual economic risks. Adequate compensation, in the form of social security provisions, was paid if the capacity to labour was jeopardized. A standard employment relation, a (predominantly male) full-time, permanent, and socially secured relationship, became the norm.

France and Germany developed more extensive legislation with regard to employment protection than Britain. In France, legislation of 1969, 1973, 1974, and 1975 subjected employers to internal and external controls over collective redundancies. In Germany, the 1972 Works Constitution Act required that in cases of dismissal at an establishment of more than 20 employees, management and the works council must negotiate a social plan which stipulates compensation for workers who lose their jobs. In the UK, The Employment Protection Act of 1975 ensured British workers received reasonable compensation for redundancies although these were much easier for the employer to obtain than in either Germany or France. In the UK 'there was still no general statutory regulation of substantive terms and conditions such as minimum wages, holidays or hours of work, but there was a marked increase in the extent to which the law sought to restrict managerial prerogative in handling the employment relationship, particularly in the areas of recruitment (through discrimination law) and dismissal' (Dickens and Hall 1995:266).

During the 1970s, economists began to argue that the greater degree of job and income security was analogous to a new form of economic feudalism, that is there were similarities to the parish and guild support of the middle ages, restricting the free play of labour markets. It was argued that this new job security could have negative consequences for economic growth. The decreasing mobility of the labour force caused by higher job security might hamper the process of structural adaptation and slow down productive growth. Job security and protection might also slow down employment growth because employers may be less willing to hire. Welfare benefits were also seen as a disincentive to work, and people who were made redundant had an easy re-entry to work and were less willing to accept conditions less favourable than their last job.

The lack of competition between workers in Europe was held to lead to employment 'rigidities' or 'Eurosclerosis'. The increasingly high levels of unemployment in Europe and the slow employment growth was contrasted with that in the USA where, between 1973 and 1986, employment grew by 28 per cent, creating 26 million new jobs. The absence of regulation in the USA with respect to hiring and firing was viewed as the reason for the boom in her employment growth (Nielsen 1991). Europe suffered a net loss of 3 million jobs between the mid-1970s and the mid-1980s. The version of 'Eurosclerosis' put forward was that wages were too high and rigid, wage differentials too small, and legally based labour rights, employment protection schemes and social security programmes had been taken too far (Nielsen 1991). The OECD was particularly active amongst those who propagated this view. (OECD 1986; see also the more recent OECD *Jobs Study* 1994c – especially for the view that economies with less flexible labour markets and greater wage rigidities are more likely to experience greater persistence in both unemployment and inflation. Proposals also include increased wage flexibility and a tightening up of benefit administrations.)

Mid-1970s to the present

From the mid-1970s, a new model of 'free market capitalism' (Lane 1989a) advocating managerial freedom in the use of capital and labour came to the fore. This was accompanied and, indeed, facilitated by the deepening of economic recession and increasing unemployment. Policy makers in Europe sought to promote industrial competitiveness in more efficient labour markets through the removal of 'rigidities', including reducing job security, weakening the social institutions surrounding the labour market and encouraging greater variety in working hours, contracts and pay.

As mentioned earlier, most European countries have pursued policies to promote more flexible labour markets from the mid-1980s. One such strategy is based on a theory of labour market reform known as 'dualism', put forward by Emerson (1988) as a response to high unemployment in Europe in the 1980s. That is, while leaving intact the job protection rights of existing job holders, the rules protecting jobs for newly hired employees are relaxed. Such a policy would promote the core–periphery model of the flexible firm identified by Atkinson (1985). In the UK this strategy, together with a more ambitious neo-liberal solution of labour market deregulation, has been pursued by Conservative governments since 1979. As we discuss below, however, in most countries in Europe the promotion of flexible work has led to more detailed regulation of such work, rather than, as in the UK, an absence of labour law (although this too is likely to change once the new Labour government signs the Social Chapter of the Maastricht Treaty).

Below we examine the nature and extent of non-standard work in our four case-study countries and then consider experiments with policies and legislation which aim to make the labour market more flexible in different European countries. However, the character of the policies has been shaped by the nature of the regulatory framework existing in each country (see Box 2.1) and in particular by the respective employment protection systems and dismissal norms in each country.

The nature and extent of non-standard employment in Germany, Spain, Sweden and the UK

As Box 2.3 shows, the trend towards flexible and non-standard forms of employment is clearly accelerating in the context of high and long-term unemployment in Europe although there are still large differences in the nature and type of non-standard employment in the member states. Table 2.1 shows the proportions in part-time, fixed-term and self-employment in 1995, and trends in these forms of employment since 1985 in selected European countries.

Box 2.3 Trends in non-standard work[1] in Europe in the 1990s

Between 1991 and 1994 numbers in employment in the EU declined by 1.5 per cent a year, and two thirds of those affected were men (this section draws on *Employment in Europe* 1996). Virtually all of the decline occurred in full-time employment and most of the additional jobs created were part-time. The year 1995 was the first year since 1991 with an increase in employment of 0.8 per cent. In Germany, Italy and Portugal, though, employment continued to decline. With the increase in employment, however, there has been a continuation of the fall in participation rates established in the early 1990s. Two-thirds of new jobs created in 1995 were taken by those previously unemployed rather than those previously inactive, reversing the trend in the 1980s. However, the trend for new jobs to be taken by women continues, with women account-ing for 62 per cent of the rise in the number employed. In Germany and Austria, however, women accounted for all the employment growth.

Of all the new jobs in 1995, 71 per cent of additional jobs for men were part-time and 85 per cent of women's new jobs were part-time. In Germany the entire increase in employ-ment was part-time for men and women, in the UK a half of men's increase and a third of women's increased jobs were part-time. In Spain about half of women's increased jobs were part-time. A high proportion of jobs created in 1995 were also temporary rather than permanent (in the period 1991–4 virtually all the increase in men's work had been temporary across the member states, except for Greece). In the UK more than half the increase in men's jobs was temporary and in Spain virtually all the increase in employment was temporary. The pattern was similar for women. Of concern was that the growth in temporary work and part-time work was occurring amongst those of prime working age. Self-employment was also an important source of employment growth for men in Germany and the UK, and for women in Germany, Spain and France.

Table 2.1　Trends in non-standard employment in selected European countries, 1985–95

	Part-time		Fixed-term contracts		Self-employment	
	1985	**1995**	**1985**	**1995**	**1985**	**1995**
	% employees		**% employees**		**% employed**	
France						
female	21.8	28.9	4.6	13.4	6.4	6.9
male	3.2	5.1	4.8	11.4	17.1	15.3
Germany						
female	29.6	33.8	11.1	11.1	5.4	5.8
male	2.0	3.6	9.2	9.9	11.7	11.9
Italy						
female	10.1	12.7	7.0	9.1	15.8	16.6
male	3.0	2.9	3.6	6.0	28.0	28.9
Netherlands						
female	51.6	67.2	10.8	14.9	4.3	8.6
male	7.7	16.8	5.9	8.9	11.6	13.3
Spain						
female	13.9	16.6	18.4	38.3	19.4	17.0
male	2.4	2.7	14.4	33.2	25.2	24.2
Sweden	[1987]					
female	46.0	43.0	14.2	14.4	4.8	5.9
male	6.9	10.3	9.6	10.5	13.1	16.3
UK						
female	44.8	44.3	8.8	7.8	6.9	7.0
male	4.4	7.7	5.7	6.2	14.7	17.8
EU 15 average						
female	27.3	31.3	9.7	12.5	9.6	9.4
male	3.4	5.2	7.6	10.7	19.1	18.8

Source: Eurostat 1996.

Note: Statistics for Germany before 1991 refer to west Germany and after 1991 include the New Lander.

Germany

In Germany part-timers account for 33.8 per cent of the labour force, but 87.4 per cent of part-timers are women and the vast majority married women (71 per cent in 1995). The pattern of women's participation in the labour market in Germany resembles that of Britain, that is there is a tendency for women to leave the labour force on the birth of a child and women start to work part-time when they then return to work (see Chapters 3 and 5 for discussion of the reasons). In contrast to mothers in the west, in the New Lander only a quarter of employed mothers with a child under 10 work part-time compared to nearly two thirds in the west (Moss 1996). As we discuss in Chapter 3, although women have suffered major job losses since unification and have had to accept west German social policies, there are continuing differences in the labour market position of the women in the two Germanies.

However, some observers consider that part-time female workers in Germany have benefited from the high degree of labour market regulation and 'the tradition of basing pay upon skills, qualifications and job content' (Rubery 1992:617; also Lane 1993). Those working under 18 hours per week, however, are excluded from unemployment insurance and those working under 15 hours per week from sickness and pensions insurance. This group of 'marginal' workers comprises just under half of part-time workers (Marullo 1995).

Evidence from Germany with respect to fixed-term contracts appears inconclusive. Table 2.1 shows a remarkable stability since 1985, at just under 10 per cent of the workforce (including the New Lander). Some studies though report a slow-down in fixed-term hirings following the 1985 Act, especially in sectors dominated by collective bargaining (Kraft 1993). Other studies have shown an increase in the hirings of young employees and blue collar workers in fixed-term employment, earning 10 per cent less than permanent workers (Rogowski and Schomann 1996). Meulders *et al.* (1994) report that fixed-term contracts have become especially important in the civil service, professions and universities, especially for those starting their careers, and for women returning to the labour force. 70 per cent of men and 74 per cent of women moving to a job from education or training moved to a fixed-term contract (*Employment in Europe* 1995).

Spain

In Spain fixed-term contract work now affects more than a third of the workforce, particularly women and young people, and virtually all new entrants to the job market. For example, in 1996 only 4 per cent of new contracts were permanent (IDS 1997). Fixed-term contract work is much more prevalent in the private sector.[2] Married women's increased participation in the labour market in the late 1980s coincided with the widespread use of fixed-term contracts and the restructuring of work. Such high levels of temporary work have led to concerns about the training and pay implications of the new employment. Employers may ignore the training and skill requirements and use the new work as a means of lowering wages (Perez Amoros and Rojo 1991). Although Spanish legislation prohibits different wage rates for permanent and fixed-term contracts, in practice Jimeno and Toharia (1994) report that fixed-term workers receive 8–11 per cent less than permanent workers.

Part-time work in Spain has been low in comparison to levels in northern Europe for reasons which we discuss below. However, in 1994 legislation was introduced to remove the legal impediments to part-time employment and such employment has increased from 11.2 per cent of female employment in 1991 to 16.6 per cent in 1995 (Table 2.1), about 60 per cent of which are fixed-term contracts (Eurostat 1996, Milner *et al.* 1995).

A further segmentation of the labour market in Spain is the submerged or informal economy. Estimates of the submerged economy ranged from 22 to 30 per cent of total employment in 1986 (Perez-Diaz and Rodriguez 1995, Cousins 1994a). In this sector there is low pay, no social security contributions and no protection from dismissal. There are, though, strong incentives for both employers and employees to continue the high levels of informal working. Since married women have access to health insurance through their husbands they have less incentive to seek jobs in which social security taxes are paid. On the demand side, social security contributions for employers are high – almost 30 per cent of wage costs – and firms which utilize married women workers prefer to go underground and face the risk of being detected and penalized rather than pay the high taxes. The Spanish labour market is therefore highly segmented into at least four different labour markets: the protected core labour market, temporary fixed-term workers, workers in the submerged economy and those who are unemployed, which in 1995 represented 22.9 per cent of the workforce (Table 2.3 below) (see also Perez-Diaz and Rodriguez 1995).

Sweden

In Sweden in 1995 43 per cent of women worked part-time, with most working three-quarters time and, evidence suggests, in less precarious jobs than many other countries, with part-timers having high levels of unionization (80 per cent), job continuity (83 per cent), and working more than 20 hours per week (Nätti 1995). In this respect women's part-time work is different from part-time work in the EU12 countries, although similar to that in Norway. Temporary fixed-term contracts, three-fifths of which are held also by women, have increased in the 1990s due to changes in legislation and the recession (see below).[3] Mahon (1996) reports however that most of the temporary jobs have employment protection and remain unionized. There has also been an increase in self-employment as employment programmes and small business start-ups have been emphasized. For men self-employment increased from 13.1 per cent in 1987 to 16.3 per cent in 1995 (see Table 2.1).

The UK

In the UK the trend towards a flexible workforce, especially part-time work, began before the deregulation policies of the Conservative government. Part-time work began increasing from the 1940s and 1950s and accelerated from the 1970s. The UK (together with the Netherlands, see Box 2.4) has the highest maternal part-time working in the EU (two-thirds of mothers with dependent children work part-time in both countries) but also the lowest average hours of work – 16.5 hours per week compared to an average 19.2 for the EU (Moss 1996). The use of a threshold for National Insurance contributions is also linked with the high incidence of part-time work in the UK. In 1993 about half of all female part-time employees earned less than the lower earning limit for National Insurance (Marullo 1995).

However, the increased participation of women in the labour market in the past decade (especially those with dependent children under five since 1990) has been associated with an equal increase of women in both full-time and part-time work (10 per cent in each case) (Sly 1996). Women's part-time work appears to have stabilized during the 1990s (see Table 2.1). The UK Labour

Box 2.4   The regulatory framework and part-time work in the Netherlands

As Table 2.1 shows, the Netherlands has the highest extent of part-time working for both men and women in Europe. Part-time employment there has also shown the highest growth rates since the 1980s of any of the member states. However, part-time work is more highly regulated than in the UK, with part-timers having the same rights as full-timers with respect to basic pay and dismissal protection. There is also a general acceptance that part-timers have the same pro rata rights to bonuses, seniority increments, holidays, holiday pay and social security benefits. However, pay equality is still an issue and many part-time female workers are not covered by a company or occupational pension scheme (Marullo 1995).

The government, employers and the trade unions are reported to favour the increased use of part-time work in order to create employment and meet changing production needs (Marullo 1995). O'Reilly (1996) also partly attributes the spectacular rise of part-time work to a policy which allows for early retirement where employers agree to take on younger workers for 32 hours a week, which counts as part-time.

As we discuss in the next chapter, labour-supply characteristics may also be important in influencing high levels of part-time work, especially for mothers. In particular tax and social security provisions, child-care facilities and a tradition of a strong male-breadwinner family model (see Chapter 5) in which women were encouraged to stay at home to look after their children have influenced women's labour market participation. There are similarities with part-time women workers in the UK. Nevertheless, as O'Reilly (1996) notes, although both countries have high levels of part-time work, part-timers in the Netherlands have better terms and conditions of employment than part-timers in Britain. As she says, this finding suggests that the regulation of part-time work does not necessarily imply a reduction in the quantity of part-time work but can seriously affect the quality of part-time jobs (O'Reilly 1996:587).

Force Survey reports a 3 per cent increase between 1990 and 1995 compared with a 29 per cent increase in the period 1979–90 (Sly 1996). Dex and McCulloch (1995) also report that employers are now seeking increased flexibility from employees, which part-time women workers with children are not in a position to offer. Men's part-time employment though has increased from 3 per cent to 6 per cent between 1985 and 1995 (Sly 1996). Men and women's self-employment and temporary working[4] have also increased between 1990 and 1995. Although from a low base, men's temporary work increased by 71 per cent and women's by 21 per cent (Sly 1996). Overall, Dex and McCulloch (1995) found that a quarter of men and one half of women were in any type of non-standard work in 1994. However, if flows into the labour market are taken into account then two-thirds of all newly filled posts were part-time or temporary in 1993 (Gregg and Wadsworth 1995).

The reasons for the high level of part-time work in the UK have been linked to cost advantages to employers, especially if workers earn less than the threshold for national insurance contributions, lack of employment protection, numerical flexibility, uneven patterns of demand, tasks that require a limited number of hours to complete, and developments in technology (Rubery and Tarling 1988). The increase in self-employment in the UK, which has been higher than most EU countries (see Table 2.1), has been linked to sectoral changes, technological advances, fragmentation of large firms, the economic cycle, demographic changes, start-up capital increases and government policies to promote self employment (Dex and McCulloch 1995).

Labour market reforms

Germany

In west Germany legislation and the legal enforcement of sectoral collective bargaining have traditionally played an important role in shaping the employment relationship. In contrast to France and the UK (see Box 2.5 and below), the employers and trade unions are given more leeway to regulate through collective bargaining employment conditions such as working hours, holidays and dismissal protection. However, throughout the 1980s and 1990s, governments and employers have argued for greater flexibility in the labour market and a reduction in the social costs associated with labour. An important difference between the UK and Germany is that the collective rights of employees have been less limited in Germany than in the UK, although there have been some legislative attempts in Germany to weaken the collective rights of employees to representation at plant level and in the case of strikes and lock-outs (Deakin and Mückenberger 1992).

Box 2.5   The regulatory framework in France

The French regulatory framework has been described as a statist model, that is there is active and direct state intervention with respect to the terms of employment and working conditions. Many terms of employment which elsewhere are the subject of collective bargaining are provided for by law, for example, minimum wages, the length of the working week, holiday periods and social security provisions. In addition the terms of employment regulation agreed by the unions and employers' associations are also influenced by government. In contrast to the UK, French law specifies what provisions a collective bargaining agreement must contain. Although trade union density is low, 10 per cent or less, collective bargaining agreements can be declared generally binding by the government to a whole industry or region.

From the mid-1980s, with growing unemployment and increased international competition, several pieces of legislation have sought to encourage part-time work, fixed-term contracts and greater flexibility in the use of working time. A five-year plan introduced in 1993 provides a new legal framework which enables companies to introduce greater working-time flexibility and extends subsidies for part-time work and job creation.

However, part-timers and workers on fixed-term contracts have the same rights pro rata as full-time and permanent workers. Employers are also obliged to inform works councils over the use of any non-standard contracts, part-time or fixed-term. Employers have, therefore, less incentive to create atypical jobs, which are cheaper and involve less protection than they do in Britain. Female workers are less likely to work part-time than in Britain, Germany or Sweden (see Table 2.1). In part this also reflects the labour-supply characteristics of women in France, that is, far more mothers with young children are able to work full-time than in either Germany or the UK. The factors affecting differing patterns of women's labour-market participation are discussed in Chapter 3.

The main piece of legislation was the Employment Promotion Act 1985,[5] now extended twice to the year 2000, which has enabled employers to relax the rules governing fixed-term contract work and more easily employ part-time workers, and has exempted firms of five or less workers from protection against dismissal. The 1985 law lengthened the duration of fixed-term contracts from six months to 18 and to 24 months for new small businesses. Prior to the 1985 Act fixed-term contracts were strictly regulated so that employers had to show good reason for so hiring employees. Since the Act employers do not have to give a reason for hiring an employee on a fixed-term contract. The Act also required that part-time work should have the same rights as full-time work.

Rogowski and Schomann (1996:635) have remarked that 'Labour law in Germany is still dominated by the view that the use of atypical employment contracts must be the exception and permanent contracts the norm'. As the authors note, the deregulation approach, therefore, leads to tensions in the traditional doctrinal view of labour law in Germany. Streeck (1992) has also remarked that 'Regulation of economic activities by law and otherwise is dense and deregulation even after a decade of conservative government is not much of an issue' (1992:51).

Nevertheless, debate on Germany's competitiveness now dominates public discussion, intensified by the reunification process. Policies oriented to more liberal market measures have been proposed several times during the 1990s. In early 1996, for example, tripartite talks between the government, employers and trade unions agreed a 50-point Action Programme to revive the economy and reduce unemployment. The plan involves reductions in public expenditure and social security contributions and a reduction of job protection in small firms. The latter proposal raises from 5 to 10 the number of workers a company may employ before rules protecting against dismissal take effect. The agreement broke down in April 1996 as the trade unions were unable to accept the plans on job protection and reductions in sick pay. The government has decided to push ahead with the reforms although the process of coalition politics, lobbying and the checks and balances of the upper and lower houses of parliament may mitigate neo-liberal solutions.

Spain

In Spain, during the Franco regime, in the context of a ban on trade unions, political parties and strikes, employment security was granted to workers by Franco to provide a modicum of political legitimacy for the regime. This protected core of the labour market still exists and contains about two-thirds of employees but only 37 per cent of total workforce (see Table 2.2). Here the rigid rules for exit and entry to the labour market have been applied for about five decades without interruption, so that employment in Spain is still highly regulated. Temporary agencies were not permitted until the December 1993 labour market reform Act, temporary, fixed-term and part-time work is regulated, and Spain is today, apart from Greece and the Netherlands, the only EC country which requires administrative authority for terminating the employment contract (or its suspension or change in hours in work) (Perez Amoros and Rojo 1991). Dismissal costs are high in comparison with other countries and compensation, depending on the size of the firm, is equivalent to 20 to 45 days' pay for each year of service. Given the low turnover of permanent staff compensation may represent up to 2 years salary.

Since 1977 employers have pressed for reforms in industrial relations which would enable them to hire and fire freely and to utilize new forms of fixed-term contracts and, more recently, part-time work. Joining the European Community in 1986 and especially the advent of the Single Market in 1992 has produced a shift in the economy from a highly protected national economy to one exposed to competition from other European countries, and industrial and agricultural producers in other parts of the industrialized and newly industrializing countries. Whilst firms

Table 2.2 Employment status of the economically active in Spain, 1995

1995	All %	Male %	Female %
Permanent core employees	37.0	40.1	32.8
Fixed-term contracts	20.0	19.9	20.0
Unemployed	22.9	18.2	30.6
Employer	3.7	5.0	1.7
Independent workers	12.2	13.9	9.6
Members of coops	0.7	0.9	0.5
Family helps	2.8	1.9	4.6
Other	0.2	0.2	0.2
Total	100	100	100

Source: *Boletin Mensual de Estadistica* 1996.

competed in the past on the basis of low wages and protective tariffs, in the 1990s this is no longer possible, especially as the wages of core workers have risen faster than inflation (one of the contradictory consequences of labour market reform, as we discuss below). Employers' calls for greater flexibility in labour markets and work organization have therefore accelerated.

The politics of labour market reform has, though, been complex, piecemeal and contradictory, as Martinez Lucio and Blyton (1995) have documented. The main orientation has been on issues of labour dismissal and its costs. The trade unions have been seen as acting defensively in seeking to protect the privileged labour market position of core workers and thereby excluding other types of workers from access to the labour market. But according to Martinez Lucio and Blyton the politics are more complex. What are now considered to be 'rigidities' in the labour market were once functional both to the dictatorship and the political transition in guaranteeing an element of labour acquiescence and stability. Unions have been concerned to protect the position of core workers in the context of limited unemployment coverage and exposure to a large submerged economy. One could add that the trade unions' concerns must also be guided by the need for families to survive in high unemployment through the employment of at least one key worker in the core labour market (see below). In the view of Martinez Lucio and Blyton the breakdown of neo-corporatist agreements since the mid-1980s has resulted in labour exclusion from state strategies of labour reform and a redefining and weakening of worker rights through temporary fixed-term contracts. Since mid-1996, however, unions have been engaged in a 'social dialogue' with employers' organizations on further labour market reforms.[6]

The main pieces of legislation to promote the use of non-standard forms of employment have been the Workers' Statute Acts of 1980, 1984, and more recently in December 1993. Some writers have argued that, strictly speaking, experiments with atypical work are not deregulation but reflect the existing employment protection system and are an amendment to it, rather than deregulation (Rogowski and Schomann 1996). Nevertheless, labour market reform has seriously eroded the principle of job security. The legislation of 1984 introduced fixed-term contracts which can be renewed for 6-month periods up to a maximum of 3 years. New employees may be contracted for a few months and then work informally before returning to legally contracted work (Miguélez Lobo 1988). Employers, especially in the small firms (firms with less than 50 workers constitute 98 per cent of all businesses), are reluctant to transform temporary contacts into permanent ones. 'They prefer to lose trained workers rather than risk one day paying the high redundancy payments' (OECD 1991/ 2a:68). The use of fixed-term contracts has grown rapidly and now constitutes more than a third of employees (see Tables 2.1 and 2.2).

The low level of part-time working in Spain appears to be due to the lack of tradition for such work. This can be traced back to restrictions placed on such contracts prior to the Workers Charter 1976, in which the worker and employer were required to pay social security contributions as if the job were full-time (Perez Amoros and Rojo 1991). The labour laws of 1980 and 1984 called for the principle of equality and proportionality between full-time and part-time work in rights conferred by the social security system and the existence of a written *contrato de trabajo a tiempo parcial* (Kravaritou-Manitakis 1988). However, in 1994 legislation was introduced to remove the legal impediments to part-time-employment, and such employment has increased for women from 11.2 per cent in 1991 to 16.6 per cent in 1995. The rights of some part-timers were reduced by the legislation. If the working time is less than 12 hours per week, the worker has no right to unemployment benefit or transitory illness payments (Milner *et al.* 1995).

Sweden

In Sweden labour radicalization in the late 1960s led to an extensive programme of labour legislation in the 1970s, to the extent that, in Kjellberg's (1992) opinion, the model of industrial relations changed from one of self-regulation to state intervention. Included in this legalization was the Protection of Employment Act of 1974, union workplace representation in 1974, codetermination in 1976, day care for children and parental leave provisions. These reforms took place in the context of the well-known features of the Swedish model, the pursuit of full employment, centralized wage bargaining and solidaristic wages policies (see Chapter 1). The result has been that as women's participation in paid work, and especially part-time work, increased from the 1970s they have been provided with a level of employment protection not available in a country such as Britain. Mahon (1996) has explained that because these jobs were not precarious the unions did not have to deal with the issue of the character of atypical work.

From the 1970s the women's movement, especially the SDP section, has campaigned for a reduction in the working day from eight hours to six hours. 'The demand for worktime reduction was particularly important if women's work was not to be defined as "atypical"' (Mahon 1996:571). However, this was continuously resisted by the blue-collar trade union confederation (LO) and the social democratic and bourgeois governments of the late 1970s. The compromise was an extension of parental leave in 1978 so that parents of young children could reduce their working day to six hours without compensation for the loss of pay. Since it has been mothers who reduce their working day, the male pattern remains that of continuous and full working time. The compromise has, therefore, been a one and three-quarters income for many two-adult households. More recently some unions have called for a reduction in the working day but in the context of high unemployment.

Reforms introduced by the conservative coalition government

of 1991 to 1994 included amendments to the Security of Employment Act 1974, whereby there was a relaxation of hiring and firing rules for employers and a removal of the prohibition on private labour exchanges[7]. Although the social democratic government elected in September 1994 repealed the 'anti-union' changes to labour law introduced by the previous conservative coalition, it has not prohibited temporary help agencies. Although most atypical jobs in Sweden are not precarious, there is no guarantee, as Mahon (1996) argues, that this will continue, especially as job growth is likely to be in the private service sector. The LO is now campaigning for rights for 'atypical' workers in a way that was previously ignored.[8]

The UK

It was noted earlier that traditionally the UK has had less extensive legislation surrounding the employment relationship than most other European countries. During the 1980s and 1990s it has been widely agreed that employment protection has also diminished faster in the UK than other EC countries. However, although there has been a refusal to sign the Social Chapter of the Maastricht Treaty in 1993 and opposition to a range of draft Directives which would have enhanced employment rights of workers in a number of Employment Acts, the UK government has had to increase employment rights in some areas to meet European Directive obligations (for example, the Sex Discrimination Act 1986, Employment Act 1989 and the Trade Union Act and Employment Rights Act 1993) (see Dickens and Hall 1995). More recently (February 1995) regulations have been brought in to give part-time workers the same protection as those working full-time after a House of Lords ruling with respect to European Union equal pay and equal treatment law. Employment protection now covers all employees with two or more years of job tenure, so that the number of hours worked per week is no longer the qualifying condition.

Dickens and Hall (1995) list 15 key Acts between 1979 and 1993 in many of which 'the scope of employment protection rights was narrowed, access to rights was made more difficult and some protections were abolished' (Dickens and Hall 1995:272). Other policies have been directed to making 'discipline to work' more effective through changes to social security and especially un-employment benefits. Notable changes also include the removal of minimum wage levels by the abolition of Wages Councils or by the Fair Wages Clause. For many writers it has been the weakening of the collective institutions of labour, the impact of changes in industrial relations legislation, the reduction in trade union members, and the reduction of those now covered by col-lective agreements which have been the most significant changes (for example, Gregg and Machin 1994, Nolan 1994).

Debate on non-standard work in the UK has focused on the flexible firm thesis, employer's labour strategies and the extent to which increases in non-standard work reflect new departures or are innovative. Studies have refuted the strong version of the flexible firm thesis, that is that employers have systematically organized their workforce in terms of a core and periphery and have argued that traditional rationales for the use of non-standard workers have remained important (for example, Hunter *et al.* 1993, Heather *et al.* 1996). However, if a weaker version of employers' strategy is used not as a 'plan' but as 'patterns' of decision making (Proctor *et al.* 1994), changes in the 1990s, in-cluding restructuring in the public sector, may produce more evidence of changing strategies.

Evaluation

One of the aims of labour market flexibility and policies to en-courage non-standard work has been to promote employment growth or a wider distribution of employment. The debate on deregulation policies and removal of 'rigidities' in European labour markets has not abated after more than a decade. Nevertheless, as O'Reilly (1996) reports, the results of employment creation from increased non-standard work have often been disappoint-ing and in many cases generate undesired consequences, such as the creation of ghettos of disadvantaged forms of employ-ment or, in the case of involuntary non-standard work, double jobbing or moonlighting. Other consequences can also be dis-cerned from our four case-study countries.

The standard employment relationship has been of particular importance in Germany, the model resulting in high levels of wages and employment protection dependent on length of service and continuity. But as Deakin and Mückenberger (1992) argue, the process is inherently selective as it is based on the use of threshold criteria to delimit this protection. The standard employment relationship therefore privileges those workers that pursue a continuous employment. Those workers who lack continuous employment, are unemployed, or fall below the number of hours for employment protection, are therefore denied insurance-related social security and have to fall back on means-tested benefits.

As we have seen, although in Germany the institutional and legal framework for deregulation of labour markets remains very different to that in Britain, and the extent of non-standard employment is not as high mainly because of lower levels of part-time work for women, non-standard employment is on the increase in the context of declining full-time employment for men. The impact of the increase in non-standard employment is, paradoxically, as Deakin and Mückenberger (1992) have argued, to limit the extent of standard employment while heightening its social and economic significance as the privileged form of wage labour. Families' livelihoods are dependent on predominantly male lifetime earnings and access to his social security benefits. Women's opportunities to work are curtailed. Such a strategy produces a society of 'insiders' and 'outsiders' with segmented labour markets.

In Spain too, core workers are also privileged within the labour market, although the core is smaller than in Germany and labour markets more segmented. With high unemployment and high levels of precarious work the family is also the key to the stability of society, with a variety of sources of incomes from different labour markets, pensions or unemployment benefits being pooled (Perez-Diaz and Rodriguez 1995). The ideal is to have one key worker located within the core labour market. Families are then dependent on the main wage earner not only for earnings but also social security benefits. Gregg and Wadsworth (1997) also note that employment in Spain is concentrated on those with dependent families, normally men aged between 20 and 40. This is shown clearly in Figure 2.1, where Spanish heads of households are the least likely to be long-term unemployed of any of our four countries (Greece, Italy and Portugal show a similar picture to Spain.). Whilst this eases the burden of unemployment for members of the family the result is that young people

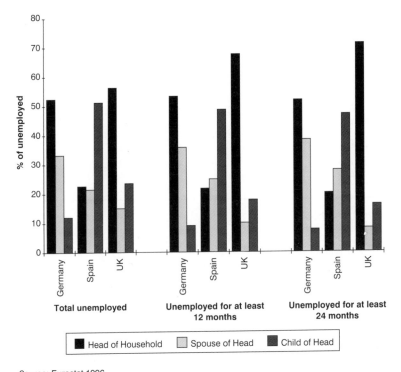

Source: Eurostat 1996
Note: data not available for Sweden

Figure 2.1   Relation to head of household of the unemployed and duration of unemployment in Germany, Spain and the UK

and women find it difficult to enter the labour market. For women such a dispersion of jobs perpetuates the traditional family structure and division of labour within it.

The widespread use of fixed-term contracts does not appear to have promoted the growth of permanent jobs. Studies report the proportion of workers hired on indefinite contracts at the end of a fixed-term contract to be small, in the order of 15 to 17 per cent (Milner *et al*. 1995, Jimeno and Toharia 1994). Further, neither the extensive informal economy nor a widespread use of fixed-term contracts has substantially modified the problem of mass unemployment, which reached 25 per cent of the working population in 1994 and was still 20.9 per cent in 1997.

Table 2.3   Unemployment in selected European countries, 1995

	Unemployment		Long-term unemployment	
	Male %	Female %	Male %	Female %
France	9.5	13.8	39.2	41.1
Germany	7.1	9.8	45.9	51.3
Italy	9.2	16.4	62.7	64.4
Netherlands	6.0	9.1	52.4	41.1
Spain	18.2	30.5	49.0	60.0
Sweden	10.1	8.2	23.4	15.9
UK	10.1	7.0	49.6	32.3

Source: Eurostat 1996.

Unemployment has become increasingly feminized and women form the major part of the worst forms of unemployment, those out of work for long periods and first-time job seekers (see Table 2.3). Fixed-term contracts do not appear to have had the effect of shortening the length of unemployment spells for first-time job seekers, which remain at the same level as in 1983 (Milner *et al.* 1995).

The findings of Bentolila and Dolado (1994) suggest that the existence of workers on fixed-term contracts has had the effect of increasing the bargained real wages of those on permanent contracts. That is, fixed-term contracts have exacerbated insider-outsider problems in Spain by internalizing such divisions within firms. Milner *et al.* (1995) summarize these findings as follows:

> Now the outsiders comprise both the unemployed and the tempor-ary workers inside the firm. Neither group's interests have much bearing on the wage bargaining behaviour of the insiders – the per-manent workers. The consequences of excessive wage demands (job losses) can now be accommodated by the buffer of temporary work-ers in the firm – whose firing costs are significantly lower for the employers (Milner *et al.* 1995:29).

The conclusions of the above writers are that the Spanish experience seems to represent a strong case against deregulation.

> On most of the crucial labour outcomes, the new permissive policy on fixed-term contracts has exacerbated the segmented labour market problem with higher wage unresponsiveness to unemployment, greater precariousness of employment, and recently, the highest unemployment level ever recorded with more than a quarter of the workforce out of work (Milner *et al.* 1995:38).

In Sweden unemployment has increased in the 1990s to 8 per cent of open unemployment in 1996 and nearly 13 per cent if workers in labour market schemes are included. If workers who are forced to retire early, those who have involuntary part-time jobs and those otherwise discouraged are included, one estimate is that some 25 per cent of the labour force is outside 'normal' full-time employment (EIRR 1996 270). Although unemployment is higher for men due to the loss of jobs in manufacturing and construction in the early 1990s, more recently (1995/6) two-thirds of job losses have been caring jobs in local authorities which have affected women workers (EIRR 1996 270). The decline of the Swedish model, decentralization of collective bargaining, increasing inequality of wages, increased unemployment, public-sector privatization and the growth of the private service sector suggest that pressures for a lessening of employment protection with an increase in non-standard work may be hard to resist. Developments in the internationalization of the economy have changed the balance of power between employers and trade unions and employers have become less interested in a compromise with domestic labour. Nevertheless, the legacies of policies of the Swedish Model have meant that a secondary labour force has not arisen to the same extent as in other countries, and at present both the trade unions and the social democratic government are resisting the lessening of employment protection.

In the UK, despite claims that labour market deregulation would enhance employment growth, there has been a persistence of unemployment and especially long-term unemployment (see Table 2.3). The UK did not do better than other countries in altering the share of long-term unemployment, and the transition from unemployment to employment worsened for men (Blanchflower and Freeman 1994). In the UK, women's lower unemployment rate (Table 2.3) may reflect a substantial under-recording of unemployment by women (see the discussion in Chapter 3). Policies have not created jobs for the unemployed; rather, the vast majority of part-time jobs are taken up by women married to men who are employed; dependants of the unemployed or the unemployed themselves are effectively prevented from doing this kind of work by loss of benefit or the 'poverty trap' (Deakin and Wilkinson 1991/2).

The picture which emerges is therefore one of polarization between households in the distribution of jobs The most common mode now is that of dual income households at about 62 per cent of households, with women's income on average representing a third of household income (Harkness *et al.* 1995, Gregg and Wadsworth 1997). The proportion of no-earner working-age households has risen from 16 per cent in 1983 to 19 per cent in 1994 (Gregg and Wadsworth 1997). As Gregg and Wadsworth (1997) note, the UK is less successful in distributing jobs among those that are unemployed. This is reflected in Figure 2.1, which shows the persistence of unemployment for heads of households in the UK. In fact the UK has the highest duration of unemployment for heads of households (male and female) in the EU: 71 per cent of unemployed heads of households had been unemployed for 2 years or more in 1995.

Conclusion

In conclusion, our examination of labour market reforms in a selected number of European countries shows increased experimentation with labour market reforms and an increased use of non-standard employment. As we noted in the Introduction, these trends seem likely to continue as policy in the European Union has also moved towards the pursuit of flexibility in the labour market in the context of rising unemployment (18 million at the end of 1997) and the advent of European monetary union. With respect to the latter, it is feared that monetary union will worsen the unemployment situation, as those member states belonging to a single currency will not be able to fine-tune their economies by altering exchange rates. Employment levels will, as a consequence, be much more vulnerable to economic downturns.

Following the change in policy emphasis of the White Paper of 1993, the Luxembourg jobs summit held in November 1997 agreed that each member state should develop national solutions to the problem of unemployment, based on guidelines issued by the Commission. These guidelines include the promotion of entrepreneurship, the creation of a culture of employability, the promotion of adaptability through more flexible forms of work which both enjoy adequate security and are compatible with the needs of business, and finally the strengthening of equal opportunities. For the European Commission it is a continuation of the compromise noted in the Introduction between its traditional emphasis on improving worker protection and a new concern with labour market flexibility (see Rhodes 1995).

So far, then, the UK (under conservative administrations) has been the sole member state that has clearly identified reduced regulation as the way forward on flexibility and jobs. Nevertheless, even in Sweden and Germany where non-standard employment remains highly protected (except for marginal part-time workers in Germany), non-standard employment is increasing together with pressures for lessening job security and employment protection. It was noted that the increase in non-standard employment in Germany was undermining the principal of insurance-related social security based on wage earners' continuous life-long employment. The Spanish experiments with labour reform suggest a case against deregulation with increasing polarization and segmentation of labour markets. The majority of the workforce are now in any form of non-standard work, in a context of very high unemployment and a considerable informal economy. Studies in the UK indicate also an increased polarization of employment conditions and experiences for both individuals and households.

However, it is not being argued here that there is a strong convergence between countries in labour-market flexibility and non-standard employment patterns associated with economic change. Although international competition, the operations of multinational companies and the diffusion of new organizational and managerial models constitute similar pressures and directions of change, as this chapter has demonstrated, these forces for change are mediated through the social, political and institutional structures within each country. One example has been the extent of labour exclusion in the UK, the lack of participation of national trade unions in proposals for labour reform, compared to the continuing role of unions, together with employers, in Germany, Spain and Sweden in national and local labour market reform agreements. However, there are signs that this will change under the New Labour government in Britain. A further example is the speed of the spread and the extent of use of fixed-term contracts in Spain, which contrasts markedly with that in West Germany where new laws permitting fixed-term contracts were introduced at the same time.

Finally there are clear differences between the countries in the extent to which non-standard employment is precarious or stable. As we discuss in the next chapter, women in Sweden benefit from 'socially acceptable' part-time work which gives them life-long continuous labour market participation. This contrasts with the precarious nature of much part-time work for women in the UK, for marginal part-time workers in Germany and fixed-term contract workers in Spain. These differences have implications not only for the gender contract in each country (which we discuss in the next chapter), but also for household coping strategies and opportunities.

Further reading

On the implications of the prolonged period of full-employment from 1950s to the early 1970s, see Bernabe 1988. For discussions of the concept of 'socially controlled welfare capitalism' and 'free market capitalism' see Sengenberger 1984 and Lane 1989a. There are many good accounts of the different regulatory frameworks surrounding the employment relation in European countries. See, for example, Rhodes 1989, Due *et al.* 1991, *Employment in Europe* 1993, Marullo 1995, and Van Ruysseveldt *et al.* 1995.

For recent trends in non-standard employment in Europe, the annual edition of *Employment in Europe* published by the European Commission is useful. For all member states of the European Unions Meulders *et al.* 1994 presents a good overview. For the UK an excellent summary is to be found in Dex and McCulloch 1995. See also *Labour Market Trends* published monthly by The Department of Education and Employment.

On labour market policies in Germany, see Deakin and Mückenberger 1992, and for Spain see Jimeno and Toharia 1994, and Cousins 1994a. For labour market reforms in Sweden see Kjellberg 1992 and Mahon

1996. For the UK good accounts of labour market reforms and their implications are to be found in Dickens and Hall 1995 and contributors to Barrell 1994. Much of the debate on labour market reform in the UK has focused on the flexible firm thesis see, for example, Atkinson 1985, Hunter *et al*. 1993, Pollert 1991, and Procter *et al*. 1994.

A recent overview and evaluation of labour market policies in Europe and other advanced countries is to be found in Schmid *et al*. 1996. For recent developments see *European Industrial Relations Review* (*EIRR*) (monthly) and *Employment in Europe* (annual).

3

Women and Employment

One of the most profound changes in employment patterns in the past two decades has been the increased participation of women in the labour market. For most European countries the increase in women's participation rates began in the 1970s, although for the UK it was from the 1960s and for Spain and Greece from the mid-1980s. As we discuss in this chapter, women's employment patterns across Europe show both convergence and cross-national differences. There is also diversity in the employment experiences of women within countries. Differences in class, educational attainment, generation, ethnicity, household formation and regional or local conditions can all affect the integration of women into the labour market.

Of importance is that women's increased labour market participation has coincided with the increased use of 'non-standard' or flexible forms of employment. As we have seen in Chapter 2 the majority of the flexible labour force is female, so that job flexibility is gendered (Walby 1997). This chapter also explores the implications of women's flexible work for gender occupational segregation and women's earnings.

In seeking to explain the diversity of women's employment patterns, both between and within European countries, we need to take into account a wide range of factors. These include differences in labour market regulation, industrial and sectoral structures and economic restructuring, familial and state supports for child rearing, social attitudes to participation and the domestic division of labour (Rubery and Fagan 1994). Supply side factors include women's caring and domestic responsibilities in the family, household forms and educational attainments. Especially important too are national differences in what, in the Scandinavian debate, has been called the 'gender contract'. As Duncan (1995) explain, the idea of the gender contract arose in Scandinavian countries in the context of a substantial change in women's roles but with the maintenance of gender divisions. Pfau-Effinger (1993), following Hirdmann (1990), defines the gender contract as a 'sociocultural consensus about the respective organization of interaction between the sexes' (1993:389). In each society and over time there develops a contract between the genders, a notion of appropriate behaviour and roles of each gender. This contract is founded, though, on an asymmetry of power in which male domains are structurally assigned a higher value. However, the use of the terms 'contract' and 'consensus' imply consent. In reality there may be little choice in accepting prevailing norms and assumptions about gender roles.

This chapter is organized in two sections. The first section examines differences in women's labour market participation with particular reference to the four case-study countries of Germany, Spain, Sweden and the UK. The second section discusses the persistence of gender inequalities by considering gender occupational segregation, women's earnings and unemployment.

Women's participation

The statistics of women's increased labour market participation are striking: between 1960 and 1990 the labour force in the European Community increased by just under 29 million, of which over 20 million were women (Rubery and Fagan 1994). In the 1980s and 1990s most of the new jobs were taken by women. For example, women accounted for three quarters of all new jobs between 1983 and 1992 in the European Community (Bulletin 1996). During the same period men's activity rates have declined as women's have increased (Figures 3.1 and 3.2 show this with respect to selected member states). The decline in men's economic activity is associated with the shift from manufacturing to service sector jobs and increased unemployment and inactivity rates. Conversely the expansion of the service sector is linked with women's jobs. However, there are significant differences between countries in the extent to which the expansion of the service sector (the structural effect) is more important than

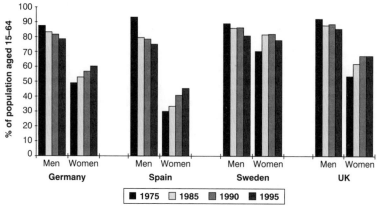

Source: Eurostat 1996

Figure 3.1   Activity rates of men and women, 1975–95, in
Germany, Spain, Sweden and the UK

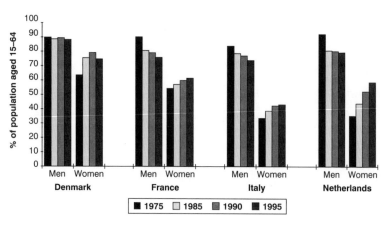

Source: Eurostat 1996

Figure 3.2   Activity rates of men and women, 1975–95, in
Denmark, France, Italy and the Netherlands

the increase in total female employment (the compositional effect). For example, the UK had the highest increase in female
employment in the 1980s in the EU 12 countries, with employment growth in the service sector accounting for 82 per cent of

total female employment growth. In contrast, in Greece most of the growth (65 per cent) was due to women increasing their share of employment (Rubery and Fagan 1994). It does not appear, though, that women have been taking 'men's jobs', as marked gender segregation is evident in all countries and women are increasing their share of already female, dominated service sectors (see the discussion below). As Rubery and Fagan (1995) note there is limited evidence of women breaking into typical male-dominated manual jobs in any of the member states. Meulders (1990) has also argued that the growth in women's economic activity has had no influence on the rise of male unemployment.

However, there is a marked diversity between the European countries in women's participation rates, especially through their lifetime, as shown in Figures 3.3 and 3.4. The profiles in the UK, Germany and the Netherlands show a similar bi-modal 'women-returner' pattern as women tend to leave work for the birth of the first child and re-enter the labour force at a later age, often in part-time work. In Sweden, Denmark and other Scandinavian countries, women's activity rate shows a similar profile to that of men with a continuity through the life-cycle. In Spain and Italy the left-handed peak of the curve shows a pattern of women leaving paid employment after the age of 25 years, a discontinuous employment pattern.

However, these distinctive profiles of women's labour market participation over their lifetime are becoming blurred as in all countries younger women, and especially those with higher education, are remaining in the labour market rather than leaving when they have children. Lower fertility rates and an increase in the average age of birth of the first child are also reducing the impact of motherhood on participation rates. Especially important here is the impact of educational attainment on participation rates. Highly qualified women have higher levels of economic activity than women with fewer qualifications and this difference persists when they become mothers (Bulletin No. 6 1995).

Germany

Women's relatively low participation rates in west Germany in comparison with other north European countries (see Fig. 3.1)

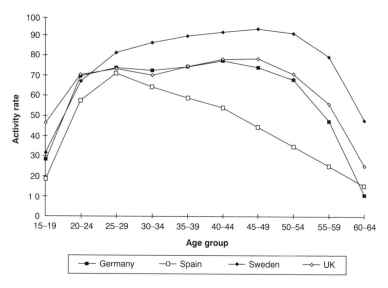

Source: Eurostat 1996

Figure 3.3   Female activity rates by age in Germany, Spain,
Sweden and the UK

has been associated with a number of unique factors. First, the
'atypical economic structure' of Germany (Erler 1988) produces
a higher contribution of manufacturing to GNP than in comparable advanced societies. This means that service (including public
welfare) and communication sectors, which are the principal job
creators for women, have not expanded to the same extent as in
other countries.[1] The lack of expansion of the public sector is
related to the nature of the welfare state in west Germany, where
it is the duty of the family to undertake caring of young children or elderly people (see Chapter 5). A second factor, therefore, is a social policy regime which favours a male-breadwinner,
and mother/housewife family model. Pfau-Effinger (1993) has
referred to the establishment of a gender contract in west Germany in which the male-breadwinner marriage provides protection for married women who do not expect to work until children
attend secondary school or have left home. As we have seen in
Chapter 2, a high proportion of part-time workers are mothers.
    School hours and insufficient provision for pre-school child

Women and Employment 77

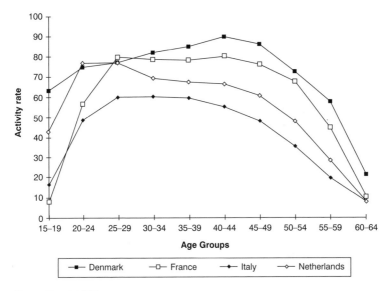

Source: Eurostat 1996

Figure 3.4   Female activity rates by age in Denmark, France,
the Netherlands and Italy, 1995

care also place enormous constraints on women's ability to work full-time. Publicly provided childcare places cater for between 65 and 70 per cent of children between the age of three and school age, but their hours are 'premised on the idea of the immobile women waiting at home with a cooked lunch. West German children are not expected to look after themselves in the afternoon but to stay in the parents' custody' (Ostner 1993:101). Women may also be responsible for their still-dependent children and for elderly relatives at the same time. As a consequence full-time employment for mothers (at 20 per cent) is one of the lowest in the European Union with only the UK (at 18 per cent) and the Netherlands (at 5 per cent) falling below Germany (Bulletin No. 5 1995).

In contrast to women in the west, women in the former GDR, including mothers, had one of the highest levels of participation in the labour market. Until unification in 1990 policies enabled women to combine paid employment and a family by full state provision of pre-school, after-school and holiday childcare facilities.

Paid work for women in east Germany was not only a normal and accepted part of women's lives but, as Kolinsky (1993) notes, it was also obligatory. However, although access to employment was taken as evidence of equality, in practice women were kept in the 'second row of society' with lower pay, lower qualifications, lower occupational status and more family obligations than men (Kolinsky 1995). We discuss below the impact of unification on women's employment opportunities.

Spain

Spain has one of the lowest participation rates for women in the EU countries (see Figure 3.1). Spain has also the highest proportion of non-employed women in OECD countries with nearly three-quarters (72.6 per cent) of working-age women being non-employed, that is either non-working or unemployed (OECD *Employment Outlook* 1991/2). In this respect Spain and Sweden (with a female non-employment rate of 23 per cent) represent polar extremes.

More recently the increase in female employment has accounted for a large part of all employment growth. As Figure 3.1 shows the proportions of women working have increased throughout the 1980s and 1990s and most of this increased participation has been amongst married women (see Espina 1989, and Cousins 1994a).[2] However, the characteristics of Spanish labour markets (see Chapter 2) has meant that women were incorporated into paid work at a time when temporary fixed-term contracts were spreading rapidly. At the same time however, the tertiary sector was expanding, especially in professional and higher-level jobs (see below), giving rise to a polarization between women's employment experiences. Rates of female activity are very dependent upon levels of educational qualification: for those with university or professional qualifications activity rates are almost equal to men but are half that rate for those with low levels of education. Female participation rates also vary significantly between the more advanced urban and the less developed agricultural regions.

Although a policy context of equal rights and opportunities has been in place since 1978, and equal pay since 1981, the reality appears to be that women have difficulty in gaining access to paid employment. Further, policies which enable women to participate in paid work and combine family and employment responsibilities, such as parental leave and child-care facilities, are at an early stage (see Frotiee 1994 and Tobio 1994). There are several reasons for this, not least the legacy of the many decades of the Franco regime in which married women were actively discouraged from taking paid work (see Chapter 5). During the expansion of the welfare state in the 1980s the long list of priorities included the national health service, benefits for the unemployed, and retirement pensions, and policies which encouraged women's paid employment came last (Tobio 1994).

Further, unemployment of over 2 million people has persisted since the mid-1980s (see below), so that there has never been the strong demand for labour which has led some countries, for example Sweden, to implement policies which encouraged married women to take paid work. Nor has there been a tradition of part-time work, which in other countries enables women to combine family and paid work (see Chapter 2).

Legislation of 1989 extended maternity leave and established parental leave, and for children between three and six years publicly provided child care is more generous than, for example, in Britain.[3] For children under 3 years, however, facilities remain inadequate and childminders are practically non-existent (Frotiee 1994). Both Frotiee (1994) and Tobio (1994) report the importance of relatives, and especially grandmothers, in looking after children while their mothers work. The majority of grandmothers and other female relatives may have never worked, but with the recent increase in female employment this form of support for working mothers will be more limited in the future.

One significant difference between women's work in Spain and northern European countries may be the importance and size of the informal economy.[4] In southern European countries informal work activities, which draw mainly on the low-paid and precarious labour of women, are a long-standing and integral aspect of the economies. Much of this work also draws on the non-declared labour of migrants from third world countries, in the case of Spain, particularly workers from north Africa.[5]

Many of the features of the labour market in Spain create favourable conditions for the increase in irregular forms of working, namely, the decline in regular, stable jobs, the increasing high unemployment, the presence of foreign immigrants from third world countries, and the subordinate position of many women in the family providing a subordinate workforce in the labour market. However, the creation of irregular work activities is still insufficient to absorb the active population and substantially reduce the high rate of unemployment (see below).

Sweden

In the 1950s and early 1960s in Sweden women's roles were seen to be sequential, first as mother and then as worker (Lewis 1992). During this period women's labour market participation remained constant at about 30 per cent, although it was lower for married women with children. Hirdmann (1990) has characterized this period as one in which a housewife gender contract existed where private patriarchy had been eroded but women's role with respect to marriage and paid work was not established (Duncan 1995). As we discuss in Chapter 5, policies introduced in the early 1970s increased incentives for women to work throughout their adult life and today the 'dual breadwinner' model has become the dominant form of family organization. As Duncan (1995) observes, an equality gender contract emerged. By 1990, 82 per cent of women between 15 and 64 years were in the labour market, almost the same proportion as men (only 4 percentage points lower) and the highest proportion in the advanced countries (Eurostat 1996). However, during the 1990s recession women's economic activity rate fell for the first time since the 1960s (to 78 per cent by 1995).

Much of women's work is part-time, especially for mothers with young children (see Chapters 2 and 5). Policies which enable mothers to combine work and a family have resulted in a high proportion of mothers with children under 6 years at work, 87 per cent in 1990. At the same time fertility rates have increased so that at 2.1 the rate is higher than most other European countries. However, Jonung and Persson (1994) argue that many Swedish mothers are in the labour market but in reality are on temporary leave looking after children while the labour market participation of women with children under seven years was about 86 per cent, their at-work rate was only 53 per cent in 1990. The distinctive feature of Sweden in this respect is that mothers with young children are paid to take leave to care for their families and are counted as being in the active labour force.

The UK

Between 1983 and 1990, the UK experienced the highest growth of female employment in Europe (followed by Spain) (Rubery and Fagan 1994). During the 1980s men's activity rate remained constant, but then fell during the recession of the early 1990s. Women fared differently, as their activity increased during the 1980s and then remained constant during the early 1990s. The falls in employment since 1990 have been caused by a reduction of full-time employees and an increase in part-time workers which, since more women work part-time, partially explains the different activity rates for men and women (Sly 1993).

Employment rates have grown more rapidly for married women with dependent children. Nevertheless labour market participation is affected by the age of the youngest child rather than the number of children (Sly 1993). The lower rate of economic activity for women in the UK with children under 4 (54 per cent compared to 67 per cent for all women between 16–59 in 1996) reflects the fact that the UK has, together with the Netherlands and Ireland, the lowest overall levels of childcare provision in Europe (Eurostat 1996, Commission of the European Communities 1991). This is undoubtedly also a reason for the high levels of part-time work amongst mothers in the UK.

Policies which enable women to participate in paid work have been, however, contradictory and ambiguous since the early 1980s (see, for example, Williams 1993, Bruegel and Perrons 1996). Equal opportunity legislation and equal pay have been in existence since the mid-1970s and equal pay for work of equal value since 1984. Initiatives such as Opportunity 2000 and company policies have also promoted equal opportunities in the larger workplaces. Yeandle (1997), for example, estimates that by 1995 approximately 30 per cent of women workers were in relatively high-status jobs. However, the deregulation and flexible labour market policies pursued by governments since 1980 have disproportionately impacted on women, especially those at the lower end of the earnings hierarchy. Further, women's freedom to engage in the labour market has been stressed but facilities to support this have been lacking. Rather, women's decision to take paid work is seen as a matter of private choice, transferring responsibility from the state to the individual. The UK is, therefore, consistent with a liberal regime in which there is formal equality to compete in the labour market but this is not accompanied by policies to support women or address inequality in a wider sense. At the same time labour market policies have promoted the market in the supply and demand for labour. Hence, in the UK there have been growing inequalities between women's experiences of employment and, as Bruegel and Perrons (1996) argue, the opportunity to be unequal not on the basis of gender, but on the basis of education.

Gender inequalities

Occupational segregation

Occupational segregation by gender continues to be a characteristic of all European labour markets. Thus women and men are most likely to be working in different types of occupations (horizontal occupational segregation) and women are more likely to work in lower-grade occupations while men occupy the higher-grade occupations (vertical segregation) (Hakim 1979).

There are a number of approaches to interpreting and measuring horizontal occupational segregation (Rubery and Fagan 1993).[6] One approach is to define gender segregation as the extent to which women work mainly with women and men mainly with men. This can be measured by the gender share or composition of the occupational structure (see Table 3.1 for the UK). A second approach is to focus on the level of concentration of women into different occupations – the distribution of the female labour force over the occupational structure. Table 3.2 shows the occupational concentration of women and men in the UK in 1995.

We can compare gender segregation, the share of women in different occupational categories, across the European member states using data from Eurostat in 1995 on the major categories of occupational groups.[7] A characteristic of these standardized occupational categories is that they are highly aggregated at the national level and will underestimate the extent of segregation for particular occupations (see below). Table 3.3 ranks the coun-

Table 3.1 Gender occupational segregation in the UK, 1995 (employees)

	Women %	Men %	Total %
Legislators and managers (1)	33.3	66.7	100
Professionals (2)	49.3	50.7	100
Technicians (3)	44.3	55.7	100
Clerks (4)	73.5	26.5	100
Service and sales workers (5)	70.4	29.6	100
Agricultural and fishery workers (6)	14.4	85.6	100
Craft and related trades workers (7)	12.1	87.9	100
Plant and machine operators (8)	17.8	82.2	100
Elementary occupations (9)	52.5	47.5	100
Armed forces (0)	5.2	94.8	100

Source: Eurostat 1996, Table 046.

Table 3.2 Concentration of women and men employees in occupational groups in the UK, 1995

	Women %	Men %
Legislators and managers (1)	9.8	17.9
Professionals (2)	15.4	14.4
Technicians (3)	7.4	8.5
Clerks (4)	28.3	9.3
Service and sales workers (5)	23.3	8.9
Agricultural and fishery workers (6)	0.2	0.9
Craft and related trades workers (7)	2.6	17.2
Plant and machine operators (8)	3.3	13.8
Elementary occupations (9)	9.6	7.9
Armed forces (0)	(0.1)	1.1
Total	100	100

Source: Eurostat 1996, Table 047.

tries according to the level of women's participation in the labour market and gender segregation. Those countries with the highest levels of female economic activity also have the highest levels of feminization of clerical and services and sales. This suggests that occupational segregation does not decline with increased rates of participation in the labour market (see also Rubery and Fagan

Table 3.3 The share of women's employment in occupational groups in Europe, 1995

	Professional and related (1–3) % female	Clerical and related (4) % female	Services and sales (5) % female	Agricultural and fishery (6) % female	Production and related (7–9) % female
Denmark	43.4	73.0	77.5	18.4	25.5
UK	42.1	73.5	70.4	14.4	26.6
Portugal	51.8	58.7	59.4	21.2	35.9
Austria	43.2	64.8	68.0	17.7	29.2
Netherlands	39.2	64.9	67.1	18.9	20.7
France	43.8	76.4	72.1	16.9	26.3
Germany	48.0	67.0	74.9	42.5	21.8
Belgium	44.6	57.0	62.6	16.7	23.4
Ireland	44.5	70.1	60.7	0	20.2
Luxembourg	36.4	48.2	57.1	0	24.6
Greece	45.1	53.8	44.3	19.1	24.1
Spain	42.0	52.8	50.1	9.2	24.1
Italy	47.1	50.7	45.8	20.9	24.9

Legend

female dominated with more than 60 per cent female
mixed occupations with 40–59 per cent females
male dominated with 20–39 per cent females and
very male dominated with less than 20 per cent females

Source: Eurostat 1996.

1993). Indeed, as we discuss below, in the Scandinavian countries, with high levels of female participation, gender segregation is at the highest levels.

Table 3.3 shows a high degree of similarity between the countries. For example, there are low proportions of women in production and manual jobs in all countries; only Portugal has a rate above 30 per cent. In the professional, technical and related group of occupations the range is from 36 per cent female in Luxembourg to 52 per cent for Portugal. It would seem that in countries with low female rates of activity, women are just as likely to have a high share of professional jobs as in countries with high participation rates. Clerical and related and service and sales jobs are also important areas of work for women in all countries, with only Greece and Italy below 50 per cent female for services and Luxembourg for clerical work.

Nevertheless, despite similarities in gender segregation between countries (and persistence over time, see Rubery and Fagan 1993) there are also clear differences between countries. For example, clerical and service occupations are far less feminized in the southern European countries compared with the very high levels of feminization in north Europe. This is consistent with the recent entry of women into the labour market in southern European countries. However, there are trends of convergence as increasing proportions of women in southern Europe entering the labour market take clerical jobs. In specific occupational groups, Rubery and Fagan (1995) found large differences between countries. One example is to be found in catering, where women in Denmark occupy 78 per cent of such jobs but only 45 and 41 per cent in France and Spain respectively. Such differences are related to differences in culture and social attitudes, in training systems and in labour market and industrial organization.

One way of analysing women's occupational concentration in occupations is to rank occupations from the most female dominated to the most male dominated for each country and categorize the continuum as follows:

very female dominated occupations with more than 80 per cent females
female dominated with 60–79 per cent female
mixed occupations with 40–59 per cent females
male dominated with 20–39 per cent females and
very male dominated with less than 20 per cent females (Rubery and Fagan 1993).

This is shown in the shading in Table 3.3. Figure 3.5 shows the concentration of women's employment, that is the share of women's employment which falls into each of the five categories in thirteen of the EU countries in 1995. The aggregate nature of the data means that no country shows very female-dominated occupations, although we know that certain occupational groups are very feminized. In the UK, for example, Walby (1997) found that 23 per cent of women were working in occupations containing more than 70 per cent women and this was considerably

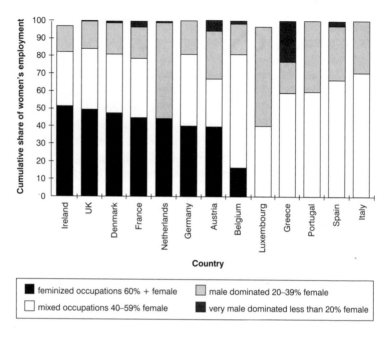

Figure 3.5   Concentration of women's employment into
segregated occupations

higher in particular localities. National levels of aggregation,
therefore, significantly underestimate the level of segregation in
given local labour markets. The experience of segregation is also
greater for men than women as men are far more likely to work
with other men (see Table 3. 1 for the UK) as women are still
effectively excluded from certain areas of work (Walby 1997).

Figure 3.5 demonstrates both a pattern of high gender segregation across the member states as well as important differences
between the countries. The north European countries have the
highest proportions of women working in feminized occupations
(over 60 per cent female), although in the southern European
countries the majority of women work in mixed occupations.
Rubery and Fagan (1993) note that in the case of southern
European countries the high share of agriculture may in part
explain these differences as the occupational classification scheme
does not differentiate male and female jobs. A further reason is

that in the southern countries many jobs, regarded as female in the north, are still seen as male domains, especially where high rates of unemployment persist.

Eurostat data does not provide us with an accurate source of information on vertical segregation as 'the nature of social prestige and pay associated with apparently similar job titles varies between countries' (Rubery and Fagan 1993:38). Nevertheless, evidence suggests that there has been some improvement over time in vertical segregation as women have gained higher qualifications and training and are increasingly entering male-dominated employment areas in higher-level jobs (Bruegel and Perrons 1996, Rubery and Fagan 1993, Walby 1997). In Spain, for example, women's increased entry into higher education coincided with an expansion of professional jobs so that women have substantially increased their share of professional and clerical jobs. As Rubery and Fagan (1993, 1995) note, however, the trends in gender segregation over time are pulling in two directions. On the one hand, women have increased their representation in higher-level jobs but, on the other, have also increased their share of lower-level clerical and service work.

There are also differences in levels of reliance on part-time workers in the different occupational sectors. In some countries such as UK, Germany and the Netherlands, with a 'women returner' employment pattern, part-time work is associated with increased levels of segregation. This is especially the case in the UK, where 85 per cent of female part-timers work mainly with other women. In the Netherlands this figure is only 42 per cent, suggesting that women part-time workers are better integrated with the male workforce (Fagan and Rubery 1996). The overall finding of these authors is that women who work part-time are less likely to work with men than full-time workers throughout all member states, but the difference is greater in some countries than others.

There are no data for Sweden in the Eurostat source, although research has shown that Sweden, together with other Scandinavian countries (see Denmark Table 3.3 and Figure 3.5), has high levels of gender segregation. In Sweden, despite the high level of women's labour market participation and the impressive policies which allow women to combine family and employment, occupational segregation by sex is one of the highest in the

advanced world (Ruggie 1988). Forsberg (1994) found that segregation in the Swedish labour market in the 1990s was largely
the same as in the 1960s. 'The labour market as a whole is nearly
as gender segregated now as then, both horizontally and verti-
cally' (1994:1239). For Forsberg it is the gender contract and
the mechanisms of gendering which sustain this. '[Things] labelled female are given one value and those labelled male get
another, higher, value. . . . Gendered mechanisms label work tasks,
educational programmes, political issues, housework, and future
plans as male or female' (1994:1253).

Other writers seeking to explain the high level of sex segregation in Sweden and other Scandinavian countries have emphasized the special role of the public sector. Commitment to full
employment in Sweden provided jobs through expansion of the
public sector, which has drawn in women in disproportionate
numbers. As Esping-Andersen (1993) shows, the occupational
structure in Sweden is extremely gender specific with the majority of men employed in the private sector and 70 per cent of
total net female employment concentrated in the welfare state.
Especially important is the employment of women at local authority level, with more than a quarter of women working in health
and social work in 1990 (Jonung and Persson 1994). Women in
the public sector tend to be highly concentrated in female-dominated occupations. Nordli Hansen (1997) has argued with respect to Norway that the public sector is attractive to women,
especially the more highly educated, as they can make inroads
into male-dominated occupations with higher earnings but with
no punishment for caring responsibilities. Men on the other hand
are more likely to be attracted to the private sector because
their expected earnings are likely to be higher.

A further reason for gender segregation is that it is mothers
who take the parental leave schemes. This may have the unan-
ticipated consequence of perpetuating women's disadvantage in
the labour market. Rosenfeld and Kalleberg (1991), for example,
have argued that despite equal-opportunity legislation women
can be channelled out of higher-level positions because of the
expectation that at some point they will be on leave. Part-time
work too may reduce 'human capital' or job choice, and reduce
earnings.

Women's earnings

One of the reasons for interest in gender segregation, both horizontal and vertical segregation, is that it is linked to gender pay
inequalities. In all European countries women's pay is lower than
that of men's (see Table 3.4) and women make up a larger proportion of the low paid. This is despite the introduction of equal
pay legislation in all member states in the past two decades (see
Table 5.1 in Chapter 5). Again, however, there are large differences between countries reflecting differences in minimum wage
protection, centralized bargaining systems and methods of job
grading. In her study of 13 OECD countries Whitehouse (1992)
found that centralized wage-fixing arrangements are strongly
associated with high relative earnings for women and that regulation under these arrangements tends to restrict processes of
casualization and feminization. Such arrangements were also found
to be more effective then equal pay legalization. However, while
national or sectoral minimum wages and the collective bargaining process are important in protecting against low pay, there
may be non-compliance with minimum wages on the part of
employers, or specific groups may be excluded, for example, young
people, trainees or part-timers on short hours (Gregory and
Sandoval 1994).

Although women in Germany comprise the majority of the
low-paid (Gregory and Sandoval 1994, Rubery *et al.* 1997), they
fare better than women in Britain in terms of the ratio of their
pay to men's (see Table 3.4). Female part-timers are also more
likely to earn similar pay levels to those of female full-time workers
(with the exception of marginal part-time workers) (Rubery 1992).
As we noted in Chapter 2, researchers consider that women in
Germany have benefited from the high degree of labour market
regulation, collective bargaining and 'the tradition of basing pay
upon skills, qualifications and job content which has led to detailed job hierarchies even in female dominated areas of work'
(Rubery 1992:617; see also Lane 1993). In contrast to the UK,
it is also more likely that women returning to the labour market
after children will experience greater protection from occupational and pay downgrading because of the importance attached
to vocational qualifications.

In Spain evidence from the Instituto de la Mujer suggests that

Table 3.4   The gender pay ratio for manual and non-manual
workers in industry, 1991[a]

	Manual workers 1991	Non-manual workers 1991
Belgium	75.6	65.2
Denmark	84.5	n.a.
Germany	73.4	67.1
Greece	79.2	68.5
Spain	72.2	60.9
France	80.25	67.2
Ireland	69.5	n.a.
Italy[b]	79.3	n.a.
Luxembourg	68.0	55.2
Netherlands	76.2	64.8
Portugal	70.8	70.7
United Kingdom	67.2	58.3

[a] As the Network of Experts on the Situation of Women in the Labour
Market note, the above data are limited by the following: the public
sector is excluded, data for manual and non-manual workers are hourly
and monthly respectively, earnings data for part-time workers are in-
consistently covered. These omissions constitute the majority of female
employment.
[b] Data for Italy is 1989 and was provided by the Italian experts for the
Network of Experts on the Situation of Women in the Labour Market.

Source: Bulletin 1994, Eurostat, 1992.

female workers earn about 30 per cent less than men although,
as Table 3.5 shows, this varies in the different sectors. Spain has
a national statutory minimum wage policy, although this is set
at a low level. There is, however, a high incidence of low pay.
On a definition of low pay as less than 40 per cent of the national
median level of earnings, 29 per cent of female employees were
low paid and 52 per cent of young people in the late 1980s
(Gregory and Sandoval 1994). The limited protection for young
people and non-compliance with the minimum wage may explain
the high incidence of low pay. The informal sector and temporary fixed-term contracts are both associated with lower wage
levels than legal work or permanent work (Jimeno and Toharia
1994).
    In Sweden, policies of wage solidarity have meant that the

Table 3.5 Average hourly earnings of men and women in selected occupational groups in Spain, 1993

	Men pesetas/hour 1993	Women pesetas/hour 1993
Industrial employees	2134	1319
Blue-collar workers	1192	863
Service sector workers	1491	1089
Construction workers	1137	1051

Source: Instituto de la Mujer 1994.

gender pay gap for full-time workers is one of the narrowest in the world. The pay gap varies by sector, being lowest for male and female blue-collar workers and highest for white-collar workers (Jenson and Mahon 1993). Most of the low-paid women are also to be found in the public sector. As we noted above, in contrast with women elsewhere, women tend not to withdraw from the labour market on the birth of their children in Sweden; they have access to training or further education and collective centralized bargaining ensures that their expected earnings are less penalized. Nevertheless, as collective bargaining becomes more fragmented in the 1990s with the disappearance of the solidarity equal-wage principle, as public sector jobs are reduced and the flexible labour force increased, women may become more at risk of lower pay with an associated increase in the gender pay gap.

In the UK there has been an improvement in the gender pay gap for female full-timers as they have improved their occupational positions over the 1980s and 1990s. Nevertheless the UK had the lowest earnings for full-time female workers among the EU 12 in 1993, with the highest gender pay gap (Rubery *et al.* 1997). Part-time female workers (who are excluded from the Eurostat data), for example, earn, on average, about 75 per cent of female full-timers' pay and there has been a worsening of this ratio over the 1990s (Rubery *et al.* 1997).

The extent of low pay for women in the UK is high. Webb *et al.* 1996 calculate that in 1994–5 around 4.6 million (22 per cent) of the workforce were low paid, using a definition of two-thirds median hourly wage. Of these workers around two-thirds were women (3.2 million).[8] As we discuss in Chapter 6 the increase in inequalities in earnings is one of the factors contributing to increased household poverty. It is the case that the earnings of the spouses of low-paid female workers lifts the household out of poverty (Webb *et al.* found that this was the case 90 per cent of low-paid married women workers). Nevertheless, it may be argued that low pay does not contribute to economic independence but rather contributes to forms of dependency 'that are inimical to the status of citizenship in contemporary society' (Siltanen 1994:100).

There a number of reasons for the extent of low pay in Britain. First, with the abolition of the Wages Councils in 1993 there is no system of minimum wage protection at national or industry level (although a minimum wage has been promised by the new Labour government). Secondly, many female workers, especially part-timers, are concentrated in firms and industries not covered by collective bargaining, for example, the retail sector, hotels and catering. These two features – the absence of a minimum wage and weak and fragmented collective bargaining in the UK – compound each other. Thirdly, as we noted above, in comparison with other European countries education and training are less directly related to pay and employment positions, employers having greater freedom to determine relative pay and grading of jobs (Rubery *et al.* 1997).

Unemployment

In most countries of Europe women's unemployment rates exceed those of men (see Table 2.3 in Chapter 2). The exceptions are the UK and Sweden for reasons which are discussed below. Men, however, were disproportionately affected by the recession of the early 1990s for, as we have seen in Chapter 2, virtually all of the job losses were male full-time jobs. Nevertheless, women's measured unemployment rates are likely to underestimate the true rate of female unemployment because unemployed women may define themselves as inactive rather than unemployed.

In Germany it is women in the east who have been most affected by unemployment. In the seven years since unification the labour market has undergone a radical upheaval. The closure and restructuring of companies has led to a loss of two million jobs. Women constituted over 60 per cent of the unemployed although in regions of textile production this proportion was even higher (Kolinsky 1996). The proportion of women in paid work fell from 80 per cent in 1990 to just over 60 per cent in 1992 (EIRR 261, 1995). The higher-qualified and professional workers were more likely to retain their jobs than blue- and white-collar workers, but many women have had to take jobs below their qualifications or previous level of competence. Although women are well qualified compared with other countries, east German women were less well qualified than men and many did not possess the skills required for a modern market economy, especially as qualifications in the east were deemed to be inferior to those in the west. Nevertheless Kolinsky (1995) maintains that east German women have not relinquished their commitment to employment and they seize every opportunity for retraining. Even if they are not looking for work they still register as unemployed rather than retreat into the housewife role, as in west Germany.

In Spain unemployment reached over 25 per cent of the working population in 1994 and was still 20.9 per cent in the second quarter of 1997. As we discussed in Chapter 2 unemployment has become increasingly feminized. In 1996 female unemployment was 29.5 per cent compared to 17.5 per cent for men, and for young women under 25 years 48.7 per cent were unemployed (Eurostat 1997). Women also form the major part of the worst forms of unemployment, those out of work for long periods (see Table 2.3. in Chapter 2) and first-time job seekers (over half of whom had been searching for work for two years or more in 1996). These statistics illustrate the profound discrimination against women in the labour market and their inability to gain access to paid employment. One reason for high female unemployment for those previously in work is the termination of temporary contracts. Once unemployed, women, and especially married women, are much less able to escape unemployment than men, the reason Jimeno and Toharia (1994) attribute to the increasing feminization of unemployment.

In Sweden, until the early 1990s female unemployment was traditionally slightly higher than the male level. In the early 1990s, though, men have suffered disproportionately from the loss of jobs in manufacturing and construction. More recently this trend has been partially reversed by labour shedding of women's jobs in the public welfare sector. As Forsberg (1994) points out, jobs cut in caring work still means that the work has to be done, so that the result is a displacement of such work from the paid to the unpaid sector.

In the UK, women's lower unemployment rate may reflect a substantial under-recording of unemployment by women. Women's invisibility in the official statistics may result from:

1. Non-entitlement to benefits. Many women still pay reduced National Insurance contributions and about 18 per cent of the earnings of working women fall below the threshold for payment (Callender 1992).
2. Not having made sufficient National Insurance contributions to be eligible for unemployment-related benefits. Women may also be ineligible for Job Seeker's Allowance if their partner is claiming the benefit himself or is working. They are therefore not classified as unemployed.
3. Not registering for work. *Employment in Europe* (1991) suggests that only 40 per cent of women in the UK recorded as being unemployed actually registered at an employment exchange.

The nature of women's unemployment in the UK may also reflect the extent and rapidity of social and economic change in the 1980s and 1990s, especially the decline of manufacturing jobs and increase in service-sector jobs (seen as more appropriate jobs for women), as well as the unequal distribution of employment among households (see also the discussions in Chapters 2 and 6). One of the consequences, though, is that unskilled male workers have suffered disproportionately higher levels of unemployment or inactivity[9] as they either do not want the lower paid, often part-time, service jobs on offer or employers do not consider them as appropriate employees.

Conclusion

Women in all European countries have been increasingly entering the labour market in the past two decades (from the 1980s for women in the south European countries). In all countries there is evidence of strong similarities in gender occupational segregation, lower pay levels and in most countries higher levels of unemployment. We cannot yet say that increased participation has led to increased equality and integration of women into European labour markets. This is despite the quite substantial achievements of legislation at the European level and at the European Court of Justice with respect to equal pay and equal treatment (see, for example, Ostner and Lewis 1995, and Hantrais 1995).

Women seem likely to continue to increase their share of employment in European labour markets especially in the expanding service sectors. However, there may be both positive and negative features associated with this. On the positive side, as women gain higher-level qualifications and training they will increasingly enter higher-level occupations (although not necessarily desegregated) with higher pay levels. However, the more feminized are these occupations the less likely it will be that their pay levels will be high relative to men. The likelihood of women entering jobs previously reserved for men depends on a wide range of factors, for example, jobs becoming less attractive to men (because of a decline in pay levels, security, prestige or working conditions), or an increasing demand which cannot be met through normal channels, or women moving ahead in the job queue through education, training or equal-opportunity policies (Rubery and Fagan 1995).

On the less positive side polarization between women workers may continue to increase as those already-feminized occupations at the lower end of the earnings hierarchy expand. The pressures for change discussed in the Introduction may increase the trend to decentralization of collective bargaining and the individualization of the employment relation, which may also impact negatively on women's pay and working conditions. Finally, the accelerating trend to 'non-standard' forms of employment also has negative consequences for women, particularly where it is associated with increased gender segregation, lower pay and less employment protection. Marked differences still persist, however, both between countries, for example, in participation rates and the nature and extent of flexible work, and within countries, for example, in the influence of education and the impact of motherhood.

Further reading

On comparative analysis of women's labour market position in the European Union member states, the series of publications by Jill Rubery and Collette Fagan as part of the Network of Experts for the European Commission is highly recommended see, for example, Rubery and Fagan 1993, 1994, 1995, and Rubery *et al.* 1997. Rubery 1988 and 1992 are also very good on differences in women's labour market participation and pay levels in selected European countries. For women and work in west and east Germany, see Ostner 1993, 1994a, Chamberlayne 1994, Kolinsky 1993, 1995, 1996. Cousins 1994a provides a comparison of women's labour market position in Spain and the UK. For Sweden, see Lewis and Åström 1992 and Forsberg 1994. Of the very large literature on women's paid work in the UK see, for example, Bruegel and Perrons 1996, Siltanen 1994, Walby 1997 and the more controversial work of Hakim (for example, 1993, 1996).

For recent trends see *Employment in Europe* published annually and *Labour Market Trends* in the UK, published monthly.

4

Industrial Change in the Regions of Europe

This chapter is concerned with new paradigms of work organization in Europe and especially the different regions of Europe. The plethora of terms used to describe the advanced countries in the last two decades – post-modern, post-industrial, post-Fordist – indicates the widespread assumption that, since the mid-1970s, we have entered a new phase of capitalist development. In this chapter we discuss one of the most commonly debated theoretical approaches to post-Fordism, namely, that of the transition from mass production to flexible specialization. Thus, we consider the renaissance of regional economies as sources of economic growth, the reorganization strategies of transnational corporations and the implications for local economies in Spain and the Baden-Württemberg region of Germany.

The proponents of flexible specialization have provided an ambitious attempt to chart changes in work organization, industrial relations, markets, state activity and the geographies of production (Tomaney 1994). The ensuing debate over a period of ten years has become very influential but also extremely polarized, with critics on one side and proponents on the other. For the critics, the flexible specialization perspective represents a 'new orthodoxy' or even 'fetish' (see Curry 1993 and Pollert 1991). From our point of view the debate is useful as it enhances our understanding of important processes of industrial change, especially changing relations between firms, pressures of international competition and the conditions of regional inequalities in Europe. The debate also stresses the tensions between national and regional institutional differences, and pressures for convergence arising out of increasing international competition and the role of transnational corporations.

The chapter is organized into two sections. The first examines dimensions of the flexible specialization thesis, the industrial district phenomena and multinational reorganization, and then critiques of this perspective. The second section considers evidence from three case studies in relation to this debate. The case studies include the industrial district phenomena in Catalonia and Baden-Württemberg in Germany, and the changing division of labour between firms in the automobile industry in Spain.

Flexible specialization

In their book *The Second Industrial Divide* (1984), Piore and Sabel distinguish two opposing poles of industrial production. First, mass production, involving standardized products, routine production with simple operations, performed by dedicated (product-specific) machines with semi-skilled workers. National social welfare programmes stabilized demand by guaranteeing minimum levels of purchasing power for those people without incomes. The second form of production is flexible specialization, involving craft production based on skilled workers who produce a variety of customized products using flexible machines.

These two types of production, according to Piore and Sabel, have coexisted throughout the modern period. In the nineteenth century however, production predominantly took place in industrial districts based on flexible specialization, for example steel and cutlery in Sheffield, cotton in Lancashire and silks in Lyon. Both France and Britain had numerous industrial districts in the nineteenth and earlier twentieth centuries. In both countries these networks disappeared during the 1960s with corporate concentration and restructuring (Lane 1995). For Piore and Sabel the first industrial divide occurred when mass production became dominant in all the advanced countries, reinforced by the Keynesian welfare state to stabilize demand. In some countries, however, with a strong craft tradition, or shop-floor control over work processes, elements of craft production continued.

The second industrial divide took place according to these writers from the mid-1970s. In the context of increased international competition, saturated and volatile markets and high costs associated with dedicated machines, regional production based on flexible specialization re-emerged as the source of economic growth. In this model, production processes reverse Taylorist and Fordist forms of deskilling and restore the dignity of labour through upskilling, and worker participation in product quality, tasks and 'know-how'. The use of advanced technology and highly flexible manufacturing systems provides further opportunities for flexible specialization, enabling small batch production without loss of economies of scale. Not all advanced regions and countries, though, are singled out as moving in the direction of flexible specialization – only those with a surviving craft tradition, and high-trust environment, for example Germany, Italy and Japan.

In the flexible specialization model two key and related developments are stressed (see Sabel 1989). First, the importance of the region as an integrated unit of production, and second, the reorganization of large multinational corporations. Each of these are discussed in turn below.

The industrial district phenomena

In the first of these developments Sabel (1989) has discerned a 'renaissance of regional economies' – new Marshallian industrial districts composed of small-firms networks. The examples, now well known, include Baden-Württemberg in Germany, Jutland in Denmark, Smaland in Sweden, Silicon Valley in the USA and the celebrated Third Italy (that is, the central and north-eastern regions of Italy: Emilia-Romagna, Friuli, the Marche, Trentino-Alto Adige, Tuscany, Umbria, Veneto).

The debate on flexible specialization and industrial districts as the source of local economic regeneration was given a further impetus by the publication of two volumes by the International Institute for Labour Studies. These volumes present conclusions of a research programme carried out by the Institute on first, the industrial district phenomena in Italy (Pyke *et al.* 1990), and secondly, the more general significance of the phenomena in Jutland in Denmark, Baden-Württemberg in Germany, and Spain (Pyke and Sengenberger 1992).

Many of these districts, it is said, have a sufficient similarity to be categorized under one generic heading 'industrial districts', which 'could combine both economic efficiency and superior standards of employment and act as a model for promotion elsewhere' (Pyke *et al.* 1990:1). 'What has captured the attention of researchers and politicians alike is their remarkable economic success' (Pyke and Sengenberger 1992:6). Box 4.1 contains the main preconditions and characteristics of the classic Italian model of industrial districts, as stated in the two volumes published by the International Institute for Labour Studies. Below we examine the industrial district phenomena with respect to regions in Germany and Spain.

Box 4.1   Pre-conditions and characteristics of industrial districts in the Third Italy

1. The organization of firms into geographically bounded, strong networks of specialization and sub-contracting. A condition of success of the district is the success of the whole network of firms, not an individual small firm. The district is characterized by a dominant type of production within one industrial sector, for example knitwear in Carpi in the Modena province of the Emilia Romagna region, and textiles in Prato in Toscana.

2. Productive decentralization. Brusco (1990:11) notes that in the Italian case a wave of decentralization took place at the end of the 1960s. Pyke and Sengenberger (1992) also note that industrial districts are emblematic of the profound industrial restructuring which has occurred in virtually all industrialized countries since 1975. This restructuring involves smaller units of production, the spread of subcontracting and geographical reorganization of the economy.

3. Economic and entrepreneurial dynamism. The reason for international interest and debate about the industrial district phenomena is said to be their remarkable economic success and vitality. For example, Emilia-Romagna, ranked in the weakest 25 per cent of European regions in 1977 had risen to the top 6 per cent by the 1990s (Rhodes 1995).

4. Cooperation between firms and between local institutions. Pyke and Sengenberger (1992) point to a readiness amongst firms for cooperation, for example, sharing information on new technologies, products or design. The sharing of information may be carried out informally or through institutions such as employers' associations, trade unions or service centres.

5. Regional governments or strong local leadership and local-level planning. 'At the regional level the local authority is an agency that can intervene to try and upgrade regions or proto-districts towards ideal dynamic social and economic conditions' (Pyke and Sengenberger 1992:25).

6. Social cohesiveness or a pre-existing cultural consensus. Becattini (1990) has called this a 'thickening of industrial and social inter-dependencies'. Pyke and Sengenberger refer to a 'social community holding supportive sets of values' and 'based on certain catalytic institutions: kinship, ethnicity, political or religious affiliation, and collective agreement' (1992:19,20).

7. A flexible labour force. 'The district's adaptability depends on a flexible labour force' (Pyke and Sengenberger 1992:23). Adaptability is required to respond to changing market demands; production is then not prone to bottlenecks and the 'sclerosis' often experienced by the large 'Fordist'-type organizations. These authors recognize, however, both 'high road' and 'low road' strategies on the part of employers. The 'high road' industrial strategy places a high value on the quality of the labour force; it necessarily involves continuous training, reskilling and labour mobility. A 'low road' response to international competition and industrial restructuring exists when firms seek competitiveness through low labour costs and a deregulated labour market environment. Such a strategy hinders investment in training, productivity, quality and stability of the workforce. As there is usually no union representation or formalized industrial relations system, employer–employee relations may be highly personalized and patriarchal.

Multinational reorganization

The second development identified by Sabel (1989) is the reorganization of multinational organizations to an emergent corporate form which blurs distinctions between large and small firms. Such reorganization has been prompted by the 'exemplary success of the new industrial districts and by fear of Japanese competitors – who are themselves perfecting systems of flexible production' (1989:31). The implication is that the branch plant of the multinationals, like small firms, will nurture the growth of industrial districts.

From the flexible specialization perspective, large bureaucratic organizations become reconstituted into smaller operating units with decentralized decision making and a shrinking headquarters unit. Use of flexible technical systems and the integration of design and production engineering promotes a broader training of workers and more collaborative industrial relations or employee participation. Relations with subcontractors change as a smaller number of subcontractors become both more and less closely integrated with the large-firm customer. On the one hand firms are expected to enter long-term contracts and engage in just-in-time, zero-defect deliveries, and on the other hand firms are expected to have contracts with other customers, as the large-firm customer imposes ceilings on the percentage of output they will buy.

Critiques

Of the many criticisms levelled against Piore and Sabel's thesis the following are deserving of attention and are salient for the discussion below on the two European regions and industries. First, trenchant criticism has come from Amin and his colleagues, who have argued that local economies are not self-contained and independent; rather, transnational companies have a powerful role in shaping localities, and the fortunes of companies within them (Amin and Malmberg 1994, Amin and Robins 1990). Further, while the European regions and cities will increasingly become tied to and shaped by powerful corporate interests, only a small number of favoured places will become hosts to more integrated transnational companies' (TNCs) investments. The less favoured regions will be left with poor economic development potential, with disembodied investment by TNC subsidiaries, external domination of local markets and a disconnection between the indigenous and non-indigenous corporate sector (Amin and Tomaney 1995). Cost-reducing incentives and 'social dumping' may attract investment in the less-favoured regions but this may promise little in terms of growth potential.

Secondly, the new customer–supplier relationship between

multinational and smaller firms also has implications for firms in the local economy. The process of externalization of production passes on risks associated with market fluctuations to suppliers (this would include reviewing quality and holding stocks). The large firm can dictate methods and profit margins (Rainnie 1993). The restructuring of relations between the large firms and their suppliers leads to a reduction in the number of suppliers and an emerging hierarchy amongst the suppliers themselves. Those who become a 'specially favoured supplier', and secure long-term contracts, develop a closer, narrower relationship with the large firms because of the necessity to monitor quality and supply flows. Others, however, may fall by the wayside, or are demoted to a lower tier, creating a widening gulf between different types of small firms (Lane 1991). We discuss this below in the case of Spain's automobile industry.

Thirdly, the flexible specialization perspective has been said to be static and short-term and ignores the evolution of these districts and the problems which they are now facing (Amin and Malmberg 1994, and see the discussion below on Baden-Württemberg). Fourthly, small firms often survive on the basis of self-exploitation, the use of family labour, evasion of tax and social security and the irregular or illegal use of cheap female and young workers (Hadjimichalis and Vaiou 1990, Amin 1989). In southern Europe in particular the informal economy is an integral part of their economies. However, in the flexible specialization perspective the use of such 'flexible' labour practices is almost celebrated and 'recast as opportunities' (Curry 1993:111; see also Pollert 1991).

Finally, the purported abrupt break between two methods of production, mass production and flexible specialization, is difficult to substantiate. Many writers have pointed to the continuation of mass production techniques, with consumer tastes being created rather than reflected (Williams *et al.* 1987, Thompson and McHugh 1995). In the services too, standardization, routinization and Taylorism are increasing in many sectors, for example fast food, retail outlets, and restaurants. The concern with quality controls and Total Quality Management has also brought standardized procedures and processes to many public and private sector services (for example, Jessop 1991a, Ritzer 1993, Thompson and McHugh 1995).

Below we consider three case studies in relation to the debate on industrial districts and multinational reorganization. The first focuses on the industrial district phenomena in Catalonia and the second on the changing division of labour between firms in the automobile industry in Spain. Thirdly, the case of Baden-Württemberg is examined as one of the successful examples of flexible specialization in Europe, but now facing strong international competition and undergoing a process of restructuring.

Evidence from three case studies

Industrial districts and industrial restructuring in Spain

A group of researchers working within the flexible specialization perspective have argued that there are regions in Spain, for instance Catalonia, Madrid and Valencia, which exhibit characteristics of industrial districts (for example, Benson 1992, Sabel 1989, Scott 1988, and Pyke and Sengenberger 1992). Similarities are to be found especially in relation to the dominance of small firms in tight subcontracting networks with dense interdependence between them.

We can consider the case of Catalonia which is one of the most prosperous regions in Spain. Barcelona, the capital city of Catalonia, has a long tradition as one of the most industrialized and dynamic cities in Spain. The revitalization of Barcelona during the period 1985–90 was partly due to the upturn in the world economy but was also due to the integration of Spain into the EC in 1986 and the city's important geostrategical position with respect to the Iberian peninsula and the rest of Europe. Increased levels of foreign investment by the transnational companies was also an important feature of this period. In 1988 the autonomous regional government of Catalonia signed a cooperation agreement with Baden-Württemberg, Rhone-Alps and Lombardy regional governments in proposing themselves as four European growth points; the 'Four Motors of Europe' (joined in 1990 by Wales).

However, with respect to the claim that Catalonia exhibits the characteristics of industrial districts, we can take the characteristics of the Italian industrial districts shown in Box 4.1 and apply them to the Catalonia region (see Box 4.2). It can be seen that there is only a superficial resemblance between the industrial structure of Catalonia and central Italy. Out of seven different criteria only the first two appear to be similar. It would, therefore, appear that subcontracting and the widespread use of the informal economy have been confused here with the phenomena of industrial districts. The supporting socio-economic conditions are quite different from either those of the Third Italy or those of Baden-Württemberg (see below). A historical legacy of impoverished institutional support for firms, a divided working class, weak trade unions and strongly paternalistic or atomized relations of production provided none of the conditions of trust and cohesiveness.

Box 4.2   Socio-economic conditions of the Catalonia industrial region

1. The organization of firms into geographically bounded, strong networks of specialization and sub-contracting. Many of the areas in and on the periphery of Barcelona are characterized by a high concentration of small firms in tight subcontracting networks and with dense interdependence between them.[1] Examples include wool production, chemicals and the metal-working industries.

2. Productive decentralization. Intense de-industrialization (see 3 below) in Catalonia during the period of economic crisis, 1974–84, led to a process of industrial diffusion from the metropolitan centre of Barcelona to the peripheral comarcas, as well as a dismantling of large firms and an increase in wider networks of subcontracting. But as Benson (1992) notes, as the intent was to lower costs, the impact of productive decentralization has been to downgrade labour conditions and depress earnings. Of particular importance was the expansion of the informal economy.

3. Economic and entrepreneurial dynamism. As a consequence of increased foreign investment in the 1980s the presence of firms with foreign capital is dominant in most of the principal branches of Catalan industry, in vehicle manufacture, electronics and electrical goods, chemicals, perfume and detergents, pharmaceuticals and plastics. These are the most dynamic

---

manufacturing sectors which use the more advanced technology, exploit scale economies, have new management and better and larger distribution networks. However, this picture masks a substantial and rapid transformation of the region's economic base. Whilst the whole of Spain was effected by the economic crisis between 1974 and 1985, the concentration of localized production in Catalonia resulted in high losses, both of employment and firms, especially in the series of industrial nuclei in Barcelona and the surrounding areas. The traditional sectors, however, are still declining. It is these sectors which are associated with weak demand, insufficient size of firm and low technological levels.

4. Cooperation between firms and between local institutions. Until 1978 there was an absence of autonomous business associations and trade unions in Spain; neither legally existed under Franco. Even after 1978 business associations were often weak in the small firm and fragmented industrial sectors.

5. Regional governments or strong local leadership and local-level planning. In Spain regional governments emerged only in the late 1970s and the regions themselves were characterized, until recently, by a lack of planning of any kind. Benson states that 'under the Franco regime local level planning even of the most rudimentary sort barely existed' (1992:77). The situation has changed now as both the City Council and the regional government have developed an extensive range of services: new technology diffusion, R & D, trade promotions, management advice, and technological parks. The socialist municipal Council in particular has attempted to integrate all groups from business management to trade unions 'in an effort to adapt to changes in the production sector (Sanchez 1992).

6. Social cohesiveness or a pre-existing cultural consensus. Modern Catalonia has 'a strong degree of national Catalan consciousness and a very distinctive culture embodied not only in the language, literature and arts, but also in the country's law, political institutions and the quality of civic life' (Giner 1980:1). In the period from the 1950s to the mid-1970s, however, the Catalan and specifically Barcelonian working class became transformed by the massive influx of immigrants from other parts of Spain.[2] In many residential areas and workplaces the working class is divided between immigrants from rural parts of Spain and indigenous workers.[3] Further, weakened trade unions and strongly paternalistic or atomized relations of production appear to provide none of the conditions of trust and cohesiveness.

7. A flexible labour force. As we discussed in Chapter 2, reforms to 'rigidities' of labour markets have given rise to a marked dualism between older permanent workers enjoying a high degree of labour protection, and temporary workers on precarious job contracts. There is also limited job mobility and a marked Taylorist emphasis in firms, with narrow job training. This applies to between one-third and one-fourth of firms, especially small and medium-sized firms (OECD 1991/2a), and negatively affects both vocational training and the introduction of new technology.

The automobile industry in Spain

The automotive industry in Spain is now wholly in the hands of foreign multinational companies. The industry is a leading one in the country with a significant contribution to exports (6 out of the top 10 exporters), and one of the major world producers of cars (Salmon 1991). Salmon estimates that in the late 1980s as many as 500 000 people worked directly and indirectly in the industry.

The period 1960–73 was a period of rapid growth for automobile production in Spain, during which foreign capital was allowed to enter local production induced by political incentives.[4] Local supplier firms with the help of alliances with foreign firms and the use of foreign technology became more involved in the production process. But Spain's economy was still isolated from the rest of Europe at this time and was unable to compete on the international economy. The period 1973 to 1986 was marked by a shift to export promotion. Large car manufacturers could invest if they exported a majority of production in return for a reduced local minimum content.[5] The strategies of the large American companies was to integrate production activities and import components through European networks. In the period 1986 to 1992, following the integration of Spain into the EC, there has been a marked reorganization of the production and supply strategies of car makers.

Lagenddijk (1994) summaries this transformation as: first, centralization of control with co-ordination of production transferred from a national to an international level; secondly, production chains have been integrated internally with increasing rationalization and specialization of local subsidiaries (this included the introduction of flexible automation systems and robots, and reductions in the size of workforces); thirdly, supply chains have been reformed and aligned to the international supply systems of the parent company. This included the substitution of foreign-owned subsidiary firms with local suppliers to implement just-in-time techniques, a reduction of the total number of suppliers and increasing imports of components from the parent company.[6]

Lagenddijk found that local firms become increasingly marginalized and there were indications of tiering and stratification among suppliers. 'Only a small number of firms have managed, often at the price of intense restructuring, to stay in the first ranks of the supply chains. Some firms have managed to acquire secondary or tertiary positions within the supply chain and many have been forced to withdraw from the automobile sector' (Lagenddijk 1994:337).

Other research carried out into the automobile industry in the Barcelona area also found that those firms who were not part of the permanent relationship of the 'favoured supplier' were converted into marginal firms covering emergency situations and specialising in marginal areas of production (Recio *et al.* 1991). It was the large firms with advanced technological knowledge and capacity and sufficient capital (or very specialized medium-sized firms) who secured the long-term contracts. The marginalized suppliers had little power or knowledge to alter their situation and in many cases had grave financial deficiencies and poor technological capacity. In the Barcelona area the emergent dual structure of component firms has given rise to distinct types of work transformation and new forms of segmentation of the labour force (Recio *et al.* 1991). Furthermore, the continued existence of the small firms, with either long-term or intermittent contracts, looks increasingly fragile as the transnational firms take decisions to relocate production elsewhere and close down local production, as in the example of Volkswagen.[7]

In other industrial sectors in Spain processes of industrial re-structuring have led to the development of hierarchical chains of sub-contracting and dependent relations. In the traditional textile sector, for example, if firms have been able to survive, it has been through the extensive use of the informal economy and more recently by the employment of temporary workers on fixed-term contracts. The employment of women and young workers in this sector has been on an increasingly precarious basis (Cousins 1994a, Recio *et al.* 1988, 1991). Thus we can say that industrial restructuring and emerging employment condi-tions vary not only between the regions but also between firms within regions, with a growing polarization between modern advanced technology firms, dominated by the transnationals, and the traditional industrial sectors still in crisis. Processes of in-dustrial restructuring have led to the development of hierarchi-cal chains of subcontracting and dependent relations between the transnationals and small and medium firms, with associated fragmentation of the workforce and labour processes.

Baden-Württemberg

Baden-Württemberg is often cited as the example of flexible specialization in Germany, and even as a Musterlandle (a model or showpiece land) (Herrigel 1996). This Lander is one of the most prosperous regions in Europe. For example, the region scores 120 compared with a European Union average of 100 for GPD per capita (CSO 1994). Although research has focused on the Baden-Württemberg region, Lane (1995) has also noted that simi-lar local networks can be found in other parts of Germany. She cites, for example, furniture in Eastern Westphalia, tool-making in Remscheid and medical products in Tuttlingen among others.

In Baden-Württemberg the main industries include the auto-motive industries, electrical engineering, and machine tools.[8] It is an area in which the 'very highest reaches of excellence have been attained' (Cooke and Morgan 1994:113). According to Herrigel (1993) the key to the success of the region is 'the abil-ity to rapidly produce high quality, specialized products, with very short product cycles while simultaneously reducing the cost gap between a standardized product and a specialized custom tailored one. It is possible to say of these producers in Baden-Württemberg that they produce an almost infinite array of special industrial products in virtually infinite variety' (Herrigel 1993:16).

Baden-Württemberg has, therefore, been seen to display the characteristics of a vertical-subcontracting network of firms, specialising in 'diversified quality production' by skilled engineers bolstered by 'the hierarchical power of the highly skilled "Meister"'. Economic success is underpinned by the firms embeddedness in a dense network of intermediary institutions which support their business and production activities. This collaborative network is based on banks, Chambers of Commerce, trade associations and regional and municipal states.[9] This is in contrast to the Italian industrial districts which, as we have seen above, are based on family, neighbourhood and political or religious ties. In both cases, however, the success of the regions is said to stem from the reliance of small and medium-sized firms on a high level of local linkages and networks to achieve competitiveness in international markets. Some writers though are sceptical of these claims. Staber (1996), for example, found little evidence to suggest business relations in Baden-Württemberg are embedded in local support structures. He found Baden-Württemberg to be diversified territorially and industrially, with leading and backward areas side by side. Some areas, such as Stuttgart, are dominated by growth industries but others, as in the Catalan example, contain declining textile and clothing firms.

By 1992 researchers report that the Baden-Württemberg region was not only suffering from the deepest recession in the post-war period, but that the job losses, bankruptcies and decline in GDP growth rate was understood as a structural crisis caused by international competition, especially from Japan (Cooke and Morgan 1994, Herrigel 1996). As Herrigel comments, 'Germany's competitors have been able to maintain their higher levels of productivity while entering German high quality production' (1996:35). Herrigel argues that it is neither high wage costs, nor the lack of modern growth-intensive industries, but rather that 'German manufacturers cannot compete in world markets using market strategies and production practices that have made them successful in the past' (Herrigel 1996:35). He cites the superiority of alternative forms of flexible production, especially of the Japanese, which enable competitors to supply high-quality customised products at lower prices.

Cooke and Morgan (1994) similarly argue that the major challenge of the 1990s has been the pressure for firms to adopt the techniques of 'lean production'. This has affected supplier relations as firms are responding by increasing the out-sourcing of components. Since many of the new suppliers are Japanese this by-passes the Mittelstand firms. This perceived long-term crisis is also exacerbated by an over-reliance on car production and other traditional sectors, technological change and high labour, land and environmental costs. The institutions of the region have been forced to restructure and to adopt new initiatives, for example new forms of cooperation between large and small firms, an increase in qualification levels and new technology and marketing policies (Cooke *et al.* 1995).

The form of regional governance displayed by regions such as Baden-Württemberg and Emilia Romagna in the Third Italy illustrate, however, the complex directions of change at the end of the 1990s. As we discussed in Chapter 1, at the national level previous neo-corporatist arrangements have been eroded as firms seek global locations and alliances with other firms. These alliances transcend the national regulatory frameworks as well as those of firms' business associations. In contrast, in regions such as Baden-Württemberg, neo-corporatism may be strengthened, in both informal and formal ways, through the networks of regional and local states, associations and institutes (Crouch and Menon 1997). However, there is some evidence that German firms may loosen their ties with the regional economy as they seek locations outside, for example, in other parts of west and east Europe. It is more likely though that employers will use the threat of relocation to another country as a means to force their workforces to accept wages and working conditions below the collective agreement standards (Flecker and Schulten 1997).

Some large firms, for example Volkswagen, and some sectors such as the postal service and the German railways, have also pulled out of their employers' associations (and large parts of the private service sector have grown up outside the collective bargaining system altogether), so that collective bargaining now devolves to company level. Many firms in east Germany too have either left the employers' associations or stayed out in the first place. Others remain members, but pay wages below the contractual minimum (Van Ruysseveldt and Visser 1996). New employer strategies, the demise of the stakeholder firm through the adoption of new methods of business organization and financing, and the tendency towards decentralization of collective bargaining are all challenges to the traditional governance of German industrial relations, the source of success in the past.

Conclusion

The success of regions such as Baden-Württemberg and Emilia Romagna has led to the emulation of their characteristics by less developed regions and to active promotion of regional policies by the European Commission as a means of promoting economic growth. The importance of the region in providing infrastructural and environmental support for firms has led some to argue that the region, rather than the nation state, is the most appropriate level for investment and economic development. New linkages and co-operative relations have been established not only between the regions but also between the regions and the European Commission. In the view of Cooke *et al.* (1997) not only are nation states experiencing a shift of economic policy-making to the supranational European level, but regional policy-making is becoming more important in some countries, especially in attracting inward investment, innovative industrial policies and support for small and medium-sized firms. In the view of these authors there is, therefore, a 'hollowing out of the nation state' (see also Jessop 1994). This adds to the complex multilevel layers of governance in the European Union, noted in the Introduction, as regions compete for international capital and European funds (Cooke *et al.* 1997, Rhodes *et al.* 1997).

However, the dynamism of regions such as Baden-Württemberg, Emilia Romagna, and the Rhone-Alps are clearly quite special rather than the rule, and dependent on 'historically rooted cultural and institutional features' (Lane 1995:115). Given the embeddedness of the economic life of firms in the social and cultural institutional structures of these regions, it is difficult for the industrial district phenomena to be transferred elsewhere. As Amin and Malmberg (1994) have argued, the gradual build up of know-how and skills, co-operative traditions, local institutional support, specialist services and infrastructure takes a long time to consolidate. The historical absence of these conditions was noted in the Catalan example. In other more centralized states regions may not even have the capacity for regional autonomy, for example in Britain, Portugal and Greece. In the automotive industry in Spain it was also found that the restructuring of the multinationals has led to growing dependent relations between large firm assemblers and 'favoured' small and medium firm supplies, as well as a polarization and hierarchy between the component supplier firms.

Regional economic development is therefore a highly uneven process in the different member states. As we noted in the Introduction, while international competition, the operations of multinational companies and the process of European integration create strong pressures for change in European economies, these are not only mediated through the specific institutional structures of each country, but are also having differential impacts within countries, both between regions and between firms within regions.

Further reading

A good introduction to the debate on post-Fordism is contained in Amin 1994. On flexible specialization see Piore and Sabel 1984, Sabel 1989, Scott 1988, Storper and Scott 1992, and the ILO studies Pyke, Becattini, and Sengenberger 1990, and Pyke and Sengenberger 1992. A cross-country comparison of the conditions for flexible specialization in France, Germany and the UK is presented by Lane 1989a, 1995. Among the many critiques of the flexible specialization thesis are Amin 1989, Amin and Robins 1990, Amin and Malmberg 1994, Amin and Tomaney 1995, Curry 1993, and Pollert 1991.

On the industrial-district phenomena in Spain, see Benson 1992. On Catalonia Balfour 1989 provides a very good account of the history of the labour movement, and see Giner 1980 for a discussion of the social structure and Sanchez 1992 on recent policy developments. On the automobile industry in Spain see Lagenddijk 1994 and Recio *et al.* 1991.

On the Baden-Württemberg region in Germany see Cooke and Morgan 1992, 1994, Cooke *et al.* 1995, Herrigel 1993, 1996, and Staber 1996.

Discussions of regional developments in Europe are to be found in Amin and Thrift 1994, Amin and Tomaney 1995, Cooke *et al.* 1997, and Rhodes 1995.

PART THREE
Issues of Social Policy

Normal expectation of women's
role within both Bri. + Ge
was and is

5

Women and Social Policies

This chapter examines the development of social policies for women in Europe with particular reference to the four countries of Britain, Germany, Spain and Sweden. In Chapter 3 we discussed the differing patterns of women's labour market participation and noted how these patterns were in part shaped by the social policies adopted in each country, especially those which encouraged or discouraged the reconciliation of paid work and family life. Chapter 6 discusses poverty and social exclusion in Europe and there we also examine how women's access to material and other resources is affected by social security policies and access to paid employment. This chapter, in contrast, focuses on the historical developments of social policies for women and the underlying assumptions of the 'normal expectations' of women's roles within each society. The chapter first considers the theoretical debates on the comparative study of welfare states and gender. This section examines recent feminist critiques of mainstream social policy and discusses a number of concepts and policy dimensions which are useful for the comparative analysis of how women fare in different welfare states. The second section focuses on the development of social policies for women in the four case-study countries.

Theoretical issues

Recent writers have stressed the need to introduce gender into a comparative analysis of welfare states, especially the relationship between paid and unpaid work and welfare. A starting point for these writers has been Esping-Andersen's (1990) typology of welfare regimes. As we discussed in the Introduction, many writers have been critical of Esping-Andersen's use of the concept of 'decommodification', which focuses mainly on the relationship between state and market. Although Esping-Andersen argues that an understanding of the welfare state must take into account how state activities are interlocked with the market's, and the family's role in the provision of welfare, many writers have pointed out that he neglects or under-analyses the family's contribution to welfare (for example, Daly 1994, Orloff 1993). However, the family remains an important provider of welfare in all welfare states, even in social-democratic regimes (Daly 1994). The relationship between the welfare state and the family – which includes the unpaid domestic and caring work of women within the family – needs, therefore, to be analysed in its own right.

Once gender is brought into the analysis the concept of decommodification presents difficulties. For example, not all demographic groups are equally commodified because of limited access to the labour market. Women, amongst other groups, are constrained in their labour market participation and quality of paid employment (O'Connor 1993). Several writers have, therefore, suggested that the concept should be supplemented or replaced with other dimensions or models (see Orloff 1993, O'Connor 1993, Langan and Ostner 1991, Lewis 1992). Orloff (1993), for example, has argued that the decommodification concept should be supplemented with an analysis of two further dimensions of welfare states. First, 'the right to be commodified', that is, policies which promote women's paid employment should be analysed since these enable access to individual economic independence. However, a strategy of women taking on more paid work and becoming more like men also has difficulties if it means that women retain the dual burden of paid and unpaid work. The problem with this is that whilst women do appear to be becoming more like men in entering paid work, 'men seem to refuse to look more like women, in that they do not take over care work to the same extent' (Bussemaker and van Kersbergen 1994). A further problem, of course, is that many women in paid work do not earn sufficient to provide for their own independence. The second dimension in Orloff's scheme is the ability of those who do most of the domestic and caring work to form and maintain autonomous households without having to marry to gain access to a breadwinner's income or benefits.

Lewis (1992, 1993) and Langan and Ostner (1991) provide an alternative to the decommodification concept. They have shown that the strength or weakness of the male-breadwinner family model and the extent to which it has been eroded in different countries can be a useful way in which to compare welfare regimes and the relation between paid and unpaid work and welfare. In the pure form of the male-breadwinner model we would expect to find that 'married women are excluded from the labour market, firmly subordinated to their husbands for purposes of social security and tax and expected to care for dependants at home without public support' (Lewis 1993:162). Lewis finds Ireland and Britain to be historically strong male-breadwinner states, France exhibits a modified operation of the model and Sweden a dual-breadwinner model. They recognize that the majority of families have never achieved the gendered division of labour that depended on men being able to earn a family wage. However, the strength or weakness of the male breadwinner family model can serve as an indicator of the way women have been treated in social security systems, of the level of social service provision and the nature of married women's position in the labour market.

Lewis (1992) and Langan and Ostner (1991) concentrate on women's relationship to the state as mothers or as workers, although it is possible to discern other roles. Sainsbury's work (1994a), for instance, makes clear that the breadwinner model is crucial to an analysis of gender and welfare states, but women's entitlements within the welfare state may be as wives, mothers, workers or as citizens. A careful analysis is therefore required to unravel the basis of entitlement in each country. A number of dimensions of the breadwinner model are used in this chapter, for example, the type of familial ideology and its influence on social policy, basis of entitlement, recipient of benefits, and division of labour within the family and employment policies (see Sainsbury 1994a).

In addition to the insights of the above writers a further dimension to the analysis of welfare states has been suggested by Walby (1994) in relation to T.H. Marshall's concept of citizenship. Walby argues that 'Marshall's concept of citizenship opens the way to discuss the degrees of citizenship obtained by different social groups at different times' (Walby 1994:381). While social citizenship is linked to, but different from, that of men, Walby considers that political citizenship is central to the transformation of gender relations and the shift from private to public patriarchy. As this chapter shows this is particularly relevant to Spain where the (re)gaining of political rights, for both men and women in the transition to democracy was especially important for women in achieving civil rights, for example, 'liberty of the person', family law and equal rights. However, as the following discussion shows, the relationship between civil, political and social citizenship rights for women is complex.

Box 5.1   Early European social policies for women

Initial programmes of social policy during the formative period of the welfare state, approximately 1880 to the onset of the First World War, were designed to fit and reinforce the family wage system, with men as breadwinners and women as dependants. Thus these earlier policies could be said to be 'paternalistic' in that they privileged the position of the breadwinner (Orloff 1993). There were 'maternalistic' policies in that by the 1930s most countries in Europe were concerned about falling birth rates and almost every country pursued 'with varying degree of vigour' pronatalist policies 'extreme in Francoist Spain, Nazi Germany and mild in Britain and Scandinavia' (Bock and Thane 1991).

Policies differed, however, between liberal democracies and dictatorships. In the liberal democracies, women, even though they had only recently gained the vote, were nevertheless able to exert some influence on the final shape of legislation (Bock and Thane 1991). As Table 5.1 shows, mothers were the beneficiaries of family allowances when they were introduced in Sweden and Britain. France, however, has followed a different pattern in that women did not achieve the vote until 1944 and family allowances, introduced in 1939, were paid to the male head of household until 1979. In contrast, the dictatorship regimes of Germany, Italy and Spain 'practised a thoroughgoing cult of masculinity striving to reinforce male authority in the family, to compensate male workers for paternity and to develop a new vision of paternity' (Bock and Thane 1991:13).

Otto Von Bismarck

Family allowances (paid to men) were introduced in Germany in 1935, in Italy in 1936, and in Spain in 1938; tax exemptions according to family size were paid to the male head of household in Italy in 1933 and Germany in 1934 and 1939; and fertility bonuses were paid to husbands in Italy in 1939 and Spain in 1943. Marriage loans were made to the male head in Germany in 1933, Italy in 1937, and Spain in 1938 (Nash 1991, Saraceno 1991 and Bock 1991).

The development of social policies for women

Germany

Welfare benefits introduced in Germany in the 1930s were similar to those introduced by other emergent European welfare states but, in common with the dictatorships of Spain and Italy, all policies privileged fathers over mothers (see Box 5.1). The regime institutionalized a cult of fatherhood in which the father was entitled to rewards from the state. Women, however, had to play a crucial role in enacting racial policies by marrying racially and eugenically correctly, bearing healthy children and policing their children's behaviour. Concern with the low birth rate had been met, for some decades, with eugenic principles to impel the 'superior' to have children and the 'inferior' to have few or no children (Bock 1984). The former was to be achieved through financial and social incentives and the latter through sterilization. Although sterilization policy had been carried out elsewhere, for example in the USA, the scale was unique in Germany in the 1930s and differed from practices in dictatorships elsewhere. It was a 'race' policy 'which put a definite, consistent and deadly limit to state welfare' (Bock and Thane 1991:15). 'The "race" policy gave National Socialism its novelty and specificity' (Bock 1992:105), and both men and women who were judged to be 'inferior' met persecution, sterilization and death.

Married women were discouraged from seeking paid employment and a policy of substituting men for their jobs became law in 1933. Women were expelled from academic or professional jobs, from the civil service and from all other jobs where men feared competition from female professional or white-collar workers. After 1936 policies were designed to draw women back

Table 5.1 Date of introduction of social policies for women and the family in selected European countries

	France	Germany	Italy	Spain	Sweden	UK
Female suffrage	1944	1919	1945	1978 (1931–6) (Second Republic)	1919	1928 (1918) (for women over 30)
Family allowances paid to fathers	1939–79	1954 (1935)	1936	1938		
paid to mothers					1947	1946
Marriage loans paid to male heads	n/k	1933	1937	1938	1937	–
Child tax allowance for fathers	n/k	1934	1933	1940s	[1952 for mothers]	1911–75
Abolition of permission of husband for wife to take paid work	1965	1977	n/k	1975	n/a	n/a
Illegitimacy as a legal status abolished	n/k	1977	1975	1981	1977	1989
Equal rights of husbands and wives written into law/constitution	1970	1977	1975	1978	1915	–
Divorce by consent	1975	1977	1970	1981	1920	1971
Contraception made legal	1967	1976	1975	1978	1938	1938
Parental leave	1977	1986	a	1989	1974	–
Abortion law reform	1975	1976	1975	1985 1975	1965	1967
Equal pay	1950	1980	1954	1975	1980	1975

[a] Parental leave in Italy is regulated by industry collective agreements, date of introduction n/k.

into paid work for production for the war effort. However, German women were unwilling recruits into the German industrial labour force, and conscripted and forced labour was more widely used. Middle-class women were not expected to work. Those who did work were from working-class backgrounds who worked in poor conditions with poor pay. As a consequence 'going out to work' was widely regard as a hardship and 'not-working' glamorized as a sign of luxury. As we discuss below, this view was still characteristic of German feminist discourse in the 1980s (Ostner 1993).

After the war the Allies suspended Nazi policies for the family. The family was now seen as an arena of privacy against the state, with a reinsertion of men's role as gatekeepers of the boundary between the public and private spheres (Ostner 1993). Despite their numerical superiority immediately after the Second World War (at 70 per cent of the electorate), women remained in the background of post-war politics. They did not 'turn their numerical strength into an effective voice of innovation or take a leading role in the social and political life of the day' (Kolinsky 1993:12). Partly this was dictated by the needs of survival in the aftermath of the war (half the population were dislocated from their usual habitat) but women had also been weakened by the decade of tutelage and social control of the Nazi regime. For stability, Germans looked to the private sphere of the family.

In the debate about family allowances or 'money for children' in the 1950s the view of the 'normal family' prevailed. Those families headed by never-married, widowed or divorced mothers were described as 'incomplete' or 'half- families' without fathers. These families were seen 'as extraordinary developments of extraordinary times' (Moeller 1989:153) which would soon disappear along with the surplus population of women. The foundation of family income was to be the male wage. 'Proposals that payments go directly to mothers were not even discussed' (Moeller 1989:153). Those not in waged work, the unemployed, those in receipt of welfare assistance and all those with one or two children were excluded. The unemployed and those on welfare assistance were included one year later. In the state's attempts to shape private relationships within the family there were striking continuities across the divide of 1945.

The adoption of the 1949 Basic Law guaranteed equal rights for men and women, but the Federal Legal Code established all decision making in the husband, a clause not annulled until 1957. Until 1977 women were presented explicitly as home-makers in the Civil Code and domestic responsibilities still recognized as the fulfilment of a legal duty. A husband also had the legal power to prevent his wife from taking paid employment or, if his income was insufficient, to force her to earn money (similar legislation existed in France until 1965 and in Spain until 1975; see Table 5.1). In 1977 in west Germany the concept of 'house-wife-marriage' was relinquished by the SPD/FDP government and legislation enacted to promote greater equality between men and women. Marriage was now seen to consist of partners who decide between them how to divide paid and unpaid work. Legislation also legitimated children born outside marriage, and liberalized divorce (Kolinsky 1993). A year earlier access to contraception and limited access to abortion on certain grounds had been made easier (see Table 5.1).

Social policy in Germany is based on the concept of subsidiarity, that is, welfare services should be provided at the lowest level, interpreted as the family as the first resort when care is needed. The high number of volunteers (mostly women) in the provision of personal social services also reinforces the view that caring work is an extension of familial caring roles and, as Wilson (1993) points out, this 'normalizes' care within the family for children and old people. One consequence has been that, unlike Sweden, there has not been an expansion of public-sector services which have provided jobs for women and in turn enabled more women to go out to work.

Social policies in west Germany have also been based on the assumption that individuals are continuously embedded in vertical and horizontal relations in gender and generation. Consequently the importance of differentiated roles for men and women (although of comparable worth) underlie social policies (Ostner 1994a). Ostner also notes that feminist discourse 'more or less explicitly supports the idea that a woman's life is shaped primarily by all sorts of unpaid caring: for her child or grandchild, for a husband, for her mother, mother-in-law, for friends and neighbours' (Ostner 1993:95).

Box 5.2   Family policy in west Germany

Family policy in west Germany is still characterized by the fact it targets the complete and legitimate family (Hantrais 1994). The fiscal and tax policies, social security policies and social policies are still based on the notion of women as the homemaker and men as the breadwinner. The dominant policy objective is to encourage women to stay at home to look after young children. The tax system is particularly favourable for a married couple with one high income and one low income or no income (Scheiwe 1994, Hantrais 1994). It therefore acts as a disincentive for married women to work.

Legislation in 1986 gave pension rights to mothers who took time out from employment to look after their child. For each child women acquired pension rights equivalent to one year's employment. However, only those women who had been employed and paid national insurance were entitled to pension rights. The same legislation also introduced a new parental leave in that either parent can choose child-rearing payments or a child-rearing vacation. From 1993 this allowance (means-tested) is available for either (working) parent for 24 months. Since 1992 a three-year period of leave brings with it the right to reinstatement of the job. In addition all parents in work are entitled to absence from work to care for children (up to 10 days per year per child, 20 days for lone parents). However, the vast majority of those who exercise their right to the allowances are mothers. Since the replacement income is low, it requires that there is another income resource available. The model is, therefore, one which assumes that someone else is providing for the family's maintenance (Scheiwe 1994).

With respect to child allowances, either parent can now choose who should be the recipient, but in practice 90 per cent of the recipients are men (Scheiwe 1994).

Feminism in west Germany is, therefore, different from other western countries in that paid work is not necessarily associated with independence. The double burden of paid work and unpaid work in the home, in this view, does not bring emancipation. The difficulties of combining paid work and a family, and the patriarchal nature of social policy in the post-war period has resulted, as Chamberlayne (1994) shows, in a curious polarization between women with and without children. 'In a perverse manner [social policy] encouraged both careerist childlessness

and traditional housewife roles' (Chamberlayne 1994:176). In the
1980s, 26 per cent of west German women were childless. However as Chamberlayne argues, the lines of fracturing are complex, with both radical and conservative feminists on either side
of the equality/difference debate. The influence of west German
feminists on social policy has, however, been more influential
than in Britain, especially through their influence on the Green
and Social Democratic political parties

For women in east Germany before unification the situation
was quite different. We have already seen in Chapter 3 the high
levels of female labour-market participation in the GDR. Rhe-
torically, economic independence was linked with emancipation
although the reality was that policies were child- and mother-
centred. The *Muttipolitik* of the state provided child-care facilities, child benefits, maternity leave and maternity benefits, housing
subsidies and a monthly day off for housework. Women tended
to marry young and have their children at a young age. In comparison with women in the west, few women wished to remain
childless and the proportion of childless couples was about 10
per cent (Kolinsky 1993). By the time of unification the divorce
rate was one of the highest in Europe and increasing numbers
of women had opted to have children without getting married.
Single motherhood was therefore an option cushioned by an array
of protective measures. However, the traditional domestic division of labour remained, with women in east Germany expected
to divide the caring work between themselves (Ostner 1994a).
Nor was there a process of public debate on, and modification
of, traditional gender roles, as in the west.

Since unification, loss of employment, and a range of social
policies and public subsidies has led most commentators to argue
that women have been the main losers. The experience of social
trauma is indicated by the decline in the birth rate (falling by
62 per cent between 1989 and 1992), a fall in marriage rates
and divorce rates and an increase in a demand for sterilizations
to enhance job prospects (Chamberlayne 1994). East German
men, on the other hand, where they are employed, have regained
roles as a husband, father and breadwinner.

Spain

In Spain the family has never been merely a part of the daily life of its citizens. It has been granted a special eminence and has always been under the control of the Church. Whilst the Church has lost control over many areas of social life, 'it never abandoned the claim that family law fell within its orbit, either directly or via the civil power' (De Ussel 1991:279). The Second Republic (1931–6), however, brought radical changes in the legal treatment of women and the family. Church and state were separated and innovatory laws such as the regulation of abortion and divorce by consent were introduced. Women also achieved suffrage in 1931. However, because the legislation was in effect for such a short time its impact may have been minimal. Nash (1991) considers that in practice inequality still characterized the social situation of Spanish women during this short period.

After the Civil War the Church called for the abolition of divorce and the return of family law to the Church; the legislation in force before 1931 was therefore restored. Equality between legitimate and illegitimate children was removed, adultery and the use of contraceptives were penalized. Religious marriage for baptised Catholics was made obligatory, the Church was given the right to adjudicate matrimonial separation and annulment, and inequality with regard to the sexes in respect of the rights outside and inside marriage was established. The state reconstituted the family and gave it a central place in the social construction of the new Spain. 'The family was the primary unit of society, a basic cell in the body politic of the state and community' (Nash 1991:170)

Francoist thought generated a pronatalist ideology which viewed women as basically mothers or potential mothers. 'Female sexuality, work and education were regulated in accordance with this social function whilst motherhood was idealised and considered a duty to the fatherland' (Nash 1991:160). The *Perfecta Casada*, the dedicated and submissive spouse and mother, was the model woman. Women were

> the key to halting national degeneration through maximum development of their reproductive capacity. . . Hence aspirations to work, education and self improvement, social activity or emancipation were a threat to women's biological destiny as forgers of the nation's future generations (Nash 1991:160, 167).

However, Spanish women took little notice of this propaganda; rather, the difficulties of survival in the immediate post-Civil-War years appear to have led to a fall in the birth rate[1]. Only when there was general improvement in the economic situation and in living standards did the birth and marriage rates begin to increase in the late 1950s and early 1960s.

A strong model of the male-breadwinner family existed under Franco. First, men were able to obtain favourable allowances as head of the family. Family allowances, introduced in 1938, were paid directly to *jefe de familia* and regarded as supplementary to his income. Family bonuses were also included in his wages. These family benefits were only available to legitimate marriages and to legitimate children and were conditional on employment. Large families were allowed numerous fringe benefits and prizes given to the largest (usually over 14 children). As in fascist Germany and Italy, all these policies rewarded and compensated for paternity, at the same time reinforcing male authority within the family.

A second feature of the male-breadwinner model was that married women were discouraged from paid work. Coercive measures were introduced which obliged women to give up work on marriage. From 1938 married women had to obtain permission from their husbands to work outside the home. Several policies acted as inducements to marriage and children, for example, *la dote* (the dowry), an economic compensation which employers gave to women when they left work to marry; nuptiality prizes given to couples; and loans granted were reduced by 25 per cent on the birth of up to four children (Nash 1991). Again these policies were similar to those introduced in Germany during the 1930s.

The legal framework established by Franco with respect to marriage and the family remained unchanged until the transition to democracy and the 1978 Constitution. However, De Ussel (1991) argues that family life and sexual and social change began as early as the 1960s. Migration from the rural to urban parts of Spain, rapid industrialization, the slow growth of women's participation in paid work and exposure to mass tourism all had their effects. Despite the illegality of contraception and the pronatalist ideology, the birth rate began to fall after 1964. De Ussel (1991) notes that during the 1960s the family as an institution

Table 5.2 The development of social policies for women in Spain after the transition to democracy: 1978–91

1978	Equal rights of men and women written into the Constitution
1978	Sale, distribution and advertisement of contraception made legal
1980	Equal pay legislation
1981	Divorce by consent
1981	Equal rights of husbands and wives
1981	Rights of children born outside marriage equalized
1985	Abortion law reform *
1989	Parental leave introduced and maternity leave extended
1989	Tax reform – wives and husbands now taxed separately
1990	Right to family entitlement extended to families previously outside the scope of social security
1991	Family allowances means-tested to those earning under 1 million pesetas per year (approx. £5000)

* The 1985 Law permits abortion under three circumstances: when there is a serious threat to the life or health of the mother; where pregnancy is the result of rape; or grounds that the foetus will be born with serious handicap.

began to be founded on personal interaction rather than the authoritarianism of the official orthodoxy and traditional values. 'Political change therefore arrived [in the late 1970s] when the behaviour and attitudes of the majority of society had already transformed the Spanish family' (1991:285). Nevertheless, despite an openness in Spanish society in the last ten years of the Franco regime, there 'were neither democratic policies nor a welfare state to provide the services women needed in order to be able to leave their homes and go out to work' (Camps 1994:56).

The transition to democracy in the late 1970s removed most of the patriarchal laws and the political, civil, personal and employment rights of women have been transformed (see Table 5.2 for the main reforms). Many feminists placed their concerns on the political agenda through the women's committees in the socialist and communist parties. As Duran and Gallego (1986) report, the period 1975 to 1985 was for many feminists 'a time of hope, euphoria and subsequent disillusion'. The period 1975–9 was one of expansion and organization of the women's movement, in which their demands and claims were recognized and incorporated into party programmes. In the second period (1979–82) the movement was divided by strong internal divisions, especially over the debate on 'equality' versus 'difference' as the principle governing policy reform. By this time most of the basic legal rights of women had been recognized (see Table 5.2) except the right to legal abortion.

The third period (1982–5) was one of decline of the women's movement and 'one in which feminism reached the institutions but lost its strength as a movement' (Duran and Gallego 1986:200). An important institution, however, was the *Instituto de la Mujer* (Institute of Women's Rights), established in 1983; it is a source of programmes and activities directed to the promotion and recognition of women. Although the Institute cannot go much further than the politics of government, its activity has been wide ranging in the years since its establishment. In Threlfall's (1989) view the Institute is an example of the machinery of state being conquered by a social movement. As a government agency, she argues, the Institute has been more successful in penetrating the social fabric of Spain than the PSOE party itself.

The first set of reforms outlined in Table 5.2 (as in other southern European countries) concerned the establishment of equal rights in the Constitution of 1978. The second set of major reforms transformed the family code and family law. While family law in the past had usually generated ideological conflict, most of the changes in the transition period were achieved without political controversy, as we have noted above. However, abortion has been a contentious issue and the Church has totally rejected the idea of authorising abortion for any reason whatsoever (Dumon 1991), although in 1985 abortion was decriminalized in three specific areas (see Table 5.2).

Fertility rates are now among the lowest in Europe at 1.2 and, in common with other southern European countries, there has been an inversion of the traditional low fertility of the north European countries compared to the high fertility rates of southern European countries. This low fertility level in Spain is said to be a reflection of changing family formation and, in particular, the postponement of marriage and the deferment of first births (Castro Martin 1992). This is related to the difficulties which young people have in gaining employment and setting up separate households.

The nuclear family of a couple and their children is now the predominant form of family in Spain. However, since divorce has only been possible since 1981 there does not yet appear to be a widespread fragmentation of the household and family structure associated with the break-up of marriages, as is now apparent in northern Europe. In 1994 5.8 per cent of households were lone parent households of whom the vast majority were headed by females (87 per cent) (Eurostat 1996).[2] The majority were separated or divorced (50 per cent) or widowed (43 per cent), rather than single (7 per cent) (Instituto de la Mujer 1994). There is minimal state financial support for lone parents and no national housing policies.

On an optimistic note, a great deal has been achieved for women in Spain in less than two decades. The pace of social, economic and political change has been so rapid that it is possible to distinguish a profound break in the experiences of different generations of women. Garrido (1992) speaks of the 'two biographies' of women in which the life experiences of younger and older women have progressively diverged. These experiences include increased equal rights and opportunities, labour market participation, education, and the decline of the birth rate.

Two forms of discrimination remain of particular importance. First, women's participation in public life, in employment, politics, trade unions and other organizations, is lower than most other European countries.[3] The second discrimination concerns 'the double working day' – paid work and unpaid work in the home. The Instituto de Mujer (1992), for example, found that work was still very unequally divided in the home: housewives spent over six hours a day on activities traditionally considered women's housework – cleaning, cooking, washing, shopping, sewing and childcare; working women spent over four hours a day on such tasks; men about an hour of their time.

Sweden

Writers on the historical background of Swedish policies for women agree that the inspiration came from the book published by Alva and Gunner Myrdal, *Crisis in the Population Question*, in 1934. Although most advanced countries were concerned about declining birth rates, Sweden had the lowest birth rate of all in western Europe in the 1930s. The Myrdals recommended that the government should subsidize the well-being of the family and promote policies which would improve the condition of all social classes, but especially the working classes. Alva Myrdal also proposed that mothers should be able to take up paid employment and urged the government to take steps to help women combine paid work with motherhood. Many of the Myrdals recommendations were followed by the Population Committee set up in 1935. In turn these recommendations influenced policies introduced by the Social Democratic government in the late 1930s.[4] The Myrdals insisted that state policies should realize the potential of each individual (Lewis 1992). They were unique, too, in suggesting that Sweden should develop a pronatalist policy which made society, rather than an individual woman, increase commitment to family life (Haas 1992).

Despite the establishment of mothers' formal rights to employment in the 1930s, the decade of the 1950s 'was the decade of the housewife' (Gustafsson 1994: 50). As we have seen in Chapter 3, few married women were employed outside the home, only 15 per cent in 1950 (Haas 1992). Myrdal and Klein's book on *Women's Two Roles* (1957) provided an influential model in the 1950s. That is, women's roles were seen to be sequential – first as a mother and then as a worker. Women's place in the 'People's Home' was firmly in the family; social policies supported them as mothers, but gave little support as workers.

In the 1960s, as elsewhere the economic boom in Sweden led to a strong demand for labour. Although foreign labour was initially employed, difficulties and the substantial costs of assimilation led the government to the view that married women were a better reserve of labour. Also important at this time were issues of women's equality, which the new women's movements began to establish on the policy agenda of the political parties. The Social Democratic Women's Federation (SSKF) has been influential, not only in promoting women into political positions in the Social Democratic government, but also in establishing women's issues within the party. In 1964 the Social Democratic party adopted a women's programme, although, as Sainsbury (1993) notes, this had little impact at the time. By contrast, the publication of an all-party document, headed by Alva Myrdal, in 1969 placed equality issues at the top of the political agenda. From the late 1960s a range of policy measures (see Box 5.3) designed to encourage women to enter the labour market and combine family and paid work were put into effect. The goal of full employment, which previously had applied only to men, was now extended to women.

Box 5.3 Parental leave in Sweden

One important factor in encouraging women into paid employment in the 1970s was the introduction of separate taxation for married women from 1970. A second factor was the introduction of a parental leave scheme in 1974, initially for 6 months and subsequently extended. From 1989 the entitlement to parental leave was 450 week-days with income replacement. A mother might take 60 days before giving birth, and the rest could be split between the parents as they wish, for example by reducing working hours. The time has to be spent before the child is eight years old (Leira 1994). Income compensation amounting to 90 per cent of the wage was given for 360 days, and for the remaining period at a reduced rate. Throughout the 1990s, however, income replacement has been progressively reduced to 80 per cent.

Entitlements to paid leave for child care are available to both parents, although it is usually the mother who takes up the entitlement (see also the discussion on Sweden in Chapter 2). Although fathers have been reluctant to take extended periods of parental leave, to combat this they are now obliged to take one month of leave which cannot be transferred to the mother.

Since 1975 parents also have the right to paid leave for 'occasional care of children' extended from 10 days in 1974 to 60 days in 1980, and 120 days in 1990 (now reduced to 90 days) per each child under 12 years (Leira 1994). Over the past two decades there has also been increased state support for child care so that by the early 1990s approximately 85 per cent of all children whose parents wanted local authority day care received a place (Sainsbury 1996). Recent legislation has also introduced the right for all parents to have access to child care for under school-age children if they wish.

An important feature of the Swedish welfare regime is that
women are incorporated as citizens on the basis of their worker
status, that is, women have the same 'right to work' as men, and
this work then gives them entitlement to welfare benefits. As we
have seen in Chapter 3 women's labour market participation is
one of the highest in the advanced countries and most two-parent
families are now dual-earner families. The transformation of
Swedish families into dual-earner families has had the effect of
decreasing the economic dependence of women on their partners. In 1981 about 13 per cent of married/cohabiting women
received almost all of their financial resources via their husband's
earnings; by 1991 that proportion had decreased to 3 per cent
(Jonung and Persson 1994).

Hernes (1987) has suggested that the family can be described
as 'going public', with the transfer of tasks traditionally carried
out in the family (socialization, education, care of the sick and
aged) to the public sector. This has gone furthest in the Scandinavian welfare states where there has been, maintains Hernes, a
shift from private dependence on men's provider status to public
dependence on the public sector, both as employees and as clients.
Hernes notes, however, that the shift from private to public
dependence has not been complete in all areas and there is still
a heavy reliance on the family to provide basic services.

Other writers confirm this, for although a high proportion of
mothers are employed they still have problems solving the contradictions between the two sets of activity, of family and work,
which they must tackle individually.

> Women have been integrated into a labour market that is still struc-
> tured by a male norm: working conditions, hours of work, and, to a
> certain degree, wages, have relied on the principle that the 'normal'
> worker has somebody else to take care of the house and care work
> within the family (Borchorst 1990:176).

We discussed in Chapter 2 how men's work pattern remains that
of continuous and full working time. Despite the most progressive legislation, which seeks to diminish the incompatibility between family responsibilities and employment, there is still a strong
division of labour by gender within the family, in which mothers
are still ascribed the role of unpaid carer.

Considerable policy reforms of the welfare state, especially benefits and allowances, have been undertaken in the 1990s. High income-replacement levels of social insurance have gradually been reduced, from 90 per cent to 80 per cent between 1990 and 1994, and 75 per cent from 1996. This applies to unemployment, sickness and parental-leave benefits. However there is still minimal reliance on means-tested benefits, as cuts have been across the population so that vulnerable groups were not disproportionately affected. Nevertheless, since benefits constitute a greater portion of women's income package than men, the cuts have had a greater impact on women. Unlike the UK, though, disentitlement and means-tested eligibility have not been policy choices (Sainsbury 1996). New developments have also included a disability law which gives the disabled the right to a personal assistant, and the twelfth month of parental leave is now dependent on the father taking some responsibility for child care.

What may be occurring in the mid and late 1990s is a new set of political realignments based on gender. This corresponds to the growing polarization between public and private sectors and the fraying of the alliances between the LO and social democratic party (SAP) which formed the basis of the Swedish model in the mid-twentieth century. Men working mainly in the private sector may have more interest in retrenchment of welfare in order to restore the competitiveness of their firms. Women, as the majority of the public welfare labour force and the major clients of the welfare state, have a clear interest in defending the People's Home and the SAP. Indeed, in the 1994 elections women constituted the majority in parliament and a third in municipal seats. As Jenson and Mahon state, women may, 'then constitute the last defence – even – saviours of the beleaguered Peoples' Home' (1993:96).

The UK

In the UK, both before and after the Second World War, the dominant idea was that the male must support his family through the family wage and that women's waged work was detrimental to the welfare of the children and the stability of the family (Lewis 1992). Britain has, thus, shown a historical commitment to the male-breadwinner model, although more recently this type of family has substantially declined. Land's work (1978, 1980) has also shown how British social security and income tax systems have been firmly based on the concept of the male breadwinner and dependent housewife and mother since their inception. Social policies before the Second World War were mainly directed towards women as mothers and wives (especially working-class women) and were concerned with increasing knowledge of health and nutrition through initially voluntary charity workers and later health visitors. Maternity and child welfare services at this time met women's real needs but at the same time served to consolidate women's place in the home (Williams 1993).[5]

The Beveridge Report saw married women as

> occupied on work which is vital though unpaid, without which their husbands could not do their paid work and without which the nation could not continue . . . the Plan for Social Security treats married women as a special class of occupied persons . . . In the next thirty years housewives as mothers have vital work to do in ensuring the adequate continuance of the British Race and British Ideals in the World (Beveridge 1942: 49, 52, quoted in Clarke *et al.* 1987).

The Beveridge Report put the insurance principle at the centre of welfare benefits, to which employees and employers would contribute. The social insurance principle of the Beveridge Report was based on three basic assumptions: first, full (male) employment; secondly, the one-earner family with a gendered division of labour between male wage-earner and female home-maker; and thirdly, the stability of the family with the unit broken only by death (Falkingham and Baldwin 1994:3). With respect to the first principle, the contribution record of full-time male employment was premised on the 'standard employment relationship' – not only full-time, but permanent, with the full range of employment and social rights. The second principle positioned married women as dependants on their husbands. It was anticipated that most women, if they worked, would pay the lower 'married women's contribution' which meant that they were not entitled to sick pay, maternity, unemployment benefits or pensions in their own right. If married women did not work they were to be dependent on the contribution record of their husband. Women did not qualify through their role as mothers or wives. The Beveridge model was therefore far from universal. The third principle, although implicit, assumed that marriage would not be broken by separation or divorce, and thus marriage would provide income security for women. It would be sufficient for the state to guarantee men's incomes only, as women would then be financially secure (Millar 1994). As many writers have commented, all three assumptions no longer apply in the 1990s.

Family allowances were introduced in 1946, payable for the second and subsequent children, and paid directly to the mother.[6] The level of family allowances when introduced was considerably below the subsistence level for children, although they were universal. Since then its real value has fallen consistently. Reform in 1975 extended the benefit to the first child and increased the rate, whilst at the same time tax allowances for children were abolished. This was conceived as a transfer from 'wallet to purse' and after campaigns by anti-poverty groups and women's organizations, the benefit was eventually payable to the mother for all her children. The benefit, however, is not index linked. During the 1980s it did not keep pace with inflation and was frozen from 1987 to 1991.

By the early 1970s, three-quarters of married women had chosen to opt out of the national insurance scheme. Married women's national insurance contribution was eventually abolished in 1978 although, because of their past exclusion, many women could never establish full contribution records, for example, for pensions. Today many women are still excluded from contributions to national insurance because their earnings are below the lower earnings limit. Lister (1994) gives a figure of 2.25 million women who earned below the lower earnings limit in 1991. There is a further estimated 1.5 million women who are working on an occasional or irregular basis (including homeworking).

In Britain the social assistance (now income support) means-tested safety net assumed women's dependence on men through the aggregation of family income as a basis of determining benefit. Thus, where husbands had an income their wife could not independently claim benefit. In 1988 means-tested benefits were reformed to permit either men or women to act as the claimant although aggregation of family income remained. Lister (1994) states, however, that only one in twenty couples has opted for the woman to be the claimant. The means-tested income support is still based on the one-breadwinner (usually male) mode, since a couple is excluded from applying for income support if one of the two is employed for 16 hours a week or more.[7] The general picture which emerges is of a 'two-tier system' where the majority of recipients of contributory benefits are men and women the majority of recipients of means-tested or non-contributory benefits (Lister 1994).

Key reforms in Britain affecting divorce, abortion, contraception and equal pay (see Table 5.1) were passed by a Labour government before second-wave feminism developed and promoted, in Chamberlayne's (1993) view, gender-neutral policies. Policies pursued in the 1980s and 1990s, however, have been described as 'gender reaffirmation', that is, 'a reaffirmation of traditional female values and roles' (Chamberlayne 1993:172). Policies on reproductive issues, such as care of children and care for elderly dependants, have sought to emphasize that these are a matter of individual or family choice and duty rather than the responsibility of the state. In the area of maternity rights Britain was the only member state in Europe where such rights diminished in the 1980s.[8] Furthermore, there is no entitlement to parental leave or working-time reduction on the birth of a child.

These policies are in contradiction, however, to a reality in which increasing numbers of married women with dependent children have entered the labour market, and to a period in which there has been a marked decline in the male-breadwinner family (see discussions on the UK in Chapters 2 and 6). Chamberlayne (1993) has suggested that the women's movement in Britain has, in contrast to feminism in many other European countries, been unable to push women's issues on to the political agenda as major electoral issues; instead they have remained off the centre stage. The causes, she suggests, may be the two-party straightjacket of British politics and the dominance of the new right from 1979 to 1997.

Conclusion

In all four countries the strength of the male-breadwinner family has been modified or eroded in the last two decades, although there are substantial differences between the countries. These differences reflect historical developments in each country and the ways in which women's life trajectories have been shaped by the 'normal expectations' of women's roles within each society. In turn these expectations have shaped the social policies adopted. At the same time women have gained new civil and social citizenship rights and in two of the countries considered here, Spain and the former east Germany, political rights have also been recently gained. Concerns with gender equality, especially for women as workers, has resulted partly from legislation at the European Community level and partly from the influence of second-wave feminist action and thinking on policy making, although we have also noted how these have differed in each country (Chamberlayne 1993, Hantrais 1995).

In Spain, as we have seen, the legal position of women has profoundly changed in less than two decades, but the strong male-breadwinner model has not yet been substantially modified. Since two-thirds of the female adult population are economically 'inactive', many will be dependent on male wages or male social security benefits. In comparison with west European welfare states, the late timing of the (re)gaining of citizenship rights is perhaps one of the most distinctive features of the Spanish welfare regime. In particular the late (re-)entry of women into the political process has meant that civil rights for women had first to be established, and social rights, especially those concerning women's economic independence (for example, policies to promote women's employment and social security rights), are at an early stage. Nevertheless, in some respects policies to enable women to combine a family and paid work are more advanced than in the UK where, although there has been a substantial erosion of the male-breadwinner model, social policies for women, and the assumptions underlying them, have not yet taken into account the profound changes which have occurred in the family and labour market.

In Germany before unification there appeared to be 'a three-way division, between "mothers" and "careerists" in the West, and "working mothers" in the East' (Chamberlayne 1994:185). Women in the New Lander have gained new political and civil rights, but many have lost their economic independence and former social citizenship rights. Ostner (1994c) has likened the situation of women in former east Germany since unification to the position of women in west Germany in the 1950s. That is, the route taken to stability and prosperity in west Germany after the war, and east Germany in the 1990s, was underpinned by the norm and model of strong male breadwinners.

In Sweden what has occurred is a shift in women's dependence on to the public sphere, both as clients and as employees, rather than on individual men. Women's continuing support for the provision of welfare has led to a realignment of political interests in Swedish society, with the majority of women now supporting the social democrats and wishing to continue the traditional high commitment to welfare.

Further reading

For the theoretical debate on the comparative study of gender and welfare states the following provide excellent accounts: Langan and Ostner 1991, Lewis 1992, 1993, Orloff 1993, O'Connor 1993, Ostner 1994a, Sainsbury 1994a, 1996a, and Walby 1994, 1997. Highly recommended on women and social policies in Europe in the earlier part of the twentieth century is Bock and Thane 1991.

On women and social policy in both west Germany and the New Lander, see Ostner 1993, 1994a, 1994b, 1994c, Kolinsky 1993, 1995, and Chamberlayne 1994. On women and social policy in Spain see Camps 1994, Cousins 1995, Nash 1991, and Threlfall 1989, 1996. There is quite a large literature available in English on women and social policy in Sweden; see, for example, Hernes 1987, Jenson and Mahon 1993, Lewis and Åström 1992, Leira 1993, 1994, and Ungerson 1990. For women and social policy in the UK see, for example, Baldwin and Falkingham 1994, Land 1985, 1995, Lister 1994, Ungerson 1990 and Williams 1993.

6

Poverty and Social Exclusion

Although the concept of poverty and research into poverty has a long tradition in the UK this is not the case in other European countries, where poverty research is much more recent. However, it is the term 'social exclusion' which is now much more widely used, initially in continental European countries but now also in the UK. This concluding chapter distinguishes between the concepts of poverty and social exclusion and discusses how social exclusion is now being used to chart the changing nature of social disadvantage in Europe. A central concern of the chapter is to link the literature on social exclusion with the debate on welfare regimes and labour market participation and mechanisms of social protection. Drawing on recent comparative analyses, this chapter also considers how women and ethnic minorities, as well as different social classes, are included or excluded in different welfare regimes.

The chapter is divided into four sections. The first considers the poverty research programmes of the European Commission. The second and third sections discuss recent literature with respect to the concept of social exclusion and relate the concepts of poverty and social exclusion to the literature on welfare regimes. Finally, in section four, different paradigms of social exclusion grounded in different conceptions of integration and citizenship are examined in the context of the social structures of the four case-study countries – Germany, Spain, Sweden and the UK. Reference is also made to France, where the concept of social exclusion has been most extensively developed and used.

Poverty research in Europe

In the context of rising unemployment and the oil crisis of the mid-1970s the then nine member states of the European Community initiated the first anti-poverty programme from 1975 to 1980 with a shared conviction that concerted action was required for disadvantaged groups (Hantrais 1995). The second programme took place between 1986 and 1989 and the third from 1989 to 1994, the findings of the latter published by Eurostat as *Poverty Statistics in the Late 1980s* (Eurostat 1994).

The statistical data produced by these programmes on poverty in Europe uses an economic definition of poverty, that is, usually 40, 50, or 60 per cent of equivalent average expenditure or income of households in each country. Measuring poverty by means of an income poverty line is though an indirect method of identifying poverty because it is not actual living conditions which are being measured but only one determinant of those conditions (Ringen 1988). In fact, the relationship between current income and measured deprivation is a complex one and is related to success or failure in accumulating resources over a long period, or access to non-monetary resources (Nolan and Whelan 1996, Hallerod 1996). However, despite this narrow measure of poverty the European Council of Ministers adopted the wider definition of poverty in 1984 as follows: 'The poor shall be taken to mean persons, families or groups of persons whose resources (material, cultural and social) are so limited as to exclude them from the minimum acceptable way of life in the member state in which they live.' This concept is more closely related to the current use of the concept of social exclusion discussed below, although in the European anti-poverty research programmes there has been as yet limited data on social and cultural resources (see Ramprakash 1994).

The Eurostat 1994 Report stresses that, given the unavoidable limitations of the data and the arbitrariness of the number of choices with respect to the definition of poverty, the statistics presented are not exact measures of the incidence of poverty.[1] One robust result though is that, using a definition of poverty as 50 per cent average equivalent expenditure, there are four member states with low rates of poverty (Denmark, Netherlands, Belgium and Luxembourg), four member states with average poverty

Table 6.1 Poverty in Europe in the late 1980s

	Per cent of households in poverty[a]
Denmark	4.2
Netherlands	6.2
Belgium	6.6
Luxembourg	9.2
Germany	12.0
France	14.9
Ireland	16.4
UK	17.0
Spain	17.5
Italy	22.0
Greece	20.8
Portugal	26.5

[a] 50 % of average household equivalent expenditure using modified OECD scale.

Source: Eurostat 1994: 185, Table 5.1.

(France, Ireland, UK and Spain) with Germany in between these two groups, two countries – Italy and Greece – with high poverty rates, and Portugal with very high poverty (see Table 6.1).

In total more than 19 million households, almost 49 million persons, were poor in the late 1980s. The five large countries, Italy, France, Germany, Spain and the UK, had 85 per cent of the poor in the European Union. However, these statistics are probably quite outdated by the late-1990s, with a deep recession from 1991 to 1994 and increasing, and in some countries still rising unemployment. We know, for example, that the proportion of households with a disposable income below 50 per cent of mean income in Sweden increased from about 5 per cent in the early 1980s to nearly 9 per cent at the beginning of the 1990s (Hallerod 1996). Britain has shown the sharpest rise in poverty: about 10 per cent received below 50 per cent of mean income in 1985, rising to about 20 per cent in the early 1990s (Nolan and Whelan 1996). Other measures of poverty such as those in receipt of means-tested social assistance also show an increase in most European countries. Again the UK shows the greatest increase, with 15 per cent of the population living in households dependent on means-tested social assistance benefits in 1992, an increase of nearly 7 percentage points since 1980, the largest increase of the OECD countries (Gough *et al.* 1997).

The European poverty research programmes also identified a change in the composition of poverty, with the emergence of new forms of poverty during the 1980s. There has been a decline in the proportions of elderly people amongst the poor and an increase in the number of unemployed (especially long-term), young people, single parents and migrant workers (see Room *et al.* 1989). For example, in 1995 almost 18 million people in the European Union countries were unemployed (just under 11 per cent of the work force), half of whom have been out of work for more than a year. In all countries there has been an increase in lone parents, especially lone mothers. In many countries young people have great difficulty in entering the labour market (for example, 49 per cent of young women aged 16–24 years failed in 1995 in Spain). As we discussed in Chapter 2, the problem is exacerbated by the fact that the new poor are generally excluded from the labour market or work intermittently and are, therefore, excluded from employment-related protection (social insurance). They therefore have to rely on inadequate means-tested social assistance schemes.

However, poverty is not just confined to those who live in households with non-working members, for some 40 per cent of the poor population of all member states in the late 1980s consisted of households with members in paid employment. The Eurostat 1994 Report concludes that in each country the size of the poor population is largely determined by the system of social security and the minimum wage rate (if any). In particular the extent of social protection for the risk group of non-working households is one of the decisive factors in determining the incidence of poverty. For example, in those countries where the poverty rate is low, social security apparently succeeds in protecting most of the households at risk from falling below the poverty thresholds.

Paradigms of social inclusion and exclusion

Recent writers have distinguished different traditions and theoretical paradigms used to conceptualize poverty and social exclusion (Room 1995a, Silver 1994). Room, for example, distinguishes between the Anglo-Saxon liberal tradition of poverty research, a product of the nineteenth century, and the notion of social exclusion as part of the continental tradition. The notion of poverty is focused on distributional issues, 'the lack of resources at the disposal of an individual or household'. The notion of social exclusion, in contrast, focuses on relational issues, that is, 'inadequate social participation, lack of social protection, lack of social integration, and lack of power' (Room 1995a:105).

The social exclusion discourse has been particularly strong in France, where it was originally coined in 1974. Gore (1995) has explained that in the 1970s in France the term was used to refer to various categories of people unprotected by social insurance, 'marginal, asocial persons and other social misfits'. In the 1980s, however, the term was used to refer to a process of social disintegration in the sense of a rupture of the relationship between the individual and society, particularly for those dislocated by the long-term transformations in the structure and organization of economic life (see also Evans *et al.* 1995). The concept influenced, for example, the *revenue minimum d'insertion* (RMI – minimum income for social integration) which some analysts have seen as 'a form of regulation of the social bond and a response to a perceived threat to social cohesion' (quoted in Silver 1994:534). From France, the discourse has spread to other European countries and the term 'social exclusion' was first used in the European Community in 1989 when the Council of Ministers requested the European Commission to study policies to combat social exclusion.

Since 1989 the term 'social exclusion' has been preferred to that of 'poverty' by the European Commission, possibly because member states expressed reservations about the word 'poverty' applied to their respective countries (Berghman 1997). The European Commission has linked the notion of social exclusion more closely with the idea of inadequate realization of social rights. Thus, social exclusion has been called 'an incomplete citizenship' due to 'deficiencies in the possession of citizenship rights and inequalities in the status of citizenship' (Gore 1995:19). The European Observatory on National Policies for Combating Social Exclusion (set up in 1990) defines social exclusion in relation to 'the social rights of citizenship ... to a basic standard of living and to participation in the major social and occupational opportunities of the society' (Room 1993:14). The principle focus of the Observatory's work has been on the effectiveness of different national, regional, and local policies. What barriers do citizens face in making realities of their rights? What consequences then follow in terms of their non-participation in the major institutions of society and their long-term disadvantage? (Room 1993).

Recent research has also made clear the series of events which trigger social exclusion, or conversely social reinsertion. Contributions to Room's (1995b) recent volume of research on social exclusion and poverty draw attention to the processes of investment and disinvestment over time, that is, the extent to which past investment (not just financial) protects (or does not) against vulnerability to poverty and exclusion. This would also include collective investments and disinvestments of local community resources and facilities.

The concept of social exclusion, though, remains 'vague, evocative, ambiguous, multidimensional and elastic' (Silver 1994:536). In the end anyone can consider themselves to be excluded from something. However, Silver also discerns that the term 'social exclusion' is now being used in ways to denote the changing nature of social disadvantage in western societies. She distinguishes a threefold typology of social exclusion based on different theoretical perspectives, political ideologies, and national discourse. These paradigms she labels 'solidarity', 'specialization' and 'monopoly'. Each is grounded in a different philosophy – Republicanism, liberalism and social democracy.

The notion of social exclusion in the French Republican tradition expresses a deficiency of solidarity as a break in the social fabric. It, therefore, represents the Durkheimian tradition of focusing on social bonds, organic solidarity and social order. Exclusion occurs when the social bond linking the individual with society breaks down. The obverse of exclusion is integration. The concept of Republic citizenship included political rights and duties and an obligation on the part of the state to aid the inclusion of the excluded.

The specialization paradigm is underpinned by Anglo-American liberalism. 'It assumes individuals differ, giving rise to specialization in the market and in social groups ... Liberalism thus conceives of the social order, like the economy and politics, as networks of voluntary exchanges between autonomous individuals with their own interests and motivations' (Silver 1994:542). In this paradigm social exclusion reflects discrimination, market failures and unenforced rights.

The monopoly paradigm, in contrast, sees exclusion and poverty as a consequence of the formation of group monopolies. 'Exclusion arises from the interplay of class, status or political power and serves the interests of the included' (Silver 1994:543). The concept of exclusion here is influenced by the writings of Weber and Marx and focuses on notions of social closure, social class and subordination. The excluded are both outsiders and dominated. Exclusion is combated through citizenship, equal membership and full participation.

Silver (1994) is adamant that the distinctions between the three paradigms should not be confused with institutional classifications such as types of welfare states. She argues that institutions are historical accretions which bear the imprint of past conflicts between ideologies and paradigms. To posit that one particular paradigm underlies a national welfare state implies that an ideological or political consensus existed at any one time. Rather, she insists that competing ideologies would have influenced the law, the welfare state and other social institutions.

Silver's analysis of the academic literature shows that the three paradigms are to be found across the advanced countries and no one paradigm is confined to any one country. For example, with respect to the solidarity paradigm, she cites the American school of flexible specialization, the Durkheimian tradition of social theory, and American conservatism. The specialization paradigm includes the British tradition of the poor law and the workhouse, American neo-classical economics, and the work of some French sociologists. Included in the monopoly paradigm are labour market segmentation theories of American radical economists, the French Regulationist school, and Marshall's formulation of citizenship rights.

However, other writers have already begun to use these three paradigms as different policy approaches which underlie different welfare states. Gore (1995), for example, argues that although the three paradigms do not constitute specific constitutional types,

> they are foundational understandings of the relationship between the individual and society on the basis of which various 'integration

regimes' develop. 'Integration regimes' are be considered analogous
to the concept of 'welfare regimes' which has usefully illuminated
discussion of welfare state systems (Gore 1995:35).

Gore finds that the concept of social exclusion is of value and
relevance for policy analysis in the following ways. First, as a
description of a state of affairs, social exclusion goes beyond
economic and social aspects of poverty to embrace political aspects such as political rights and citizenship which outline a relationship between the individual and the state. Secondly, as a
means of understanding analytically the inter-relationships between poverty, employment and social integration. Thirdly, social
exclusion can be understood as a normative concept, raising
questions about social justice.

Silver and Wilkinson (1995) have also contrasted French and
British insertion policies as exemplars of the solidarity and specialization paradigms of social exclusion (see also Evans *et al.*
1995). Hence they compare social security benefits, training programmes for the unemployed, economic policies and locality-
based urban programmes. They find that there are considerable
differences in the approach of the two countries. For example,
in Britain social policy discourse has used the terminology of
'long-term dependency', 'new-poverty' and 'underclass'; problems
which are to be combated with 'self reliance', 'enterprise' and
'opportunity'. In France, in contrast, the new policies of the 1980s
and 1990s reflected goals of 'insertion', 'integration', 'cohesion'
and 'solidarity'. The RMI, as mentioned earlier, is a policy intended to re-attach individuals who face the risk of permanent
exclusion to a social programme woven around work, training,
associational and community activities. In Britain, however, means-
tested programmes for residual categories of the unemployed
fight poverty through passive receipt of social assistance (although,
as we note below, the introduction of the Job Seeker's Allowance introduces a stronger 'discipline' to work and in the more
recent 'Welfare to Work' policy for young people the passive
receipt of benefit is no longer an option). However, for those in
receipt of Job Seeker's Allowance or Income Support the minimum level of this benefit excludes the recipients from the costs
of social obligations or exceptional expenses (Silver and Wilkinson
1995).

Both Silver and Esping-Andersen have also argued that a further paradigm of exclusion and inclusion can be distinguished. Esping-Andersen (1990) has discussed the similarities in the development of welfare in the authoritarian dictatorships of Germany, Spain, Italy and Portugal. As he notes, in both the Catholic Church and the states of the Fascist dictators corporatism was a way of upholding 'traditional society in the unfolding capitalist economy; as a means to integrate the individual into an organic entity, protected from the individualization and competitiveness of the market and removed from class opposition' (Esping-Andersen 1990:40). Silver has also differentiated the three paradigms of social exclusion discussed above from what she calls 'organic' approaches to social integration. In Silver's view organic approaches are distinguished by the pursuit of a social order based on groups, which may be vertical, functional or primordial groups (that is, regional, religious, ethnic or linguistic groups). Functional groups are privileged over groups based on primordial identities. Principles of a harmonious community, denial of class conflict and subsidiarity are stressed. Exclusion occurs because some groups are privileged over others, resulting in the exclusion of those not integrated into civil society, which in turn is strongly shaped by the state. In the post-war or post-transition periods the organicist thought of the authoritarian, fascist regimes has been tempered by a Christian Democratic or societal corporatism which introduced individual rights and tolerated rival ideologies or religious beliefs.

Poverty, exclusion and welfare regimes

Room (1995a) has pointed to the lack of fit between the poverty literature on the one hand and the debate on welfare regimes (see the Introduction to this book) on the other. The two sets of literature appear to have an almost complete insulation from one another. As Room notes, the welfare regime debate is part of the classic sociological debate with liberalism. The commodification of labour which occurs in capitalist society has been mitigated to varying extents by decommodified welfare rights. The varying extents of decommodification are captured in Esping-Andersen's (1990) work in his typology of liberal, conservative and social democratic regimes. Room (1995a) suggests that the concept of social exclusion is central to the continental vision (or conservative-corporatist in Esping-Andersen's terminology) of social security and social policies, while the liberal vision of society has inspired the Anglo-Saxon concern with poverty.

However, it may be more useful to differentiate the countries included in Esping-Andersen's 'conservative-corporatist' welfare regime, especially France and Germany according to the schema set out by Silver. Policy forums in Germany could, therefore, be characterized as representative of a neo-organic paradigm and France as representative of a solidarity paradigm. These could be contrasted with the UK as a liberal regime informed by the specialization model. The monopoly model has underpinned not only the tradition of academic research into poverty in Britain, but has influenced the egalitarian social policies pursued in Scandinavian countries, and Sweden in particular.

We can, therefore, point to four paradigms which have underpinned conceptions of social justice and the relationship between the individual and society in each country. What light do these paradigms throw on differences in exclusion, integration and citizenship in European countries? An attempt is made below to sketch some of the key aspects of processes of inclusion and exclusion in our four case-study countries. Spain and Germany are represented as examples of neo-organic regimes. However, although there are similarities between Germany and Spain, as we discuss below, there are also considerable differences in labour market structures and outcomes and access to social security benefits. This suggests that the paradigms outlined by Silver may be useful but not sufficient for our understanding of social exclusion in different European societies.

There is also the problem of relating the different paradigms of social exclusion to Esping-Andersen's concepts of commodification and decommodification (see Introduction). In Esping-Andersen's view the concept of decommodification 'refers to the degree to which individuals or families can uphold a socially acceptable standard of living independently of market participation' (Esping-Andersen 1990:37). In order to test the usefulness of the paradigms, therefore, labour market participation and mechanisms of social protection are examined with respect to patterns of exclusion and inclusion in each country. This necessarily narrows the following discussion of social exclusion to only two dimensions, namely access or lack of access to the labour market and social protection. Possibilities for further comparative research therefore include analyses of exclusion from the democratic and legal system (which promotes civic integration) or exclusion from family or community (which promotes interpersonal integration) (see Berghman 1997) or other forms of exclusion such as homelessness or illiteracy.

In the following discussion, it is also recognized that patterns of exclusion in each country are the result of complex systems of interaction of groups and institutional mechanisms which may in turn give rise to their own contradictions. Moreover, there is not necessarily a consensus with respect to a particular paradigm at any one time and different groups within each country may espouse competing ideologies.

The analysis of social exclusion and commodification/decommodification also needs to take into account how women and ethnic minorities, as well as different social classes, have fared under different welfare regimes (see Chapter 5). As Ostner (1994a) has argued, decommodifying social rights gained can counteract unequal bargaining power between capital and labour but such social policies can produce new inequalities which can operate to exclude women or ethnic minority groups. In Chapter 5 we discussed the work of other writers who have suggested that the concept of decommodification should be replaced or supplemented to take account of gender divisions. Comparative analyses of ethnic minorities and the construction of different policy regimes have also recently been undertaken, for example, Castles and Miller (1993), Faist (1995), Ginsberg (1992, 1994), and Williams (1995). These studies demonstrate that in different countries migrant workers and their families have experienced 'similar structural outcomes with similar processes of labour market segmentation, residential segregation and ethnic group formation' (Castles and Miller 1993:196). Following Castles and Miller, Williams (1995) finds that the important explanatory variables in welfare state differences are state policies on immigration, settlement, citizenship and cultural pluralism. Space in this chapter does not permit an in-depth comparative analyses of all these areas; rather, the following discussion considers some of these variables in relation to the paradigms of exclusion set out above.

Paradigms of social exclusion

The neo-organic paradigm of social exclusion: Germany and Spain

The origins of social policy in Germany and Spain were laid by the etatist paternalistic tradition of Bismarck and the corporatist fascist regime of Franco. In both cases social insurance schemes were introduced as alternatives to full political and civil rights. They were top-down schemes intended to integrate and incorporate groups of workers in an hierarchical ordering of society and state. Policies of inclusion, however, became a source of exclusion for others. The Catholic Church's principle of subsidiarity promoted the male-breadwinner family model and families' livelihoods were dependent on predominantly male lifetime earnings and access to his social security benefits. Nevertheless, although writers have identified a common organic tradition of social integration, in post-war Germany and post-transition Spain there are considerable differences between the two countries.

Germany

Both Germany and Spain have protected core labour markets but, as we have seen in Chapters 2 and 3, there are significant differences in labour market structures and outcomes for men and women and especially young people. In Germany the large protected core labour markets are associated with the education and training system so that job entry is defined by credentials and certification and the 'dual-system' of industrial training discussed in Chapter 1. Esping-Andersen (1993) finds that for those with skills the labour market is characterized by high levels of mobility. Skilled workers have good chances of upward mobility into technical, semi-professional and managerial positions. The high-wage, high-skill profile has, though, resulted in strong insider/outsider divisions, so that Germany exhibits one of the strongest dual-market structures in Europe, with very rigid barriers between unskilled and skilled workers. Hence those lacking in skills will automatically find themselves in secondary, unskilled and closed labour markets from which they find it difficult to escape.

In February 1997 Germany's unemployment rate reached a post-war record of 4.3 million, affecting 11.2 per cent of the labour force nation-wide and 17.2 per cent in the New Lander, with almost half of the unemployed in long-term unemployment (see also Chapter 2). Germany's strategy to combat unemployment has been early retirement, but in Esping-Andersen's (1996a) view this has enhanced the 'insider-outsider' divide with a small, predominantly male, 'insider' workforce enjoying high wages, job security and social rights but a growing population of 'outsiders', including early retirees, the unemployed, women, and ethnic minorities.

In Germany social security insurance has predominated, paid through lifetime earnings for all social classes and benefits have reflected contributions made. Welfare benefits have, therefore, preserved class and occupational status. Offe (1991) has referred to five classes of benefit recipients in German society. The most privileged are tenured public-sector employees and the least are those who do not qualify as citizens (for example, refugees and asylum seekers), who receive social assistance on the basis of need rather than as citizens. Privileged groups, therefore, have greater degrees of commodification and decommodification, but it is difficult for excluded groups to gain either and they have to rely on the 'detached periphery of social assistance' (Bruckner 1995). 'Along with unequal access to the labour market goes unequal access to entitlements to insurance systems' (Bruckner 1995:321). Applicants for social assistance have to prove that they have no other way of surviving and are treated with mistrust by those administering the benefit. 'The amount received is often insufficient as payments do not meet demands necessary for a dignified life' (Bruckner 1995:319).

As we discussed in Chapter 2, record levels of unemployment in the mid-1990s have resulted in falling employment rates for full-time male jobs and additional new jobs have been non-standard jobs for both men and women. Non-standard employment undermines the principle of insurance-related social security based on life-long employment and increases the number of those who have to rely on means-tested benefits. Researchers report that the proportion of the population receiving social assistance was 6.8 per cent in 1992, with a sharp rise to 16 per cent among non-Germans. The majority, 62 per cent, of recipients are women. In west Germany the unemployed comprise one third of social assistance recipients and a third of claimants are non-Germans.

In the New Lander, the difficulties of the transition to a market economy, recession, and especially high unemployment have meant that since 1990 living conditions have been widely determined by social security benefits, with up to two-thirds of households depending completely or mainly on them (Clasen 1994, Gough *et al.* 1997, Mangen 1996).

Since the social policy regime in Germany is organized around 'the male worker's life course with life-long gainful employment' (Bruckner 1995:317) policies in Germany are still underpinned by a strong male-breadwinner family model (see Chapter 5). Recognition is given to women as wives and mothers, for example, in the tax system and parental leave legislation. In Ostner's view 'social catholic family policies encourage women to fulfil their potential to live a different but equal existence with different obligations and occupations' (Ostner 1994b:41). Lone mothers, however, fare less well in a social policy regime based on life-time earnings and marital status (see also Chapter 5).

Germany comes close to what has been called an 'ethno-cultural political exclusion' model of immigrant status (Faist 1995) or in Castles and Miller's (1993) terminology an 'exclusionary citizenship' model. The pattern of migration was as guest-workers but permanent residence has left immigrants with an undefined status as 'foreigners'. As workers and tax payers, immigrants are integrated into an economic community. However, access to full citizenship is difficult because the definition of rights to citizenship and therefore membership of the German nation is based on the principle of *ius sanguinis* – of birth and descent. As a consequence a negligible proportion of post-war German immigrants – except for ethnic Germans – has German citizenship (Brubaker 1992). Faist (1995) makes clear that in Germany a preferential treatment of immigrant groups is based on German citizenship law. Ethnic Germans have a privileged access to citizenship. However, other groups, who may have been resident for many years in Germany, do not have the same rights of membership.

Spain

The historical legacy of the 'organic' paradigm, as in Germany, has privileged core workers in their labour market status and income maintenance. As we have seen in Chapter 2, one of the legacies of the Franco era is the protected core of the labour market containing about two-thirds of the official employed workforce but only 37 per cent of total workforce (see Table 2.2). Perez-Diaz and Rodriguez (1995) and Ferrera (1996) maintain that the defence of the privileged core by trade unions and patronage-oriented parties in the 1980s prevented the development of universal benefits, although – as discussed in Chapter 2 – the politics of reform have been complex. The persistence of the core has also been a determining factor in the creation of other quite different labour markets, each with its own rules (Perez-Diaz and Rodriguez 1995). That is, a second labour market which contains those on temporary-fixed-term contracts, a third labour market consisting of those workers in even more precarious work in the underground economy. In this sector there is low pay, no social security payment and no protection from dismissal. The fourth sector is that of the officially ex-employed or unemployed population, which reached 25 per cent of the working population in 1994 and was still 20.9 per cent in the second quarter of 1997 (see Chapters 1 and 2).

Social insurance organized along Bismarckian lines predominates for those in work with a high degree of fragmentation for the different occupational groups. As in Germany cash benefits rather than services play an important role. Spain differs from Germany, however, in the persistence of clientelism and the formation of fairly elaborated 'patronage machines' for the selective distribution of cash subsidies (see Ferrera 1996). However, it is the polarized character of social protection in Spain (and other southern European states) which marks one of the most significant departures from Bismarckian or continental welfare (Ferrera 1996). For those who occupy the core sectors of the labour market there is generous social protection, but for others in weak labour market positions there are only meagre benefits. Spain provides no national minimum income.

About 80 per cent of the unemployed in Spain have entitlement to benefits (although if agriculture is included the proportion covered drops to 63 per cent) (see Ayala 1994). Only those unemployed people who are eligible to receive unemployment benefits can receive additional benefits under the social assistance principle. Thus unemployed people without previous work experience are not entitled to receive benefits (Jimeno and Toharia 1994). Unemployed women and young people are more likely to be seeking their first job and thus will not be eligible for benefits. The conditions of eligibility for unemployment insurance may also be difficult to achieve for those who have temporary fixed-term contracts or who have been taken on for short periods of illegal work. In a country which now has one of the most 'flexible' labour markets in Europe the unemployment protection system still founded on the principle of stable employment appears inadequate.

Since 1991, new schemes of means-tested social assistance have been introduced. In addition to the contributory system, there is now a means-tested system of non-contributory benefits for family allowances, pensions and invalidity benefits.[2] However, the proportion of the population in receipt of social assistance is lower than the other three countries at 2.7 per cent, with categorical assistance for specific groups being more important than general programmes (Gough *et al.* 1997).

More recently (since 1989), in the context of lack of universal provision, a solidaristic conception of exclusion has entered policy debate and practice through the introduction of minimum income schemes by the autonomous communities. This is similar to the RMI in France, but administered on a regional basis, as central government has consistently opposed the introduction of a minimum income scheme on a national basis. Average benefits are low, about half of the poverty line. Although the benefit aims to reinsert people back into the labour market Ayala (1994) considers that this has been unsuccessful.

As in Germany, the privileging of the (male) life-time worker in Spain has produced a strong male-breadwinner family model which has underpinned social policy (see Chapter 5). Although the legal position of women has profoundly changed in the two decades since the transition to democracy, the strong male-breadwinner model has not been substantially modified. The route to financial independence for women is still difficult, especially in the context of high unemployment, temporary work or precarious work.[3] Lone mothers, although as yet a small proportion of households, receive no social security benefits on a national basis. It is difficult for lone mothers to form autonomous households.

Until the early 1970s Spain was a country of emigration. Economic growth in the late 1980s has, however, attracted migrant workers from third world countries, north Africa and eastern Europe.[4] Many of the immigrants are working irregularly, without identification papers or contracts; working in agriculture, catering and tourism. Women may take poorly paid work in the service sector such as cleaning or as maids, and men in low-paid construction work. As Rea (1995) has remarked, the form of migration in Spain, as in other southern European countries, is characterized by the existence of a genuine 'culture of clandestinity'. The existence of a large informal economy also provides opportunities for employment as the occasional 'amnesties' or 'regularizations' of illegal immigration have brought into the open.

The monopolistic paradigm of exclusion: the case of Sweden

Sweden can be characterized as having a 'monopoly' concept of social exclusion, that is, exclusion has been seen to arise from the 'interplay of class, status and political power and serves the interests of the included'. As Therborn (1991) has noted, since the turn of the twentieth century, Sweden has shown institutionalized class divisions within the political parties and one of the highest scores of class voting. Exclusion has been combated through policies pursued by the social democrats and trade unions to promote citizenship, equal membership and full participation.

The aims of economic and social policy (at the height of the 'Swedish model') were to give all citizens the opportunity to work and to keep unemployment as low as possible. The policies of the Swedish model – centralized collective bargaining, wage solidarity and active labour market policies – succeeded in these aims until the 1980s. The result has been very high employment rates for both men and women (see Figure 3.1 in Chapter 3). The expansion of public sector employment until recently has meant that women's employment rates are higher than that of men in many other European countries. These policies have also meant that a secondary labour market (as a form of social closure[5] and economic inequality) did not arise to the same extent as in other countries.

Economic policies pursued in the 1980s and 1990s have been

considered by some to have undermined the Rehn-Meidner equilibrium (for example, Ryner 1994; see also Chapter 1). In the 1990s there has been a rapid increase in unemployment, to 8 per cent in 1996 of open unemployment and nearly 13 per cent if workers in labour market schemes are included. Men have suffered disproportionately from the loss of jobs in manufacturing and construction, although more recently this trend has been partially reversed by labour shedding of women's jobs in the public welfare sector. The impact of Sweden's active labour market policies and the recent adoption of more stringent workfare policies is reflected, however, in the much lower proportion of the unemployed who are long-term unemployed compared with other European countries (see Chapter 3).

The achievements of Sweden's public policies have been citizenship rights based on universal, high income-replacement benefits with broad coverage and liberal qualifying conditions. Decommodification is high and citizenship rather than labour market participation or position still provides the basis to entitlement to goods and the extensive publicly provided services (Stephens 1996). Inequality of income distribution declined in the post-war period until the 1980s and, indeed, Sweden has been regarded as exceptional in the extent of social equality among the advanced nations. Since the early 1980s, however, income inequality has risen and the basic aim of the Swedish income maintenance programme to combat poverty has more recently been called into question (Hallerod 1995). The numbers of households dependent on social assistance increased from 4 per cent in 1980 to 8 per cent in 1993, and eligibility rules have been tightened and benefits cut (Clasen and Gould 1995). Considerable policy reforms of the welfare state have already been undertaken, although this has been carried out in a particularly Swedish way with a commitment to across-the-board cuts in social security so that no one group is disadvantaged. As Esping-Andersen (1996a) has argued, the drift of recent reforms is one of marginal adjustments not a paradigmatic shift away from the basic principles of the Swedish welfare state. In mid-1997 the Social Democratic government has also promised to increase public spending on child benefits and student grants, ease sickness benefit rules and give precedence to full employment.

The Swedish model favours those who participate in the labour market, and individuals who cannot or will not participate receive less generous flat-rate compensation. New work-welfare measures introduced in the 1990s seem likely to speed up the process of permanent exclusion of some from the labour market (Lindqvist and Marklund 1995).[6] As we noted in Chapter 2, one estimate is that some 25 per cent of the labour force are now outside 'normal' full-time employment. This includes workers forced to retire early, those who have involuntary part-time jobs and those otherwise discouraged workers (EIRR 270, 1996).

In Jenson and Mahon's (1993) view, if the well-known features of the Swedish model reinforced class identity and helped to reproduce important inter-class alliances, this was not the case for gender relations. Between the 1930s and 1960s social policies reinforced separate spheres for women and men (see Chapter 5). Women had a part to play in the 'People's Home', but as wives and mothers, and they were largely absent from the public sphere. As we have seen in Chapter 5, in the 1960s and 1970s women's demands for equality became central to the social democratic reform programme, leading to important legislation which enabled women to combine paid work with a family. There are therefore greater opportunities for women to become commodified and hence also decommodified than in our other three countries. Although many commentators argue there is still not an 'equality contract', women's options have been extended and they have become more economically independent. Most two-adult households are dual earner and lone parents are able to combine child care and paid work to a greater extent than lone parents in most other European countries.

Immigration policy since 1975 has been based on multiculturalism and a rejection of the *gastarbeiter* strategy of Germany. Policy goals are in line with the monopoly paradigm of integration in that exclusion has been combated through policies which promote citizenship, equal membership and full participation in Swedish society. Immigration policy has been termed 'multicultural' by Castles and Miller (1993) and 'pluralist political inclusion' by Faist (1995). The pattern of immigration was initially for employment but since restrictions in 1967 immigration has been family reunion and political refugees.[7] The aim, however, has been inclusion in citizenship rights through permanent settlement. Policies therefore pursue principles of equality between

immigrants and Swedes, 'freedom of cultural choice' for immigrants and cooperation and solidarity between Swedish people
and the various ethnic minorities (The Swedish Institute 1994).
Policies aim to provide foreigners with the same legal and social
rights as Swedish citizens and an acceptance by the general public
of multiculturalism.[8] Commentators have reported, however, that
there are disjunctions between a multicultural ideology and reality,
and Swedish multiculturalism involves a high degree of social
control (Alund and Schierup 1993, Castles and Miller 1993).
Despite these progressive policies non-European immigrants
especially have high levels of unemployment and disproportionately low occupational status (Trehorning 1993).

The specialization paradigm of social exclusion: the UK

As Silver (1994) has remarked, it is no accident that both liberal political economy and the idea of poverty emerged from
the transformations of the industrial revolution in Britain from
the early nineteenth century. Liberal assumptions are also reflected historically in narrow conceptions and measurements of
poverty based on subsistence levels which, in turn, have influenced minimum levels of social security. Britain could, therefore, be said to have a strong specialization concept of exclusion.
However, more recent poverty research has been analysed from
within the monopoly paradigm in a strong academic tradition
(for example, Townsend 1979). The monopoly paradigm has also
influenced action by a welfare rights movement to combat poverty, leading to some success in the late 1960s and the 1970s
(Ginsberg 1992).

In the labour market there has been a severe and prolonged
decline of manufacturing jobs since the early 1980s, with an increase in service-sector jobs which have favoured part-time jobs,
especially for women. There has been an increase in both higher-
and lower-earning service jobs which has contributed to growing
income inequality. Other factors which have affected increased
wage inequality have been a tendency for the earnings of the
higher paid to grow more rapidly than those of the low paid
and the decline or abolition of labour market institutions such
as trade unions or wages councils (Michie 1995, Gregg and Machin
1994). In comparison with other EU countries Britain is a country

with a high incidence of low pay for full-time and part-time workers (Gregory and Sandoval 1994).

As we have argued in Chapter 2, despite claims that labour market deregulation would enhance employment growth, there has been a persistence of unemployment and especially long-term unemployment. The UK has been less successful in distributing jobs among the working population with a resulting polarization between 'work-rich' and 'work-poor' households (Gregg 1993), that is those households with two or more people in work and those where no one is in work. Inequalities between wage earners and those in receipt of benefits have widened since benefit increases have been in line with prices rather than wage levels at a time when many of those in work have seen their real wage increase.

The undermining of the principle of social insurance in Britain now means that about a quarter of the population are in households partially or entirely dependent on means-tested social assistance benefits (Rowntree Foundation 1995a). In Alcock's view

> The experience of protection in return for contributions paid has thus been undermined for many of the new poor who get little or no support from insurance benefits ... Entitlement to social insurance has thus become an issue of exclusion from protection, rather than integration within it (Alcock 1996:44).

For those who are dependent on means-tested benefits, low waged and insecure jobs do not provide opportunities and incentives to re-enter employment. Decommodification is therefore at a minimum level of subsistence, and this in turn brings poverty and exclusion from standards of living and participation which other members of society have been able to achieve.

The specialization paradigm, however, associates dependency on welfare, long-term unemployment and the 'underclass' with failings of personal characteristics. Recent social policies in the UK have targeted the most disadvantaged groups and increasingly used a 'discipline to work' in unemployment benefit. The new Job Seeker's Allowance is even more punitive and refusal to work, or leaving a job voluntarily without good cause, could result in loss of any support.

As many writers have demonstrated, Britain has shown a

historical commitment to the male-breadwinner family model, although more recently this family type has substantially declined (see Chapter 5). Increasing numbers of women, especially mothers, have entered the labour market in the past two decades. However, as Lewis has said: 'If women enter the public sphere as workers, they must do so on terms very similar to men. It is assumed that the family (women) will provide child care and minimal provision is made for maternity leave, pay and the right to reinstatement' (1992:164). In the 1980s and 1990s, the notion of 'individual choice' – whether it be choice to have children, choice of a mother to enter the workforce or decisions about a child's education and welfare – have become the dominant neo-liberal ideology underpinning social policies (Brannen 1992). The consequence of making parenthood and childhood one of 'individual choice' is the transfer of responsibility from the state to parents. Accordingly, it is not the state's responsibility to provide facilities and policies to enable women to combine a family and paid work. Lone mothers especially find it difficult to be financially independent through paid work. ✗

In the specialization paradigm exclusion results from discrimination. Liberal reforms in the 1970s attempted to combat the exclusion of women and ethnic minorities through anti-sex and anti-'race' discrimination legislation. Some writers consider that such liberal policies provide better opportunities than those based on the neo-organic paradigm (or conservative corporatist welfare regimes)(for example, Ostner 1994a). Bruegel and Perrons (1996) have documented the complex and contradictory effects of equal opportunities which limit gender discrimination but which operate in increasingly deregulated labour markets. The outcomes have been that an increasing number of women have moved into professional and managerial jobs with higher incomes, but earnings for women at the lower end of the employment hierarchy have remained static relative to that of men.

✗ Immigration policy in Britain differs from other European countries in a number of respects. Castles and Miller (1993) describe Britain (until the Nationality Act of 1981) as an Imperial Model, that is, a definition of citizenship of belonging to the nation in terms of being a subject of the same power or ruler. The pattern of migration was post-colonial, recruiting from former colonial countries. Immigrants who came to Britain before

1971, however, have had full citizenship rights although in practice the entitlement to formal rights has not been enjoyed on a substantive basis, especially in the areas of employment, housing and welfare services (Mitchell and Russell 1994). Immigration Acts since 1962 have substantially restricted immigration, and since 1971 have established through the 'patrial' principle (those with parents or grandparents who had lived in the UK) a form of institutionalized racism. Political mobilization on the part of Britain's black communities led, however, in the 1970s to anti-discrimination legislation and anti-racist strategies at the level of the local state. Those who have status as full citizens of the UK have been able to struggle for anti-racist policies which are unknown in the EU, bringing about real, if limited, changes for members of these communities (Mitchell and Russell 1994).

Conclusion

The processes of change currently affecting the economies of Europe were identified in the Introduction as increased international competition, the shift to neo-liberal policies and European integration. These changes are associated with constant restructuring of regional and local economies, high and long-term unemployment, an increase in flexible work and an increase in the proportion of non-working households in Europe. It was also noted in Chapter 2 that European monetary integration in particular could increase unemployment and that in order to qualify for membership of the single currency, as well as promote their competitiveness, member states may reduce social expenditure, taxation and social charges (especially on employers). As Rhodes (1996) has argued, there has already been convergence between national welfare states with respect to the modification of funding arrangements, tightening regulations and qualifying conditions for benefits, an increase in the targeting of benefits, and an increase in the privatization and marketization of welfare provision. These policy directions are likely to increase poverty and the risks of social exclusion, especially for the more vulnerable groups.

At the same time, however, the European Commission has been decisive in the introduction of the concept of social exclusion and its dissemination and, as noted in the Introduction and the earlier part of this chapter, has been involved in direct action (albeit limited) in relation to poverty programmes and policies to combat social exclusion. The White Papers 1993 and 1994 and the Luxembourg Jobs Summit 1997 give a central importance to combating unemployment and promoting reinsertion in the labour market. On the other hand the shift in policy emphasis (see the Introduction and the conclusion to Chapter 2) at the European level towards more flexible labour markets and reduced social charges could increase the levels of precarious employment and the risks of exclusion.

It is against this background that this chapter has shown that much of the discourse in the European Union on social exclusion borrows from the French solidarity paradigm. In this paradigm exclusion is to be combated through policies which promote solidarity and aim to integrate the individual in society primarily through employment. As we have seen, this paradigm is influenced by a Durkheimian tradition of social theory in which social divisions result from an abnormal breakdown in social cohesion which should be maintained by the division of labour. However, this chapter has attempted to demonstrate that other paradigms of exclusion are useful in analysing patterns of inclusion and exclusion in different European countries. Silver's typology of paradigms, it was suggested, could be seen as underpinning conceptions of the relationship between the individual and society in different European countries. Central to this was an analysis which linked the paradigms of exclusion with the debate on welfare regimes with its emphasis on forms of commodification and decommodification.

Germany and Spain were considered as representative of the neo-organic paradigm outlined by Silver (1994). As we noted, there is a common organic tradition of social integration in Germany and Spain and similarities in their contemporary societies. In this paradigm certain groups in the occupational hierarchy are favoured but in turn this is a source of exclusion for others. In both countries families' livelihoods are dependent on predominantly male lifetime earnings and access to his social security benefits. Women's opportunities to work are curtailed. However, there are considerable differences between the two countries. The incidence of exclusion from the labour market through unemployment, especially youth and female unemployment, is much higher in Spain than in Germany. The extent of precarious employment, either fixed-term temporary work or work in the submerged economy, is also much greater in Spain. A notable feature of Spanish social protection is the polarization between those in the protected core labour market with generous social security benefits (a minority of the workforce) and those outside the core (the majority), who may receive meagre benefits or no benefits at all. In contrast, German income maintenance has a smaller spread between high- and low-income replacement levels and a much larger proportion of beneficiaries of high protection (Ferrera 1996). It would appear to be appropriate to consider Spain as a separate employment and welfare regime, with perhaps more in common with other southern European countries (see Ferrera 1996).

In Sweden the monopoly paradigm, where social exclusion is combated by citizenship, equal membership and full participation, has been a dominant paradigm since the 1930s. The effect has been to integrate into employment and give access to social protection many of those who may be excluded in other countries, for example, women, lone parents, and the long-term unemployed. Consensus around this paradigm does now appear to be under threat as a different discourse, especially from Sweden's business and employers' organizations, has become more dominant in the 1980s and 1990s. Nevertheless by including as many as possible in the labour market, poverty has been reduced through increased earnings in each household.

If Britain in the mid-twentieth century moved towards a monopoly concept of inclusion through civil, political and social citizenship rights, from the 1980s Britain promoted a predominantly liberal or specialization conception of social integration and exclusion. Policies have pursued labour market and wage deregulation, a reduction in the social wage and the abolition of the Wage Councils minimum wage. Narrow conceptions and measurements of poverty based on subsistence levels have influenced minimum levels of social security. Benefit recipients have been more narrowly targeted and associated with an increased coercion or discipline to work for those unemployed. In comparison with Germany or Sweden a far higher proportion of the population are dependent on minimum levels of means-tested benefits, but unlike Spain there are less that receive no state support

whatsoever. Paradoxically, however, anti-discrimination legislation has provided the chance to participate for some, though
not all, women and ethnic minorities in Britain.

In conclusion it seems clear that different conceptions of social
integration can influence the different forms of social exclusion
that develop, and some groups are excluded in some countries
but not in others. The countries examined here suggest that the
four paradigms outlined by Silver, solidarity, specialization, monopoly and neo-organic are useful for our understanding of the
divergent foundations of the welfare states of Europe and the
ways in which different groups in each society are included or
excluded. However, as this chapter has demonstrated with respect to Germany and Spain, although there are similarities between these two countries as representatives of the neo-organic
paradigm, there are also considerable differences between them
in labour market structures and access to social security benefits. This suggests that the paradigms outlined by Silver may be
useful but not sufficient for our understanding of structures and
processes of social exclusion in different European countries.

Further reading

On the poverty programmes of the European Commission, see Hantrais
1995, Room *et al.* 1989, Ramprakash 1994, Teekens and Zaidi 1990,
and Eurostat 1994. For poverty studies in specific countries, see Bruckner
1995 for Germany, Ayala 1994 for Spain, Hallerod 1995, 1996 for Sweden
and The Rowntree Foundation 1995a for the UK.
For recent discussions of the concept of social exclusion, see Berghman
1997, Evans *et al.* 1995, Room 1995a, 1995b, Silver 1994 and Gore
1995.

Conclusion

The previous chapters have reviewed cross-national similarities and differences and pressures for convergence and divergence in selected European countries, focusing on the changing relationship between work and welfare. Convergence between countries in all the substantive issues of work and employment considered in Part Two of the book was clearly evident – in labour market policies, in women's increased labour market participation, in the operations of multinational companies, and in new production techniques. As we have also seen, though, there remain substantial divergences between countries in the extent and nature of the directions of change. In Part Three, with respect to women and social policies and social exclusion, there are also similarities between countries, for example in the recent entry of women into the public sphere and the gaining of citizenship rights, and the groups at risk of poverty or exclusion. But cross-national differences also remain significant here, especially with respect to the different development of social policies for women, the extent of the erosion of the male-breadwinner family model, and the different understanding of integration, citizenship, and exclusion in each country.

In the Introduction we discussed some of the pressures for change affecting European countries. The evidence reviewed in previous chapters suggests that these changes are accelerating convergence between countries which means that all will experience a continuing 'lack of fit' between employment conditions and welfare systems developed under different conditions of accumulation and regulation in the earlier post-war period. One useful way to analyse possible future trajectories of the different European countries, and different solutions to this 'lack of fit' is, drawing on the recent work of Esping-Andersen (1996a) and

Gough (1996), to consider the interrelationships between welfare, labour markets and family/household structures in each regime type. The perspective of Esping-Andersen and Gough is one which suggests that each regime type has generated different solutions or responses to similar economic problems, producing different outcomes with respect to, for example, employment opportunities, equality, or gender relations. In turn, these outcomes have generated further dilemmas or contradictions for each country which have to be addressed.

In the UK a neo-liberal solution has generated dominant threats of inequality, problems of social polarization, instability of demand and low-quality education and training. Unemployment is currently falling, although the problem of long-term unemployment and those who are excluded, or exclude themselves, from social assistance benefits remain. As we have seen in previous chapters, in the neo-liberal route, there has been pursuit of labour market and wage deregulation, a reduction in the social wage and in the minimum wage. It is easier to gain access to work but low wages are earned by unskilled, young and non-unionized workers with consequent poverty in work. Many jobs available are, therefore, low paid, less secure and protected. Women often have to seek work to supplement men's wages, but in the context of an insufficiency of policies to combine employment and family life, and especially a lack of affordable child care, women become available as a flexible (and for a large proportion a low-paid) labour force. Households often survive through one and a half wages. A feature in the UK, however, is that if one partner is unemployed it is likely that the other is also unemployed. As Esping-Andersen (1996a) has argued, there is a double jeopardy in that social assistance to vulnerable groups is the highest of the European countries but this in turn produces poverty traps and disincentives to work.

Germany in the 1990s appears to be in a period of transition exacerbated by the unification process, high costs of the welfare state and threats of international competition. Increasing unemployment and jobless growth are two of the major problems now facing Germany. Unemployment has been tackled through labour reduction, especially through early retirement, but with a continuation of social insurance for those in work. In labour markets, core workers with high earnings and social protection are privileged, but the result has been divisions between core and periphery workforces and between men and women. Families' livelihoods are dependent on predominantly male life-time earnings and access to his social security benefits. One solution to low employment levels, the familialist model of welfare and the aspirations of women would be to encourage women to augment their participation in paid work. However, this threatens the 'insiders', the prime-age male workers, as well as strong trade union and employers' interests, and the breadwinner model of welfare which underpins these corporatist arrangements.

In Spain as we have seen there are similarities with Germany, and indeed Esping-Andersen (1996b) has included Spain in the group of continental European countries in his recent work. However, the discussions throughout the previous chapters have demonstrated that Spain is a distinctive socio-economic formation in terms of historical and political developments, labour market structures and unemployment, the dominance of foreign investment, the position of women in paid work and the family, the nature of social protection and the extent of social exclusion. Of the four countries discussed in this book Spain has shown the most profound transformation of its social structures in the past two decades. Policy reforms since the transition to democracy have been layered on top of previous social structures to create new divisions and forms of social exclusion. This has been most evident in the far-reaching experiments of labour market reform to combat the very high levels of unemployment.

In Sweden in the 1990s, major problems are rising unemployment and the costs of the welfare state. The earlier route of employment expansion in the public sector (which has been particularly favourable to women) has therefore reached its limit. Employment growth is likely to be only in private services which could accelerate wage differentials and increase less secure and protected jobs. As we have seen, of particular importance in Sweden is the emergence of new gender divisions and alliances, as the earlier class-based alliances and hegemony of the LO are eroded. The high participation of women in politics and in the labour market, and women's ability to combine family and paid work with increased financial independence, suggest that women are likely to defend these gains through new strategies. This in turn, however, exacerbates existing tensions and contradictions between the provision of an extensive welfare state and the needs of increasingly internationally oriented Swedish employers.

Notes

Introduction

1. The Regulationist school of writers considers that since the mid-1970s we have entered a new phase of capitalism, a transition to a new post-Fordist regime. Their perspective has enabled us to understand how the Keynesian welfare state played a key role in underpinning the virtuous circle of growth in the economies of the advanced countries established after the Second World War (see for example, Jessop 1992a, 1994 and Lipietz 1992). The Keynesian welfare state provided a system of welfare guaranteeing a minimum social wage, regulated collective bargaining, and managed full employment in relatively closed economies. In turn the expansion of the welfare state undermined the conditions which had sustained both itself and the mode of accumulation.

2. Due *et al.* (1991) suggest that we can distinguish three principal traditions of legal regulation of industrial relations across the member states of the European community:

   (i) The Romano-German system in which the state plays a central role in industrial relations and the constitution guarantees 'a core of fundamental rights and freedoms, constituting the foundation of national industrial relations'. Examples include Belgium, France, Germany, Italy and the Netherlands.

   (ii) The Anglo-Irish system in which the role of the state is limited and there is little legislation conferring basic rights. Traditionally the state has absented itself from regulation of labour markets and the relationship between employer and employee. Paradoxically, however (as we discuss in Chapters 1 and 2), in the UK since 1979 the state has intervened more in industrial relations and labour markets than in any other country. As Visser (1996) has remarked, the limited legal framework makes industrial relations in Britain more sensitive to the prevailing balance of economic or political power.

   (iii) The Nordic system of the Scandinavian states in which the state plays a limited role in industrial relations, but agreements concluded between employers and unions provide the foundation.

   Esping-Andersen's (1990) typology of welfare regimes, the social democratic, conservative-corporatist and liberal, are now well known. Briefly, in Esping-Andersen's scheme the liberal welfare state provides means-tested social assistance and modest social insurance. Benefits cater for low-income clients and benefit entitlement rules are strict and are associated with a 'discipline to work'. Welfare clients are stigmatized. 'The state encourages the market, either passively – by guaranteeing only a minimum – or actively – by subsidising private welfare schemes' (Esping-Andersen 1990:27). The main examples are the USA, Canada, and Australia.

The conservative-corporatist welfare regime includes Austria, France, Germany and Italy. Social insurance predominates, paid through lifetime earnings for all social classes, and benefits reflect contributions made. Welfare benefits, therefore, preserve class and occupational status. Social policies are strongly influenced by the Church and committed to the preservation of the traditional family. The principle of subsidiarity ensures that the family carries out the caring of young children and elderly people (see for example Spicker 1991).

The social-democratic welfare regime includes Sweden and other Scandinavian countries. In these countries social-democratic governments have been the dominant force behind social policy reform and have pursued a welfare state which promotes an equality of the highest standard, and not an equality of minimal needs as elsewhere. The state socializes the costs of familyhood and social policies allow women to choose work rather than the household. There is a commitment to full-employment and the 'right to work'. The egalitarian, universal welfare state requires most people to be working, and the fewest possible living off social transfers (Esping-Andersen 1990:27, 28).

3. The degree of decommodification in the advanced countries is one dimension which Esping-Andersen uses to identify clusters of countries which form his typology of welfare regimes. There are two other dimensions, the first being the relation between the state and market in providing welfare. This concerns the range, or domain, of human needs that are satisfied by either social policies or the market. The second dimension is the stratification dimension, in which the welfare state is seen to be a system of stratification in its own right, an active force in the ordering of social relations (see the introduction to Esping-Andersen 1990 and Orloff 1993).

1 National Diversity: Germany, Spain, Sweden and the UK

1. Where the companies are small, worker representatives have only a third of the seats on the supervisory board, but in large joint-stock companies (over 2000 employees) workers have equal representation.
2. In 1938 the Employers' Association 'made peace with social Keynesianism' when it concluded a pact with the trade unions in the 'historic compromise' between capital and labour (Korpi 1983) The pact, known as the 'Saltsjobaden Agreement', initiated the corporatist system of centralized wage negotiations outside direct state regulations, which ensured increased stability in industrial

relations for several decades to follow. The underlying principle was that both labour and capital could contribute to increasing economic growth and efficiency.

3. The Swedish active labour-market policies are characterized by the 'right to work' model rather than the 'right to an income' model. Unlike many other countries all vacancies and planned lay-offs have to be notified to the employment service. If the service cannot find a job a training programme is organized and hard-to-place workers sent on high-quality training courses, even before they become unemployed in some cases. If workers have not been placed within six months employers are offered 50 per cent wage subsidy over a six-month period. Finally, if none of these measures works workers are entitled to unemployment benefit paid only for 300 days maximum and are subject to a strict work test, that is, if the recipient refuses to take a job or training the benefit is stopped. If all these measures fail the public sector, mainly local authorities, acts as an employer of last resort, mostly in construction or caring jobs. Anyone whose benefit has run out is entitled to such work by law.

4. In the mid 1980s the top marginal rate of income tax was 88 per cent, although this has been progressively reduced since, so that from 1991 the top rate was reduced to 50 per cent and the tax base broadened.

5. More recently the unions 'have hijacked the initiative from employers and the government on a key issue of public debate' (*Financial Times*, 23 January 1996). This concerns the proposal of Klaus Zwickel, President of IG Metall, to deliver wage restraint in return for the creation of 300 000 new jobs by 1998.

6. The *Treuhand* was installed as a holding institution for all east German *Kombinate* (centrally controlled industrial enterprises). The aim of the *Treuhand* (which became the world's largest holding company) was to organize a process of restructuring under the supervision of managers and bankers of west Germany. By the end of January 1993, 4998 enterprises had been fully privatized and of the remaining about 1800 were to be liquidated and the balance of these companies were still to be fully privatized (Owen Smith 1994:481).

7. The new middle classes (which Giner, writing in 1973, considered to be one of the outstanding features of Spanish society) increased by 86 per cent between 1964 and 1988 (Tezanos 1990). Giner (1973) speaks of the old middle class consisting of small merchants, civil servants, administrators, teachers, military officers. The new middle class in contrast are those university educated, professional, technical, scientific and managerial 'new' occupations associated with rapid industrialization and especially expansion of the service class in the last two decades.

8. Ryner (1994) argues that the polices pursued by the social democrats contradicted the Rehn-Meidner model. Too-high profits led to higher wages in the high-profit industries, leading to a conflict of interests between different unions in different sectors. Increased

wage differentials were exacerbated by the increased size of the public sector and tertiary sector, which were less constrained by the competitive conditions of the world economy in their wage demands. Public sector jobs expanded to over 35 per cent of the workforce and it became more difficult for the export-tradable goods sector to set the wage levels and prevent inflation or wage drift. Both the public sector unions and white collar unions were more interested in their members' relative positions whereas, to an extent, the stability of industrial relations in Sweden had traditionally been based on the awareness, on the part of the manual, export-oriented unions, of the effects of international competition on unit labour costs and therefore wage moderation.

9. The financial position of the government rapidly deteriorated. In 1989 the general government budget was in surplus by 5.5 per cent of GDP, the largest surplus in the OECD area. By 1993 the budget deficit was the largest deficit in the OECD area at 14.5 per cent of GDP (OECD 1994b:19). In the 3-year period 1990 to 1993 GDP fell by 5 per cent, industrial output fell by 13 per cent and for the first time since the 1930s unemployment reached 9.3 per cent at the end of 1993 (and if those on training programmes are included, over 14 per cent, with youth unemployment at 21 per cent) (Freeman *et al.* 1995).

10. Reviewing the evidence for explanations of this decline, Waddington and Whitson (1995) found that fluctuations in the business cycle and the effect of changes in the composition of employment to be the most effective explanations, especially at the beginning of the 1980s. The rise in real earnings at the beginning of the 1980s, especially for white collar workers, inhibited recruitment, and high levels of unemployment restricted opportunities for workers to unionize. The high loss of manufacturing also meant that employment contracted where unionism was most concentrated. In the late 1980s the authors consider, however, that legislation passed during the decade, as well as employers' practices, became more important, as unions failed to secure recognition and membership in the expanding private sectors.

2 Labour Market Reform and 'Non-Standard' Employment

1. The statistics used in this chapter are taken from the Eurostat Labour Force Survey. The definition of part-time workers relies on how workers interviewed classified themselves. A self-employed worker is defined as in business on her or his own account. Eurostat figures would appear to include employers with one or more employees as well as self-employed with no employees.

2. The use of fixed-term workers varies by size of firm, with small and newly started firms having the highest proportions and large firms the lowest. Sectors employing more than a third of fixed-term workers are agriculture, construction, shoe and leather industries, hotels and

restaurants (Milner *et al.* 1995). Higher uses of fixed-term workers are also to be found in the secondary sector of multinational firms, retailing firms, contracted-out work in the public sector and small local firms (Recio 1992).

3. However, EIRR 1996: 270 reports that in the year to May 1996 temporary employment fell by 18 000 jobs as local authorities cut their workforces and failed to renew temporary contracts.

4. Temporary work in the UK can be fixed-term contracts, interim work, seasonal work, and casual work. 3 per cent of the male workforce and 4 per cent of the female workforce were on fixed-term contracts in 1994. The use of fixed-term contracts has been increasing, especially in the public sector, and such workers are often more highly qualified (Dex and McCulloch 1995).

5. Employers and trade unions have also pursued flexibility in other ways, employers seeking to increase productivity and flexibility of working time and the unions pursuing strategies of a more 'skill oriented', training path together with a reduced working week (Mahnkopf 1992). In the ten years since the 1985 Act, working time reductions, flexible work and extended operating hours at work have continued to be important collective-bargaining issues. In the 1990s agreements were reached on reductions in working hours so that Germany now has one of the shortest contractual working weeks in the world.

6. Labour market reform in 1994 accelerated the process of repealing the labour ordinances, many of which date back to the Franco period and which regulate a wide range of employment conditions. The unions and employers' confederation signed an agreement in 1994 to replace the existing labour ordinances, and now negotiation of a variety of employment conditions passes to collective bargaining at sectoral or company levels. The union UGT is reported to have found that on the whole collective bargaining in 1995 was effective in maintaining employment rights and minimizing the possible deregulatory effects of the labour reforms (EIRR 1996:268).

7. The reforms included an extension of the right for an employer to hire a worker on probationary terms from six months to a year, a relaxation of the stringent 'last-in-first-out' seniority rules which applied when implementing redundancies, and a much greater freedom to hire and fire for small employers.

8. Debate on relaxation of job security legislation is currently underway and proposals include increased temporary working and a system whereby sectoral collective agreements can adjust employment security legislation to conditions in each industry. However, unions fear that employers will put pressure on local unions by threatening workforce reductions if disagreements arise. National unions will therefore be involved in plant-level negotiations (EIRR 1997:276:13).

3 Women and Employment

1. For example, in 1995 only 60.8 per cent of all the employed (male and female) worked in the service sector in Germany, compared to 70.5 per cent and 71 per cent in the UK and Sweden respectively (Eurostat 1996) . Between 1983 and 1989 women's employment growth in the service sector was 12 per cent in Germany compared to 23.9 per cent in the UK (Meulders *et al.* 1993).

2. In 1976, for young women aged 20 to 39 years, there were 45 percentage points difference between single and married women's participation in paid work (67 per cent and 22 per cent respectively). By 1991 this gap had declined to 13 points (50 per cent and 37 per cent respectively) (Garrido 1992).

3. Probably about 70 per cent of 3–5 year-olds attend some type of publicly funded school/nursery, compared to about 37 per cent of children in this age group in the UK (Commission of the European Communities 1991).

4. The term 'informal activities' has been defined by Hadjimichalis and Vaiou as 'legal or illegal practices which present a number of common characteristics: they are not officially recorded, thereby evading taxation; they are 'invisible' by ordinary inspection; they absorb low paid, usually female, labour; they avoid the ever-increasing reach of the state, especially with regard to the enforcement of safety and insurance legislation or the observation of collective bargaining agreements' (Hadjimichalis and Vaiou 1990: 81). These authors argue that informal work derives from both traditional and modern productive activities. Informal activities can be found in the traditional forms of production in rural areas, for example, construction, petty trade, handicraft industries, or in areas where there is a high demand for seasonal labour such as harvesting or tourism.

5. Miguélez Lobo (1988) has suggested that such activity in Spain may be about 20 per cent of all active workers in the late 1980s, although in some regional and local economies it is much higher. For example, in the textile area of Sabadell near Barcelona informal work could be generating between 30 and 50 per cent of the city's wealth and in the toy-making and footwear industries in Valencia more than 90 per cent of firms use some degree of informal labour, and the irregular work of women far exceeds that of women's legal work.

6. There are a number of measures of occupational segregation. One widely used measure is an index of dissimilarity. Another measure is the index of desegregation developed by Siltanen *et al.* (1992). These authors argue that the measure of segregation needs to be based on an assumption of symmetry between the segregation of men and women in the labour market. That is, for the purpose of an indicator male and female segregation should be treated as the same. However, Walby (1997) has argued that segregation is not a symmetrical process between men and women but one centrally structured by inequalities of power. As she says, 'The concentration of

men in, say, senior management is not symmetrical with a concentration of women among, say, cleaners' (Walby 1997:103). Further problems involve the variability in boundaries and sizes of occupations or industrial units over time and across countries, and in the different definitions of occupational terms in different countries.

7. This and the following data uses a new classification of occupational groups introduced in 1992 (ISCO-88(COM)) which means it is not directly comparable to the earlier work of the European Network of Experts on Women in the European Community (see Rubery and Fagan 1993, and Rubery and Fagan 1995).

8. The level of low pay among women has been stable over the 1980s and 1990s (at about a third) although for men the proportion who are low paid has increased sharply from around 8 per cent in the 1970s to 13 per cent in the mid-1990s.

9. For example, the employment rates of men with no formal qualifications fell by 21 per cent between 1977 and 1992, for women with no formal qualifications the fall was only 3 per cent (Balls and Gregg 1993).

4   Industrial Change in the Regions of Europe

1. For example, in the textile industry in Catalonia in mid-1980s 62 per cent of firms employed less than 25 workers and 88 per cent of firms employed less than 100 workers; only 12 firms had more than 500 workers (Homs 1988). In the town of Sabadell in the Valles Occidental in 1989, 68.5 per cent of firms employed less than 5 workers, 97.8 per cent employed less than 50 and only 5 firms employed more than 500 workers (Farriol and Valette 1989).

2. Over the 20-year period 1950 to 1970 the city of Barcelona grew from one million inhabitants to one and three-quarter million inhabitants.

3. In the textile industry the workers remained Catalan and were mainly women, in construction and transport workers were mainly immigrants, whilst workers in the service industries and non-manual sector were Catalan. Later the immigrant workers made up the bulk of the workforce in chemicals and engineering, especially in the SEAT factory in Zona Franca (Balfour 1989).

4. Citroen in 1957, Morris in the late 1960s, Chrysler in 1967. From 1964 onwards a minimum local content was introduced, boosting the local component industry. Multinational component firms were also allowed to invest from the late 1950s.

5. For example, Ford was allowed to set up production in Valencia with a minimum local content of 50 per cent and a minimum export rate of 67 per cent. In 1979 General Motors set up near Zaragoza with a 55 per cent local content and 65 per cent export rate.

6. For example, Renault decreased the number of suppliers from 500 to 270 by the early 1990s, Ford from 450 in 1976 to 125 in the late 1980s and Nissan from about 1000 to 450 in the late 1980s. In 1986

in Barcelona, for example, SEAT limited long-term contracts to a group of 50 firms compared to more than 400 who had supplied them before (Recio *et al.* 1991). All these firms are procuring the large majority of components from external sources.

7. Volkswagen in 1993 decided to close down the SEAT plant in Zona Franca and relocate production at its Matorell factory from 1994. Of the 9000 workers in the SEAT plant in Zona Franca, 3000 will take early retirement, 1400 will not have a renewal of temporary contracts, and the dismissal compensation will be applied to 4600 workers (*La Vanguardia* 23 October 1993).

8. Firms include Daimler-Benz, Porsche, Audit Bosch Sony, IBM, Hewlett-Packard and in machine tools Heidelberg, Trumpf and Traub. The latter are examples of the region's Mittelstand, that is, small to medium-sized firms (SMEs) employing between 50 and 1000 employees. These make up 99.4 per cent of manufacturing establishments in Baden-Württemberg and 57.9 per cent of manufacturing employment (Herrigel 1993). The machine tool industry employs some 46 000 workers in 391 firms and the automotive industries has 237 000 employees with 8000 supplier firms (Cooke and Morgan 1994).

9. These include 211 university, research and training institutes (the most extensive in Germany), agencies for the promotion of trade, cooperation and finance, 13 Chambers of industry and commerce, trade unions and employers' associations, and the role played by the regional government (Cooke and Morgan 1994).

5 Women and Social Policies

1. The birth rate declined from 3.22 in 1935 to 2.46 in 1950 in Spain, and in Catalonia from 1.91 to 1.72 in the same period (Nash 1991:164).

2. The majority of these lone-parent households contain at least one child over 16, that is, 5.1 per cent of households compared with 0.7 per cent of households where the lone parent has at least one child under 16 (Eurostat 1996).

3. However, in 1994 three women were members of the PSOE government's 17 ministers, and 12.9 per cent of top level central government positions were held by women. In the legislature of 1993–1997, 15.7 per cent of the Congress of Deputies and 12.5 per cent of Senators were women (Instituto de la Mujer 1994).

4. For example, in 1937 a law was introduced to prohibit employers from dismissing women for getting married or pregnant. Women were also granted three months' unpaid maternity leave. In addition, public housing schemes for large families, rent rebates according to family size, child tax allowances, marriage loans, and guaranteed maintenance for lone mothers were also introduced (Ginsberg 1992:192).

5. Population decline was also of importance in national debate in the 1930s and 1940s. *The Times*, for example, drew attention to the pronatalist policies of Germany and Italy (Land 1985). The

government's reaction was the establishment of the Population Investigation Committee in 1936 which included an investigation of
family allowances in its terms of reference.

6. The success in achieving the payment of family allowances, and the
fact that they were paid to the mother, has been ascribed to the
long-running campaign of Eleanor Rathbone for the endowment of
motherhood. She argued that family allowances paid to mother would
encourage equal pay by undermining the case of family wage (Lister
1994). However, by the end of the 1930s support for family allowances was different from the earlier feminist advocates who wished
to improve the status of women and provide a source of independent income. Rather, new converts to the allowances wished to abolish
poverty among children and halt the decline in the birth rate (Land
1985). Lewis (1991) has argued that when allowances were introduced in 1945 they were used as part of a substitute for men's wages.

7. A further means-tested benefit is family credit, which is paid as a
supplement to low wages. McLaughlin (1994) has argued that it was
the failure, inadequacy and inefficiency of the traditional family wage
for men, which, combined with the inadequancies of family allowances and child tax allowances, led to the adoption in the mid-1970s
of the principle of publicly-funded supplements to low wages. At
the same time, she argues, wages for men at the lower end of the
earnings scale have been declining throughout the 1980s, 'eroding
the capacity of these wages to meet household and family needs'
(1994:19). Family credit can, therefore, act as a poverty trap and
reduce incentives for wives to seek work, as this would mean that
the couple would be beyond the threshold of family credit benefit.

8. In all countries in Europe maternity leave is a universal right for
employed women, with the full period of leave covered by earnings-
related payments (of 70–100 per cent) (Commission of the European Communities 1991). The UK, however, is the exception as only
6 weeks' leave is covered by earnings-related payments and a large
number of women are excluded from eligibility conditions. These
conditions were restricted in the 1980s, requiring 5 years, continuous employment with the same employer for part-timers working
between 8 to 16 hours, and 2 years for those working more than 16
hours per week. The maternity grant was also eroded in the 1986
Social Security Act, in which the universal grant was abolished and
a means-tested £80 grant allowed for those women targeted as in
need. However, as a result of an EU Directive, the 1993 Trade Union
Reform and Employment Rights Act gives new legal rights to women
for maternity leave and pay regardless of length of service. Under
this Act all women employees have a right to 14 weeks' leave regardless of the hours they work, length of service, type of employment contract or how many people an employer employs. However,
there is no right to maternity pay for those who have worked for
less than six months or earn less than £57 a week (in 1994).

6 Poverty and Social Exclusion

1. Room, who was the co-ordinator of the second European poverty research programme, notes that consultants were allowed to use whatever definition of the poor was current in their countries. As a result 'it is difficult to draw any firm comparisons between countries' (Room *et al.* 1989:167) See also Teekens and Zaidi (1990) for further problems associated with the second poverty study.

2. In Spain, on average, two-thirds of insurance-benefits benefit recipients are men and almost 50 per cent of social assistance recipients are women (Blanchard *et al.* 1995).

3. For those women in the labour market, a high proportion – over half in 1994 – did not have access to stable or secure incomes by reason of unemployment or temporary contracts, and if illegal work is included this proportion would be even higher (Cousins 1995).

4. Estimates of the number of immigrants in the late 1980s was about 720 000 with approximately 300 000 illegal aliens (Instituto de la Mujer 1992). Of these, 8 per cent are political exiles and over 50 per cent come from the third world.

5. The term 'social closure' is used here in the Weberian sense to refer to a process by which social groups seek to maximize rewards by restricting access to resources and opportunities to a limited circle of eligibles. Professional groups, trade unions, and occupational groups may operate strategies of social closure to obtain and maintain a more privileged place within the division of labour (see, for example, Cousins 1987, Chapter 5).

6. New work-welfare measures include policies to utilize the residual work capacity of unemployed people (the Swedish version of workfare – for example, work in voluntary projects or pressures to find work while on social assistance). There is also an emphasis on work rehabilitation to combat the costs and numbers of early retirees and those on sickness absence (Lindqvist and Marklund 1995). This has taken the form of active rehabilitation in the workplace for chronically ill people. Lindqvist and Marklund (1995) have argued, however, that this tends to speed up early retirement, as a faster decision will have to be made as to whether a claimant is to become an early retiree or successfully rehabilitated. In the view of these authors, however, this speeds up the process of permanent exclusion from the labour market.

7. In a few decades Sweden changed from a monolingual and ethnically homogeneous society to a multilingual society with a number of ethnic minorities. Sweden now has a high proportion of immigrants, comprising 13 per cent of the Swedish population, and foreign citizens 5.7 per cent in 1993 (The Swedish Institute 1994, Alund and Schierup 1993). Nordic immigrants from Finland, Norway and Denmark comprise 40 per cent of immigrants. Employment motivated immigration predominated in the period from the end of the Second World War to the early 1970s, in response to the strong

demand for labour. Immigrants came principally from other Nordic countries but also Yugoslavia and Greece. However, since the introduction of strict immigration controls in 1967, non-Nordic immigration virtually came to an end by 1974.

8. Foreign citizens have been able to vote in local and regional elections since 1975. An important policy has been home language tuition in efforts to encourage bilingualism, so that ethnic minorities can retain their own ethnic identity and language but also speak Swedish. Although there is no equivalent of the Commission for Racial Equality in Britain, in 1986 an Act against Ethnic Discrimination came into force and an Ombudsman Against Ethnic Discrimination appointed.

Bibliography

Adnett, N. (1995) 'Social Dumping and European Economic Integration', *Journal of Social Policy*, 5 (1): 1–12.

Alcock, P. (1996) 'The Advantages and Disadvantages of the Contribution Base in Targeting Benefits: A Social Analysis of the Insurance Scheme in the United Kingdom', *International Social Security Review*, 49 (1): 31–49.

Alund, A. and Schierup, C. (1993) 'The Thorny Road to Europe: Swedish Immigration Policy in Transition' in J. Wrench and J. Solomos (eds) *Racism and Migration in Western Europe*, Oxford: Berg.

Amin, A. (1989) 'Flexible Specialisation and Small Firms in Italy: Myth and Realities', *Antipode* 21 (1): 13–34.

Amin, A. (1994) 'Post-Fordism: Models, Fantasies and Phantoms of Transition', in A. Amin (ed.) *Post-Fordism: A Reader*, Oxford: Blackwell.

Amin, A. and Malmberg, A. (1994) 'Competing Structural and Institutional Influences on the Geography of Production in Europe', in A. Amin (ed.) *Post-Fordism: A Reader*, Oxford: Blackwell.

Amin, A. and Robins, K. (1990) 'The Re-emergence of Regional Economies? The Mythical Geography of Flexible Accumulation', *Society and Space*, 8: 7–34.

Amin, A. and Thrift, N. (1994) 'Living in the Global', in A. Amin and N. Thrift (eds) *Globalisation, Institutions and Regional Development in Europe*, Oxford: Oxford University Press.

Amin, A. and Tomaney, J. (1995) 'The Challenge of Cohesion', in A. Amin and J. Tomaney (eds) *Behind the Myth of the European Union: Prospects for Cohesion*, London: Routledge.

Atkinson, J. (1985) *Flexibility, Uncertainty and Manpower Management*, Brighton: Institute of Manpower Studies.

Ayala, L. (1994) 'Social Needs, Inequality and the Welfare State in Spain: Trends and Prospects', *Journal of European Social Policy*, 4 (3): 159–79.

Baldwin, S. and Falkingham, J. (eds) (1994) *Social Security and Social Change: New Challenges to the Beveridge Model*, London: Harvester Wheatsheaf.

Balfour, S. (1989) *Dictatorship, Workers and the City: Labour in Barcelona since 1939*, Oxford: Clarendon Press.

Balls, E. and Gregg, P. (1993) *Work and Welfare*, London: IPPR.

181

Barrell, R. (ed.) (1994) *The UK Labour Market: Comparative Aspects and Institutional Developments*, Cambridge: Cambridge University Press.

Becattini, G. (1990) 'The Marshallian Industrial District as a Socio-economic Notion', in Pyke, F., Becattini, G. and Sengenberger, W. (eds) *Industrial Districts, Inter-firm Co-operation in Italy*, Geneva: International Institute for Labour Studies – ILO.

Benson, L. (1992) 'The Emergence of Industrial Districts in Spain: Industrial Restructuring and Diverging Regional Responses', in Pyke, F., Sengenberger, W. (eds), *Industrial Districts and Local Economic Regeneration*, Geneva: International Institute for Labour Studies – ILO.

Bentolila, S and Dolado, J. (1994) 'Spanish Labour Markets', *Economic Policy*, April: 53–99.

Berghman, J. (1997) 'The Resurgence of Poverty and the Struggle against Social Exclusion: A New Challenge for Social Security in Europe?' *International Social Security Review*, 50 (1): 3–20.

Bernabe, F. (1988) 'The Labour Market and Unemployment', in A. Boltho (ed.) *The European Economy: Growth and Crisis*, Oxford: Oxford University Press.

Blanchard, O. *et al.* (1995) *Spanish Unemployment: Is there a Solution?* Centre for Economic Policy Research, London School of Economics.

Blanchflower, D.G. and Freeman, R.B. (1994) 'Did the Thatcher Reforms Change British Labour Market Performance?' in R.Barrell (ed.) *The UK Labour Market: Comparative and Institutional Developments*, Cambridge: Cambridge University Press.

Bock, G. (1984) 'Racism and Sexism in Nazi Germany: Motherhood, Compulsory Sterilisation and the State', in R.Bridenthal, A. Grossman and M. Kaplan (eds) *When Biology Became Destiny: Women in Weimar and Nazi Germany*, New York: Monthly Review Press.

Bock, G. (1991) 'Antinatalism, Maternity and Paternity In National Socialist Racism', in Bock, G. and Thane, P. (eds) *Maternity and Gender Policies: Women and the Rise of the European Welfare States 1880s–1950s*, London: Routledge.

Bock, G. (1992) 'Equality and Difference in National Socialist Racism', in G. Bock and S. James (eds) *Beyond Equality and Difference: Citizenship, Feminist Politics and Female Subjectivity*, London: Routledge.

Bock, G. and Thane, P. (1991) 'Editors' Introduction', in G. Bock and P. Thane (eds) *Maternity and Gender Policies: Women and the Rise of the European Welfare States 1880s–1950s*, London: Routledge.

Boletín Mensual de Estadística (1993) (1994) Madrid: Instituto Nacional de Estadística.

Borchorst, A. (1990) 'Political Motherhood and Child Care Policies: A Comparative Approach to Britain and Scandinavia', in C. Ungerson (ed.) *Gender and Caring: Work and Welfare in Britain and Scandinavia*, Hemel Hempstead: Harvester Wheatsheaf.

Brannen, J. (1992) 'British Parenthood in the Wake of the New Right: Some Contradictions and Changes', in U. Bjornberg (ed.) *European*

Parents in the 1990s: Contradictions and Comparisons, New Brunswick: Transaction Publishers.

Brubaker, R. (1992) *Citizenship and Nationhood in France and Germany*, Cambridge, Massachusetts: Harvard University Press.

Bruckner, H. (1995) 'Research on the Dynamics of Poverty in Germany', *Journal of European Social Policy*, 5 (4): 317–22.

Bruegel, I. and Hegewisch, A. (1992) *Flexibilization and Part-time Work in Europe*, Cranford School of Management Paper SWP19/92.

Bruegel, I. and Perrons, D. (1996) *Deregulation and Women's Employment: The Diverse Experience of Women in Britain*, London: Gender Institute, London School of Economics.

Brusco, S. (1990) 'The Idea of the Industrial District: Its Genesis', in Pyke, F., Becattini, G. and Sengenberger, W. (eds) *Industrial Districts, Inter-firm Co-operation in Italy*, Geneva: International Institute for Labour Studies – ILO.

Bulletin (1994) (1995) (1996) *Bulletin on Women and Employment in the EU*, Brussels, European Commission Director General for Employment, Industrial Relations and Social Affairs.

Bussemaker, J. and van Kersbergen, K. (1994) 'Gender and Welfare States: Some Theoretical Reflections', in D. Sainsbury (ed.) *Gendering Welfare States*, London: Sage.

Callender, C. (1992) 'Redundancy, Unemployment and Poverty', in Glendinning, C. and Millar, J. (eds) *Women and Poverty in Britain: the 1990s*, London: Harvester Wheatsheaf.

Camps, V. (1994) 'The Changing Role of Women in Spanish Society', London: *RSA Journal*, August/September, CXLII (5452).

Carr, R. and Fusi, J.P. (1987) *Spain: Dictatorship to Democracy*, 2nd Edition, London: Allen and Unwin.

Castles, S. and Miller, M.J. (1993) *The Age of Migration: International Population Movements in the Modern World*, London: Macmillan.

Castro Martin, T. (1992) 'Delayed Childbearing in Contemporary Spain: Trends and Differentials', *European Journal of Population*, 8: 217–46.

Chamberlayne, P. (1993) 'Women and the State: Changes in Roles and Rights in France, West Germany, Italy and Britain', in J. Lewis (ed.) *Women and Social Policies in Europe*, Aldershot: Edward Elgar.

Chamberlayne, P. (1994) 'Women and Social Policy', in J. Clasen and R. Freeman (eds) *Social Policy in Germany*, Hemel Hempstead: Harvester Wheatsheaf.

Cheshire, P. (1995) 'European Integration and Regional Responses', in M. Rhodes (ed.) *The Regions and the New Europe: Patterns in Core and Periphery Development*, Manchester: Manchester University Press.

Clarke, J., Cochrane, A. and Smart, C. (1987) *Ideologies of Welfare: From Dreams to Disillusion*, London: Hutchinson.

Clasen, J. (1994) 'Social Security – the Core of the German Employment-Centered Social State', in J. Clasen and R. Freeman (eds) *Social Policy in Germany*, Hemel Hempstead: Harvester Wheatsheaf.

Clasen, J. and Freeman, R. (eds) (1994) *Social Policy in Germany*, Hemel Hempstead: Harvester Wheatsheaf.

Clasen, J. and Gould, A. (1995) 'Stability and Change in Welfare States: Germany and Sweden in the 1990s', *Policy and Politics*, 23 (3): 189–201.

Commission of the European Communities (1991) *Women of Europe Supplement: the Position of Women in the Labour Market*, Brussels: Commission of the European Communities Women's Information Service.

Commission of the European Communities (1993) *White Paper: Growth, Competitiveness, Employment: The Challenges and Ways Forward into the 21st Century*, Bulletin of the European Communities, Supplement 6/93, Luxembourg: Office for Official Publications of the European Communities.

Commission of the European Communities (1994) *White Paper on European Social Policy – a Way Forward for the Union*, Luxembourg: Office for Official Publications of the European Communities.

Commission of the European Communities *Employment in Europe* (Annual) DG for Employment, Industrial Relations and Social Affairs, Luxembourg: Office for Official Publications of the European Communities.

Cooke, P., Christiansen, T. and Schienstock, G. (1997) 'Regional Economic Policy and a Europe of the Regions', in M. Rhodes, P. Heywood and V. Wright (eds) *Developments in West European Politics*, London: Macmillan.

Cooke, P. and Morgan, K. (1994) 'Growth Regions under Duress; Renewal Strategies in Baden-Württemberg and Emilia Romagna', in A. Amin and N. Thrift (eds) *Globalisation, Institutions and Regional Development in Europe*, Oxford: Oxford University Press.

Cooke, P., Price, A. and Morgan, K. (1995) 'Regulating Regional Economies: Wales and Baden-Württemberg in Transition', in M. Rhodes (ed.) *The Regions and the New Europe: Patterns in Core and Periphery Development*, Manchester: Manchester University Press.

Cousins, C. (1987) *Controlling Social Welfare: A Sociology of State Welfare Work and Organisations*, Sussex: Wheatsheaf.

Cousins, C. (1994a) 'A Comparison of the Labour Market Position of Women in Spain and the UK with Reference to the "Flexible" Labour Debate', *Work, Employment and Society*, 8 (1): 45–67.

Cousins, C. (1994b) 'Industrial Districts and Industrial Restructuring: Evidence from the Barcelona Region', Paper presented to 12th Annual International Labour Process Conference, March, Aston University.

Cousins, C. (1995) 'Women and Social Policy in Spain: The Development of a Gendered Welfare Regime', *Journal of European Social Policy*, 5 (3): 175–97.

Cressey, P. and Jones, B. (eds) (1995) *Work and Employment in Europe: A New Convergence?*, London: Routledge.

Crouch, C. (1995) 'The State, Economic Management and Incomes Policy', in P. Edwards (ed.) *Industrial Relations: Theory and Practice in Britain*, Oxford: Blackwell.

Crouch, C. (1997) *Class Conflict and Industrial Relations Crisis*, London: Heinemann.

Crouch, C. and Menon, A. (1997) 'Organised Interests and the State', in M. Rhodes, P. Heywood and V. Wright (eds) *Developments in West European Politics*, London: Macmillan.

Curry, J. (1993) 'The Flexibility Fetish', *Capital and Class*, Summer: 99–126.

Cutler, T., Williams, K. and Williams, J. (1986) *Keynes, Beveridge and Beyond*, London: Routledge and Kegan Paul.

Daly, M. (1994) 'Comparing Welfare States: Towards a Gender Friendly Approach', in D. Sainsbury (ed.) *Gendering Welfare States*, Sage, London.

De Ussel, J.I. (1991) 'Family Ideology and Political Transition in Spain', *International Journal of Law and the Family*, 5: 277–95.

Deakin, S. and Mückenberger, U. (1992) 'Deregulation and European Labour Markets', in A. Castro *et al.*, *International Integration and Labour Market Organisation*, London: Academic Press.

Deakin, S. and Wilkinson, F. (1991/2) 'Social Policy and Economic Efficiency: The deregulation of the labour market in Britain', *Critical Social Policy*, Winter, 33: 40–61.

Delsen, L. and van Veen, T. (1992) 'The Swedish Model: Relevant for Other Countries?' *British Journal of Industrial Relations*, 30 (1): 83–105.

Dex, S. and McCulloch, A.(1995) *Flexible Employment in Britain: A Statistical Analysis*, London: Equal Opportunities Commission.

Dickens, L. and Hall, M. (1995) 'The State: Labour Law and Industrial Relations', in P. Edwards (ed.) *Industrial Relations: Theory and Practice in Britain*, Oxford: Blackwell.

Due, J., Madsen, J.S. and Jensen, C.S. (1991) 'The Social Dimension: Convergence or Divergence in the Single European Market?', *Industrial Relations Journal*, 22 (2).

Dumon, W. (1991) *Families and Policies: Evolutions and Trends in 1989/90*, European Observatory on Family Policy, Luxembourg: Commission of the European Community.

Duncan, S. (1995) 'Theorizing European Gender Systems', *Journal of European Social Policy*, 5 (4): 263–84.

Duran, M.A. and Gallego, M.T. (1986) 'The Women's Movement in Spain and the New Spanish Democracy', in D. Daherup (ed.) *The New Women's Movement: Feminism and Political Power in Europe and the USA*, London: Sage.

Edwards, P. (ed.) (1995) *Industrial Relations: Theory and Practice in Britain*, Oxford: Blackwell.

EIRR *European Industrial Relations Review* – monthly.

Emerson, M. (1988) 'Regulation or Deregulation of the Labour Market?', *European Economic Review*, 32 (4): 775–818.

Employment in Europe (annual) see Commission of the European Communities.

Erler, G. (1988) 'The German Paradox', in J. Jenson, E. Hagen and C.

186 *Bibliography*

Reddy (eds) *Feminization of the Labour Force: Paradoxes and Promises*, Oxford: Polity Press.

Espina, A. (1989) 'La Mujer en el Nuevo Mercado de Trabajo', *Revista de Economia y Sociologia del Trabajo*, 6 October: 19–38.

Esping-Andersen, G. (1985) *Politics Against the Market: The Social Democratic Road to Power*, Princeton NJ: Princeton University Press.

Esping-Andersen, G. (1990) *The Three Worlds of Welfare Capitalism*, Cambridge: Polity Press.

Esping-Andersen, G. (ed.) (1993) *Changing Classes: Stratification and Mobility in Post-Industrial Societies*, London: Sage.

Esping-Andersen, G. (ed.) (1996a) *Welfare States in Transition: National Adaptations in Global Economies*, London: Sage.

Esping-Andersen, G. (1996b) 'Welfare States Without Work: The Impasse of Labour Shedding and Familialism In Continental European Social Policy', in G. Esping-Andersen (ed.) *Welfare States in Transition: National Adaptations in Global Economies*, London: Sage.

Eurostat (1990a) *Family Budgets: Comparative Tables, FRG, Spain, France, Ireland, Italy and the Netherlands*, Luxembourg: Office for Official Publications of the European Communities.

Eurostat (1990b) *Poverty in Figures: Europe in the Early 1980s*, Luxembourg: Office for Official Publications of the European Communities.

Eurostat (1992) *Earnings: Indentity and Services*, Luxembourg: Office for Official Publications of the European Communities.

Eurostat (1993) *Digest of Statistics on Social Protection in Europe, Vol. 4 Family*, Luxembourg: Office for Official Publications of the European Communities.

Eurostat (1994) *Poverty Statistics in the Late 1980s: Research Based on Micro-data*, Luxembourg: Office for Official Publications of the European Communities.

Eurostat, *Labour Force Survey Results* (1989) (1991) (1994a) (1995) (1996) (1997) Luxembourg: Office for Official Publications of the European Communities.

Evans, M., Paugam, S. and Prelis, J. A. (1995) *Chunnel Vision: Poverty, Social Exclusion and the Debate on Social Welfare in France and Britain*, STICERD Welfare State Programme Discussion Paper WSP/115, London: London School of Economics.

Fagan, C. and Rubery, J. (1996) 'The Salience of the Part-time Divide in the European Union', *European Sociological Review*, 12 (3): 227–50.

Faist, T. (1995) 'Boundaries of Welfare States: Immigrants and Social Rights on the National and Supranational Level', in J. Miles and D. Thranhardt, *Migration and European Integration: The Dynamics of Inclusion and Exclusion*, London: Pinter.

Falkingham J. and Baldwin, S. (1994) 'Introduction', in Baldwin, S. and Falkingham, J. (eds) *Social Security and Social Change: New Challenges to the Beveridge Model*, Hemel Hempstead: Harvester Wheatsheaf.

Farriol, J. and Valette, M. (1989) *Sabadell Mercat de Treball 1989*, Barcelona: Ajuntament de Sabadell.

Ferrera, M. (1996) 'The "Southern Model" of Welfare in Social Europe', *Journal of European Social Policy*, 6 (1): 17–37.

Flecker, J. and Schulten, T. (1997) 'The End of Institutional Stability: What Future for the German Model?' Paper presented to the 15th Annual International Labour Process Conference, April, Edinburgh University.

Forsberg, G. (1994) 'Occupational and Sex Segregation in a Woman-friendly Society – The Case of Sweden', *Environment and Planning*, 26 (8): 1235–56.

Freeman, R.B., Swedenborg, B. and Topel, R. (1995) *Economic Troubles in Sweden's Welfare State: Introduction, Summary and Conclusions*, Occasional Paper No. 69, Stockholm: Centre for Business and Policy Studies.

Frotiee, B. (1994) 'A French Perspective on Family and Employment in Spain', in M. Letablier and L. Hantrais (eds) *The Family–Employment Relationship*, Cross-National Research Papers, Fourth Series, Loughborough University: European Research Centre.

Fulcher, J. (1987) 'Labour Movement Theory Versus Corporatism: Social Democracy in Sweden', *Sociology*, 21 (2): 231–52.

Fulcher, J. (1991) *Labour Movements, Employers and the State*, Oxford: Clarendon Press.

Gamble, A. (1991) *Britain in Decline*, London: Macmillan.

Gamble, A. (1994) *The Free Economy and the Strong State: The Politics of Thatcherism*, Second Edition, London: Macmillan.

Garrido, J.G. (1992) *Las Dos Biografías de la Mujer en España*, Instituto de la Mujer, 33, Madrid: Ministerio de Asuntos Sociales.

Gillespie, R. (1990) 'The Break-up of the "Socialist Family" Party-Union Relations in Spain 1982–89', *West European Politics*, 13:147–62.

Giner, S. (1973) 'Spain', in M.S. Archer and S. Giner (eds) *Contemporary Europe: Class, Status and Power*, London: Weidenfeld and Nicolson.

Giner, S. (1980) *The Social Structure of Catalonia*, Anglo-Catalan Society, University of Sheffield Printing Unit.

Giner S. (1985) 'Political Economy, Legitimation and the State in Southern Europe', in R. Hudson and J. Lewis (eds) *Uneven Development in Southern Europe: Studies of Accumulation, Class Migration and the State*, London: Methuen.

Giner, S. and Sevilla, E. (1984) 'From Corporatism to Corporatism: The Political Transition in Spain', in A. Williams (ed.) *Southern Europe Transformed*, London: Harper and Row.

Ginsberg, N. (1992) *Divisions of Welfare*, London: Sage.

Ginsberg, N. (1994) 'Ethnic Minorities and Social Policy', in J. Clasen and R. Freeman (eds) *Social Policy in Germany*, Hemel Hempstead: Harvester Wheatsheaf.

Gore, C. (1995) 'Introduction: Markets, Citizenship and Social Exclusion', in G. Rodgers, C. Gore and J.B. Figueiredo (eds), *Social Exclusion: Rhetoric, Reality, Responses*, Geneva: International Institute for Labour Studies.

Gough, I. (1996) 'Social Welfare and Competitiveness', *New Political Economy*, 1 (2): 209–32.

188   *Bibliography*

Gough, I., Bradshaw, J., Ditch, J., Eardly, T. and Whiteford, P. (1997) 'Social Assistance in OECD Countries', *Journal of European Social Policy*, 7 (1): 17–43.

Gregg, P. (1993) 'Jobs and Justice', in E. Balls and P. Gregg, *Work and Welfare; Tackling the Jobs Deficit*, London: Institute for Public Policy Research.

Gregg, P. and Machin, S. (1994) 'Is the UK Rise in Inequality Different?' in R. Barrell (ed.) *The UK Labour Market: Comparative and Institutional Developments*, Cambridge: Cambridge University Press.

Gregg, P. and Wadsworth, J. (1995) 'A Short History of Labour Turnover, Job Tenure and Job Security 1975–93', *Oxford Review of Economic Policy*, 11 (1): 73–90.

Gregg, P. and Wadsworth, J. (1997) 'Prosperity Begins at Home', *Financial Times*, 8 January 1997.

Gregory, A. and O'Reilly, J. (1996) 'Checking Out and Cashing Up: The Prospects and Paradoxes of Regulating Part-time Work in Europe', in R. Crompton, D. Gallie and K. Purcell (eds) *Changing Forms of Employment: Organisations, Skills and Gender*, Routledge, London.

Gregory, M. and Sandoval, V. (1994) 'Low Pay and Minimum Wage Protection in Britain and the EC', in R. Barrell (ed.) *The UK Labour Market: Comparative and Institutional Developments*, Cambridge: Cambridge University Press.

Greve, B. (1996) 'Indications of Social Policy Convergence in Europe' *Social Policy and Administration* 30 (4): 348–67.

Guillen, A.M. (1992) 'Social Policy in Spain: From Dictatorship to Democracy (1939–1982)', in Z. Ferge and J.E. Kolberg (eds) *Social Policy in a Changing Europe*, European Centre for Social Welfare Policy and Research, Frankfurt: Campus Verlag.

Gustafsson, S. (1994) 'Childcare and Types of Welfare State', in D. Sainsbury (ed.) *Gendering Welfare States*, London: Sage.

Haas, L. (1992) *Equal Parenthood and Social Policy: A Study of Parental Leave in Sweden*, Albany: State University of New York Press.

Hadjimichalis, C. and Vaiou, D. (1990) 'Whose Flexibility? The Politics of Informalisation in Southern Europe', *Capital and Class*, 42 (Winter): 79–106.

Hakim, C. (1979) *Occupational Segregation: a Comparative Study of the Degree and Pattern of Differentiation between Men and Women's Work in Britain, the US and Other Countries*, Department of Employment Research Paper No. 9, London: HMSO.

Hakim, C. (1990) 'Workforce Restructuring in Europe in the 1980s', *The International Journal of Comparative Labour Law and Industrial Relations*, 5 (4): 167–203.

Hakim, C. (1993) 'The Myth of Rising Female Employment', *Work, Employment and Society*, 7 (1): 97–120.

Hakim, C. (1996) *Key Issues in Women's Work: Female Heterogeneity and the Polarisation of Women's Employment*, London: Athlone Press.

Hallerod, B. (1995) 'Making Ends Meet: Perceptions of Poverty in Sweden', *Scandinavian Journal of Social Welfare*, 4: 174–89.

Hallerod, B. (1996) 'Deprivation and Poverty: A Comparative Analysis of Sweden and Great Britain', *Acta Sociologica*, 39:141–68.

Hantrais, L. (1994) 'Comparing Family Policy in Britain, France and Germany', *Journal of Social Policy*, 23 (2): 135–60.

Hantrais, L. (1995) *Social Policy in the European Union*, London: Macmillan Press.

Harkness, S, Machin, S. and Waldfogel, J. (1995) *Evaluating the Pin Money Hypothesis: The Relationship Between Women's Labour Market Activity, Family Income and Poverty in Britain*, STICERD Welfare State Programme Discussion Paper WSP/108, London: London School of Economics.

Harris, C.C. (1990) 'The State and the Market' in P. Brown and R. Sparks (eds) *Beyond Thatcherism: Social Policy, Politics and Society*, Milton Keynes: Open University Press.

Hauser, R. and Semerau, P. (1990) 'Trends in Poverty and Low Income in the Federal Republic of Germany 1962/3–1987', in R. Teekens and M.S. van Praag (eds) *Analysing Poverty in the EC*, Eurostat News, Special Edition, Luxembourg: Office for Official Publications of the European Communities.

Hay, C. (1996) *Re-stating Political and Social Change*, Buckingham: Open University Press.

Heather, J., Rick, J., Atkinson, J. and Morris, S. (1996) 'Employers' Use of Temporary Workers', *Labour Market Trends*, September: 403–11.

Hernes, H.M. (1987) *Welfare State and Women Power*, Oslo: Norwegian University Press.

Herrigel, G. (1993) 'Large Firms, Small Firms and the Governance of Flexible Specialisation: The Case of Baden-Württemberg', in B. Kogut (ed.) *Country Competitiveness: Technology and the Organising of Work*, Oxford: Oxford University Press.

Herrigel, G. (1996) 'Crisis in German Decentralised Production: Unexpected Rigidity and the Challenge of an Alternative Form of Flexible Organisation in Baden-Württemberg', *European Urban and Regional Studies*, 3 (1): 33–52.

Heywood, P. (1995) *The Government and Politics of Spain*, London: Macmillan.

Hills, J. (1993) *The Future of Welfare: A Guide to the Debate*, London: Joseph Rowntree Foundation.

Hirdmann, Y. (1990) 'Genussystemet' in Statens Offentliga Utredningar, *Demokrati och Makt i Sverige*, Stockholm: SOU.

Hirst, P. (1994) *Associative Democracy: New Forms of Economic and Social Governance*, Cambridge: Polity Press.

Hirst, P. and Thompson, G. (1996) 'Globalisation' *Soundings*, 4 Autumn: 47–66.

Hobson, B. (1994) 'Solo Mothers, Social Policy Regimes and the Logics of Gender', in D. Sainsbury (ed.) *Gendering Welfare States*, London: Sage.

Homs, O. (1988) *Training in the Spanish Textile and Clothing Industry:*

the situation in Catalonia and the Autonomous Community of Valencia, European Centre for the Development of Vocational Training, Luxembourg: Office for Official Publications of the European Commission.

Humphries, J. and Rubery, J. (1988) 'Recession and Exploitation', in Jenson, J., Hagen, E. and Reddy, C. (eds) *The Feminization of the Labour Force: Paradoxes and Promises*, Oxford: Polity Press.

Hunter, L., McGregor, A., MacInnes, J. and Sproull, A. (1993) 'The "Flexible Firm": Strategy and Segmentation', *British Journal of Industrial Relations*, 31 (3): 383–407.

Hutton, W. (1996) *The State We're In*, London: Vintage.

Hyman, R. (1989) *The Political Economy of Industrial Relations: Theory and Practice in a Cold Climate*, London: Macmillan.

Hyman, R. (1991) 'Plus ça change? The Theory of Production and the Production of Theory', in A. Pollert (ed.) *Farewell to Flexibility?* Oxford: Blackwell.

Hyman, R. (1994) 'Introduction: Economic Restructuring, Market Liberalism and the Future of National Industrial Relations Systems', in Hyman, R. and Ferner, A. (1994) (eds) *New Frontiers in European Industrial Relations*, Oxford: Blackwell.

Hyman, R. and Ferner A. (1994) *New Market in European Industrial Relations*, Oxford: Blackwell.

IDS (Income Data Services) (1997) 'Spain: Will Labour Reform Dent Unemployment?', *Employment Europe*, 425, May: 27–8.

ILO (1994–5) *Bulletin of Labour Statistics*, Geneva: International Labour Office.

Instituto de la Mujer (1992) *Las Mujeres en España: Todos Los Datos*, Numero 1, Madrid: Ministerio de Asuntos Sociales.

Instituto de la Mujer (1994) *Spanish Women on the Threshold of the Twenty-first Century: Report Submitted to the Fourth World Conference on Women, Beijing 1995*, Madrid: Ministerio de Asuntos Sociales.

Jenson, J. and Mahon, R. (1993) 'Representing Solidarity: Class, Gender and the Crisis in Social-Democratic Sweden', *New Left Review*, 201: 76–100.

Jessop, B. (1988) *Conservative Regimes and the Transition to Post-Fordism: The cases of Britain and West Germany*, Essex Papers in Politics and Government, Essex: University of Essex.

Jessop, B. (1991a) 'Thatcherism and Flexibility: The White Heat of a Post-Fordist Revolution', in Jessop, B., Kasendiek, H., Nielsen, K. and Pedersen, O. (eds) *The Politics of Flexibility: Restructuring State and Industry in Britain, Germany and Sweden*, Aldershot: Edward Elgar.

Jessop, B. (1991b) 'The Welfare State in the Transition from Fordism to Post-Fordism' in Jessop, B., Kasendiek, H., Nielsen, K. and Pedersen, O. (eds) *The Politics of Flexibility: Restructuring State and Industry in Britain, Germany and Sweden*, Aldershot: Edward Elgar.

Jessop, B. (1992a) 'Fordism and Post-Fordism: A critical Reformulation', in M. Storper and A. J. Scott (eds) *Pathways to Industrialisation and Regional Development*, London: Routledge.

Jessop, B. (1992b) 'Fordism in Britain and Europe', in J. Allen, P. Braham and P. Lewis (eds) *Political and Economic Forms of Modernity*, Cambridge: Polity Press/Open University.

Jessop, B. (1994) 'Post-Fordism and the State', in A. Amin (ed.) *Post-Fordism: A Reader*, Oxford: Blackwell.

Jessop, B., Bonnett, K., Bromley, S. and Ling, T. (1988) *Thatcherism*, Cambridge: Polity Press.

Jimeno, J. and Toharia, L. (1994) *Unemployment and Labour Market Flexibility: Spain*, Geneva: ILO.

Jonung, C. and Persson, I. (1994) 'Combining Market Work and Family', in T. Bengtsson (ed.) *Population, Economy and Welfare in Sweden*, Berlin: Springer-Verlag.

Kerr, C., Dunlop, J.J., Harbison, F.H. and Mayers, C.A. (1960) *Industrialism and Industrial Man*, Cambridge, Mass.: Harvard University Press.

Kjellberg, A. (1992) 'Sweden: Can the Model Survive ?' in A. Ferner and R. Hyman (eds) *Industrial Relations in the New Europe*, Oxford: Blackwell.

Kolinsky, E. (1993) *Women in Contemporary Germany: Life, Work and Politics*, Oxford: Berg.

Kolinsky, E. (1995) 'Everyday Life Transformed: An Introduction', in E. Kolinsky (ed.) *Between Hope and Fear: Everyday Life in Post-unification East Germany*, Keele: Keele University Press.

Kolinsky, E. (1996) 'Women in the New Germany', in G. Smith *et al.* (eds) *Developments in German Politics 2*, London: Macmillan.

Korpi, W. (1983) *The Democratic Class Struggle*, London: Routledge and Kegan Paul.

Kraft, K. (1993) 'Eurosclerosis Reconsidered: Employment Protection and Work Force Adjustment in West Germany', in C.F. Büchtemann (ed.) *Employment Security and Labor Market Behaviour*, Ithaca/New York: ILR Press.

Kravaritou-Manitakis, Y. (1988) *New Forms of Work: Labour Law and Social Security aspects in the European community*, Luxembourg: European Foundation for the Improvement of Living and Working Conditions.

Kurth, J. (1993) 'A Tale of Four Countries: Parallel Politics in Southern Europe 1815–1990', in J. Kurth and J. Petras (eds) *Mediterranean Paradoxes*, Oxford: Berg.

Labour Market Trends (monthly) London: The Stationery Office.

Lagenddijk, A. (1994) 'The Impact of Internationalisation and Rationalisation of Production on the Spanish Automobile Industry 1950–90', *Environment and Planning*, 26: 321–43.

Land, H. (1978) 'Who cares for the Family?' *Journal of Social Policy*, 7 (3): 257–84.

Land, H. (1980) 'The Family Wage', *Feminist Review*, 6: 55–78.

Land, H. (1985) 'Who Still Cares for the Family? Recent Developments in Income Maintenance, Taxation and Family Law', in C. Ungerson (ed.) *Women and Social Policy: A Reader*, London: Macmillan.

Land, H. (1995) 'Families and the Law', in J. Muncie, M. Wetherell, R. Dallos and A.Cochrane (eds) *Understanding the Family*, London: Sage.

Lane, C. (1989a) 'From "Welfare Capitalism" to "Market Capitalism": A Comparative Review of Trends Towards Employment Flexibility in the Labour Markets of Three Major European Societies', *Sociology*, 25 (4): 583–610.

Lane, C. (1989b) *Management and Labour in Europe*, Aldershot: Edward Elgar.

Lane, C. (1991) 'Industrial Reorganisation in Europe: Patterns of Convergence and Divergence in Germany, France and Britain', *Work, Employment and Society*, 5 (4): 515–39.

Lane, C. (1993) 'Gender and the Labour Market in Europe: Britain, Germany and France Compared', *The Sociological Review*, 14 (2): 274–301.

Lane, C. (1994) 'Is Germany following the British Path: a Comparative Analysis of Stability and Change', *Industrial Relations Journal*, 25 (3): 187–98.

Lane, C. (1995) *Industry and Society in Europe: Stability and Change in Britain, Germany and France*, Aldershot: Edward Elgar.

Langan, M. and Ostner, I. (1991) 'Gender and Welfare: Towards a Comparative Framework', in G. Room (ed.) *Towards a European Welfare State?*, Bristol: SAUS/SPA.

Leibfried, S. (1993) 'Towards a European Welfare State', in C. Jones (ed.) *New perspectives on the Welfare State in Europe*, London: Routledge.

Leibfried, S. and Pierson, P. (1995) 'Semisovereign Welfare States: Social Policy in a Multitiered Europe', in S. Leibfried and P. Pierson (eds) *European Social Policy: Between Fragmentation and Integration*, Washington DC: The Brookings Institute.

Leira, A. (1993) 'Mothers, Markets and the State: A Scandinavian Model', *Journal of Social Policy*, 22 (3): 329–47.

Leira, A. (1994) 'Combining Work and Family: Working Mothers in Scandinavia and the European Community', in P. Brown and R. Crompton (eds) *A New Europe? Economic Restructuring and Social Exclusion*, London: University College London.

Lewis, J. (1991) 'Models of Equality for Women: The Case of State Support for Children in Twentieth Century Britain', in Bock, G. and Thane, P. (eds) *Maternity and Gender Policies: Women and the Rise of the European Welfare States 1880s–1950s*, London: Routledge.

Lewis, J. (1992) 'Gender and the Development of Welfare Regimes', *Journal of European Social Policy*, 2 (3): 159–73.

Lewis, J. (1993) 'Introduction', in J. Lewis (ed.) *Women and Social Policies in Europe*, Aldershot: Edward Elgar.

Lewis, J. and Åström, G. (1992) 'Equality, Difference and State Welfare: Labour Market and Family Policies in Sweden', *Feminist Studies*, 1891:59–87.

Lindqvist, R. and Marklund, S. (1995) 'Forced to Work and Liberated from Work: A Historical Perspective on Work and Welfare in Sweden', *Scandinavian Journal of Social Welfare*, 4: 224–37.

Lipietz, A. (1992) *Towards a New Economic Order*, Cambridge: Polity Press.

Lister, R. (1994) 'She has other duties – Women, Citizenship and Social Security', in Baldwin, S. and Falkingham, J. (eds) *Social Security and Social Change: New Challenges to the Beveridge Model*, Hemel Hempstead: Harvester Wheatsheaf.

Machin, S. and Waldfogel, J. (1994) *The Decline of the Male Breadwinner: Changing Shares of Husband's and Wives' Earnings in Family Income*, STICERD Welfare State Programme Discussion Paper WSP/103, London: London School of Economics.

Mahnkopf, B. (1992) 'The "Skill-oriented' Strategies of German Trade Unions: Their Impact on Efficiency and Equality Objectives', *British Journal of Industrial Relations*, 30 (1): 61–81.

Mahon, R. (1996) 'Women Wage Earners and The Future of Swedish Unions, *Economic and Industrial Democracy*, 17: 545–86.

Mangen, S. (1996) 'German Welfare and Social Citizenship' in G. Smith *et al.* (eds) *Developments in German Politics 2*, London: Macmillan.

Marsh, D. (1992) *The New Politics of British Trade Unionism: Union Power and the Thatcher Legacy*, London: Macmillan.

Marsh, D., and Rhodes, R.A.W. (1992) *Implementing Thatcherite Policies: Audit of an Era*, Buckingham: Open University Press.

Marshall, T.H. (1950) *Citizenship and Social Class and Other Essays*, Cambridge: Cambridge University Press.

Martinez Lucio, M. (1991) 'Employer Identity and the Politics of the Labour Market in Spain', *West European Politics*, 14 (1): 41–55.

Martinez Lucio, M. and Blyton, P. (1995) 'Constructing the Post-Fordist State? The Politics of Labour Market Flexibility in Spain', *West European Politics*, 18 (2): 340–60.

Marullo, S. (1995) *Comparison of Regulations on Part-Time and Temporary Employment in Europe: A Briefing Paper*, Research Series No. 52, Sheffield: Employment Department.

McLaughlin, E. (1994) *Flexibility in Work and Benefits*, London: Institute for Public Policy Research.

Meulders, D. (1990) *The Position of Women in the Labour Market: Trends and Developments in the Twelve Member States of the European Community, 1983–1990*, Brussels: Commission of the European Communities Women's Information Service.

Meulders, D., Plasman, O. and Plasman, R. (1994) *Atypical Employment in the EC*, Aldershot: Dartmouth.

Meulders, D., Plasman, R. and Vander Strict, V. (1993) *Position of Women on the Labour Market in the European Community*, Aldershot: Dartmouth.

Michie, J. (1995) 'Unemployment in Europe', in Amin, A. and Tomaney, J. (eds) *Behind the Myth of the European Union: Prospects for Cohesion*, London: Routledge.

Michie, J. and Grieve Smith, J.G. (eds) (1994) *Unemployment in Europe*, London: Academic Press.

Miguélez Lobo, F.M. (1988) 'Irregular Work in Spain', in EEC Survey *Underground Economy and Irregular Forms of Employment, Final Report*, Brussels.

Miguélez Lobo, F.M. (1990) 'Estructuración de Clases y Desgualidad: La España de Los Años 70 y 80', *Papers Revista de Sociologia* 33: 21–34.

Millar, J. (1994) 'Lone Parents and Social Security Policy in the UK', in S. Baldwin and J. Falkingham (eds) *Social Security and Social Change: New Challenges to the Beveridge Model*, London: Harvester Wheatsheaf.

Milner, S., Metcalf, D. and Nombela, G. (1995) *Employment Protection Legislation and Labour Market Outcomes in Spain*, London: Centre for Economic Performance, London School of Economics.

Mitchell, M. and Russell, D. (1994) 'Race, Citizenship and Fortress Europe', in P. Brown and R. Crompton (eds) *A New Europe? Economic Restructuring and Social Exclusion*, London: University College, London.

Moeller, P.G. (1989) 'Reconstructing the Family in Reconstruction Germany – Women and Social Policy in the Federal Republic, 1949–1955', *Feminist Studies*, 15 (1): 137–69.

Moss, P. (1996) 'Parental Employment in the European Union, 1985–1993', *Labour Market Trends*, December: 517–22.

Mückenberger, U. (1989) 'Non-standard Forms of Work and the Role of Changes in the Labour and Social Security Regulation', *International Journal of the Sociology of Law*, 17: 381–402.

Mückenberger, U. (1994) 'Social Integration or Anomie ? The Welfare State Challenged by Individualism', in Ferris, J. and Page, R. (eds) *Social Policy in Transition: Anglo-German Perspectives in the New European Community*, Aldershot: Avebury.

Myrdal, A. and Klein, V. (1957) *Women's Two Roles*, London: Routledge and Kegan Paul.

Nash, M. (1991) 'Pronatalism and Motherhood in Franco's Spain', in Bock, G. and Thane, P. (eds) *Maternity and Gender Policies: Women and the Rise of the European Welfare States, 1880s–1950s*, London: Routledge.

Nätti, J. (1995) 'Part-time Work in the Nordic Countries: A Trap for Women?' *Labour*, 9 (2): 343–57.

Nielsen, K. (1991) 'Towards a Flexible Future', in Jessop, B., Kasendiek, H., Nielsen, K. and Pedersen, O. (eds) *The Politics of Flexibility: Restucturing State and Industry in Britain, Germany and Scandinavia*, Aldershot: Edward Elgar.

Nolan, B. and Whelan, C.T. (1996) *Resources, Deprivation and Poverty*, Oxford: Clarendon Press.

Nolan, P. (1994) 'Labour Market Institutions, Industrial Restructuring and Unemployment in Europe', in J. Michie and J.G. Grieve Smith (eds) *Unemployment in Europe*, London: Academic Press.

Nolan, P. and Walsh, J. (1995) 'The Structure of the Economy and Labour Market', in P. Edwards (ed.) *Industrial Relations: Theory and Practice in Britain*, Oxford: Blackwell.

Nordli Hansen, M. (1997) 'The Scandinavian Welfare Model: The Impact of the Public Sector on Gender Equality', *Work, Employment and Society*, 11 (1): 83–99.

O'Connor, J.S. (1993) 'Gender, Class and Citizenship in the Comparative Analysis of Welfare State Regimes: Theoretical and Methodological Issues', *British Journal of Sociology*, 44 (3): 501–18.

OECD (1977) *Economic Survey: Spain*, Paris: OECD.

OECD (1986) *Flexibility in the Labour Market*, Paris: OECD.

OECD (1989) *Economic Survey: Spain*, Paris: OECD.

OECD (1990/1) *Economic Surveys: Germany*, Paris: OECD.

OECD (1991) *Historical Statistics, 1960–1990*, Paris: OECD.

OECD (1991/2a) *Economic Survey: Spain*, Paris: OECD.

OECD (1991/2b) *Employment Outlook*, Paris: OECD.

OECD (1994a) *Economic Survey: Spain*, Paris: OECD.

OECD (1994b) *Economic Survey: Sweden*, Paris: OECD.

OECD (1994c) *The OECD Jobs Study: Evidence and Explanations*, Parts 1 and 2, Paris: OECD.

Offe, C. (1991) 'Smooth Consolidation in the West German Welfare State: Structural Change, Fiscal Policies and Populist Politics' in F. Fox Piven (ed.) *Labor Parties in Post-industrial Societies*, Cambridge: Polity Press.

Olsson, S.E. (1990) *Social Policy and Welfare State in Sweden*, Lund: Arkiv.

O'Reilly, J. (1996) 'Labour Adjustments through Part-time Work', in G. Schmid *et al. International Handbook of Labour Market Policy and Evaluation*, Cheltenham: Edward Elgar.

Orloff, A.S. (1993) 'Gender and the Social Rights of Citizenship: The Comparative Analysis of Gender Relations and Welfare States', *American Sociological Review*, 58 (June): 303–28.

Ostner, I. (1993) 'Slow motion: Women, Work and the Family in Germany' in J. Lewis (ed.) *Women and Social Policies in Europe*, Aldershot: Edward Elgar.

Ostner, I. (1994a) 'Independence and Dependency: Options and Constraints for Women Over the Life Course', *Women's Studies International Forum*, 17 (2/3): 12939.

Ostner, I. (1994b) 'The Women and Welfare Debate', in L. Hantrais and S. Mangen (eds) *Family Policy and the Welfare of Women*, Cross-National Research Papers, Loughborough: Loughborough University.

Ostner, I. (1994c) 'Back to the Fifties: Gender and Welfare in Unified Germany', *Social Politics*, Spring.

Ostner, I. and Lewis, J. (1995) 'Gender and the Evolution of European Social Policies', in S. Leibfried and P. Pierson (eds) *European Social Policy: Between Fragmentation and Integration*, Washington DC: The Brookings Institute.

Owen Smith, E. (1994) *The German Economy*, London: Routledge.

Paugam, S. (1995) 'The Spiral of Precariousness: A Multidimensional Approach to the Process of Social Disqualification in France', in G.

Room (ed.) *Beyond the Threshold: The Measurement and Analysis of Social Exclusion*, Bristol: The Policy Press, University of Bristol.

Perez Amoros, F. and Rojo, E, (1991) 'Implications of the Single Market for Labour and Social Policy in Spain', *International Labour Review*, 130 (3): 359–72.

Perez-Diaz, V. (1987) 'Economic Policies and Social Pacts in Spain During the Transition', in I. Scholton (ed.) *Political Stability and Neo-corporatism*, London: Sage.

Perez-Diaz, V. and Rodriguez, J.C. (1995) 'Inertial Choices: An Overview of Spanish Human Resources, Practices and Policies', in R. Locke, T. Kochan and M. Piore (eds) *Employment Relations in a Changing World Economy*, Cambridge, Mass.: The MIT Press.

Pestoff, V.A. (1993) 'Towards a New Swedish Model', in Hauser, J., Jessop, B. and Neilsen, K. (eds) *Institutional Frameworks of Market Economies: Scandinavian and Eastern European Perspectives*, Aldershot: Avebury.

Petras, J. (1993) 'Spanish Socialism: The Politics of Neo-liberalism', in J. Kurth and J. Petras (eds) *Mediterranean Paradoxes*, Oxford: Berg.

Pfau-Effinger, B. (1993) 'Modernisation, Culture and Part-time Employment: The Example of Finland and West Germany', *Work, Employment and Society*, 7 (3): 383–410.

Phizacklea, A. (1990) *Unpacking the Fashion Industry: Gender, Racism and Class in Production*, London: Routledge.

Phizacklea, A. and Miles, R. (1980) *Labour and Racism*, London: Routledge and Kegan Paul.

Piore, M. and Sabel, C. (1984) *The Second Industrial Divide: Possibilities for Prosperity*, New York: Basic Books.

Pollert, A. (1991) 'The Orthodoxy of Flexibility', in Pollert, A. (ed.) *Farewell to Flexibility*? Oxford: Basil Blackwell.

Pridham, G. (1989) 'Southern European Socialists and the State: Consolidation of Party Rule or Consolidation of Democracy?' in T. Gallagher and A.M. Williams (eds) *Southern European Socialism*, Manchester: Manchester University Press.

Procter, S.J., Rowlinson, M., McArdle, L., Massard, J. and Forrester, P. (1994) 'Flexibility, Politics and Strategy: In Defence of the Model of the Flexible Firm', *Work, Employment and Society*, 8 (2): 221–42.

Pyke, F., Becattini, G. and Sengenberger, W. (eds) (1990) *Industrial Districts, Inter-firm Co-operation in Italy*, Geneva: International Institute for Labour Studies – ILO.

Pyke, F. and Sengenberger, W. (eds) (1992) *Industrial Districts and Local Economic Regeneration*, Geneva: International Institute for Labour Studies – ILO.

Rainnie, A. (1993) 'The Reorganisation of Large Firm Sub-contracting: Myth and Reality', *Capital and Class*, 49: 53–75.

Ramprakash, D. (1994) 'Poverty in the Countries of the European Union: A Synthesis of Eurostat's Statistical Research on Poverty', *Journal of European Social Policy*, 4 (2): 117–28.

Rea, A. (1995) 'Social Citizenship and Ethnic Minorities in the European Union', in M. Martiniello (ed.) *Migration, Citizenship and Ethno-National Identities in the European Union*, Aldershot: Avebury.

Recio, A. (1991) 'La Segmentación del Mercado de Trabajo en España', in Miguelez, F. and Prieto, C. *Las Relaciónes Laborales en España*, Madrid: Siglo XXI.

Recio, A. (1992) 'Economic Internationalisation and the Labour Market in Spain', in A. Castro, P. Mehaut and J. Rubery (eds) *International Integration and Labour Market Organisation*, London: Academic Press.

Recio, A., Miguelez, F. and Alos, R. (1988) *La Industria Textil Lanera del Valles Occidental*, Barcelona: Centre d'Estudis i Recerca Sindicals, Comissio Obrera Nacional de Catalunya (Ceres-CONC).

Recio, A. Miguelez, F., Alos, R. (1991) *Decentralización Productiva y Cambio Technico en la Industria Auxiliar de la Automocion*, Barcelona: Centre d'Estudis i Recerca Sindicals, Comissio Obrera Nacional de Catalunya (Ceres-CONC).

Rex, J. (1992) 'Race and Ethnicity in Europe', in J. Bailey (ed.) *Social Europe*, Longman, Harlow.

Rhodes, M. (1989) 'Whither regulation? Disorganized Capitalism and the West European Labour Market', in L. Hancher and M. Moran (eds) *Capitalism, Culture and Economic Regulation*, Oxford: Clarendon Press.

Rhodes, M. (1995) 'A Regulatory Conundrum: Industrial Relations and the Social Dimension', in S. Leibfried and P. Pierson (eds) *European Social Policy: Between Fragmentation and Integration*, Washington DC: The Brookings Institute.

Rhodes, M. (ed.) (1995) *The Regions and the New Europe: Studies in Core and Periphery Development*, Manchester: Manchester University Press.

Rhodes, M. (1996) 'Globalization and West European Welfare States: A Critical Review of Recent Debates', *Journal of European Social Policy*, 6 (4): 305–27.

Rhodes, M., Heywood, P. and Wright, V. (1997) 'Towards a New Europe?' in M. Rhodes, P. Heywood and V. Wright (eds) *Developments in West European Politics*, London: Macmillan.

Ringen, S. (1988) 'Direct and Indirect Measures of Poverty', *Journal of Social Policy*, 17 (3): 351–65.

Ritzer, G. (1993) *The McDonaldization of Society*, London: Pine Forge Press.

Rogowski, R. and Schomann, K. (1996) 'Legal Regulation and Flexibility of Employment Contracts', in G. Schmid *et al.*, *International Handbook of Labour Market Policy and Evaluation*, Cheltenham: Edward Elgar.

Room, G. (1993) *Agencies, Institutions and Programmes: Their Inter-relationships and Coordination in Efforts to Combat Social Exclusion*, European Observatory on National Policies to Combat Social Exclusion, Luxembourg: Office for Official Publications of the European Communities.

Room, G. (ed.) (1995a) *Beyond the Threshold: The Measurement and Analysis of Social Exclusion*, Bristol: The Policy Press, University of Bristol.

Room, G. (1995b) 'Poverty in Europe: Competing Paradigms of Analysis', *Policy and Politics*, 23 (2): 103–13.

Room, G., Lawson, R. and Laczko, F. (1989) '"New Poverty" in the European Community', *Policy and Politics*, 17 (2): 165–76.

Rosenfeld, R. A. and Kalleberg, A. L. (1991) 'Gender Inequality in the Labour Market: A Cross-National Perspective', *Acta Sociologica*, 34: 207–25.

Ross, G. (1995) 'Assessing the Delors Era and Social Policy', in S. Leibfried and P. Pierson (eds) *European Social Policy: Between Fragmentation and Integration*, Washington DC: The Brookings Institute.

Rowntree Foundation (1995a) *Inquiry into Income and Wealth*, Vol. 1, York: Joseph Rowntree Foundation.

Rowntree Foundation (1995b) *Inquiry into Income and Wealth*, Vol. 2, York: Joseph Rowntree Foundation.

Rubery, J. (1988) 'Women and Recession: A Comparative Perspective' in J. Rubery (ed.) *Women and Recession*, London: Routledge and Kegan Paul.

Rubery, J. (1992) 'Pay, Gender and the Social Dimension in Europe', *British Journal of Industrial Relations*, 30 (4): 605–21.

Rubery, J., Bettio, F., Fagan, C., Maier, F., Quack, S. and Villa, P. (1997) 'Payment Structures and Gender Pay Differentials: Some Societal Effects', *The International Journal of Human Resource Management*, 8 (3): 131–49.

Rubery, J. and Fagan, C. (1993) *Occupational Segregation of Women and Men in the European Community*, Social Europe Supplement 3/93, Luxembourg: Official Publications of the European Community.

Rubery, J. and Fagan, C. (1994) 'Does Feminization mean a Flexible Labour Force?' in R. Hyman and A. Ferner (eds) *New Frontiers in European Industrial Relations*, Oxford: Blackwell.

Rubery, J. and Fagan, C. (1995) 'Gender Segregation in Societal Context', *Work, Employment and Society*, 9 (2): 213–40.

Rubery, J. and Tarling, R. (1988) 'Women's Employment in Declining Britain', in J. Rubery (ed.) *Women and Recession*, London: Routledge and Kegan Paul.

Ruggie, M. (1988) 'Gender, Work and Social Progress', in J. Jenson, E. Hagen and C. Reddy (eds) *Feminization of the Labour Force: Paradoxes and Promises*, Oxford: Polity Press.

Ryner, M. (1994) 'Assessing SAP's Economic Policy in the 1980s: The "Third Way", the Swedish Model and the Transition from Fordism to Post-Fordism', *Economic and Industrial Democracy*, 15: 385–428.

Sabel, F. C. (1989) 'Flexible Specialisation and the Re-emergence of Regional Economies' in Hirst, P. and Zeitlin, J. (eds) *Reversing Industrial Decline? Industrial Structure and Policies in Britain and her Competitors*, Oxford: Berg.

Sainsbury, D. (1993) 'The Politics of Increased Women's Representation: The Swedish case', in J. Lovenduski and P. Norris (eds) *Gender and Party Politics*, London: Sage.

Sainsbury, D. (1994a) 'Women's and Men's Social Rights; Gendering Dimensions of Welfare States', in D. Sainsbury (ed.) *Gendering Welfare States*, London: Sage.

Sainsbury, D. (ed.) (1994b) *Gendering Welfare States*, London: Sage.

Sainsbury, D. (1996) *Gender, Equality and Welfare States*, Cambridge: Cambridge University Press.

Salmon, K. G. (1991) *The Modern Spanish Economy: Transformation and Integration into Europe*, London: Pinter Publishers.

Sanchez, J. (1992) 'Societal Responses to Changes in the Production System: The Case of Barcelona Metropolitan Region', *Urban Studies*, 29 (6): 949–64.

Sapelli, G. (1995) *Southern Europe Since 1945: Tradition and Modernity in Portugal, Spain, Italy Greece and Turkey*, London: Longman.

Saraceno, C. (1991) 'Redefining Maternity and Paternity; Gender, Pronatalism and Social Policies in Fascist Italy', in Bock, G. and Thane, P. (eds) *Maternity and Gender Policies: Women and the Rise of the European Welfare States, 1880s–1950s*, London: Routledge.

Scheiwe, K. (1994) 'Labour Market, Welfare State and Family Institutions: The Links to Mothers' Poverty Risks', *Journal of European Social Policy*, 4 (3): 201–24.

Schmid, G., O'Reilly, J. and Schomann, K. (eds) (1996) *International Handbook of Labour Market Policy and Evaluation*, Cheltenham: Edward Elgar.

Scott, A. J. (1988) 'Flexible Production Systems and Regional Development: the rise of new industrial spaces in North America and Western Europe', *International Journal of Urban and Regional Research*, 12: 171–85.

Sengenberger, W. (1984) 'West German Employment Policy: Restoring Worker Competition', *Industrial Relations*, 23 (3): 323–43.

Share, D. (1989) *Dilemmas of Social Democracy: The Spanish Socialist Workers Party in the 1980s*, Westport: Greenwood.

Shubert, A. (1991) *A Social History of Modern Spain*, London: Unwin and Hyman.

Siaroff, A. (1994) 'Work, Welfare and Gender Equality: A New Typology', in D. Sainsbury (ed.) *Gendering Welfare States*, London: Sage.

Siltanen, J. (1994) *Locating Gender: Occupational Segregation, Wages and Domestic Responsibilities*, London: UCL Press.

Siltanen, J., Jarman, J. and Blackburn, R. M. (1992) *Gender Inequality in the Labour Market: Occupational Concentration and Segregation, a Manual on Methodology*, Geneva: ILO.

Silver, H. (1994) 'Social Exclusion and Social Solidarity: Three Paradigms', *International Labour Review*, 133 (5–6): 531–78.

Silver, H. and Wilkinson, F. (1995) 'Policies to Combat Social Exclusion: A French–British Comparison', in G. Rodgers, C. Gore and J. B. Figueiredo (eds), *Social Exclusion: Rhetoric, Reality, Responses*, Geneva: ILO, International Institute for Labour Studies.

Sly, F. (1993) 'Women in the Labour Market', *Employment Gazette*, November: 483–93, London: HMSO.

Sly, F. (1994) 'Mothers in the Labour Market', *Employment Gazette*, November: 403–13, London: HMSO.

Sly, F. (1996) 'Women in the Labour Market: Results from the Spring 1995 Labour Force Survey', *Labour Market Trends*, March: 91–113.

Smith, G., Paterson, W. E. and Padgett, S. (eds) (1996) *Developments in German Politics 2*, London: Macmillan.

Spicker, P. (1991) 'Solidarity', in G. Room (ed.) *Towards a European Welfare State?*, Bristol: SAUS/SPA.

Spicker, P. (1996) 'Social Policy in a Federal Europe', *Social Policy and Administration* 30 (4): 293–304.

Staber, U. (1996) 'Accounting for Variations in the Performance of Industrial Districts: The Case of Baden-Württemberg', *International Journal of Urban and Regional Research*, 20 (2): 299–316.

Stephens, J. D. (1979) *The Transition from Capitalism to Socialism*, London: Macmillan.

Stephens, J. D. (1996) 'The Scandinavian Welfare States: Achievements, Crisis and Prospects', in G. Esping-Andersen (ed.) *Welfare States in Transition: National Adaptations in Global Economies*, London: Sage.

Storper, M. and Scott, A. J. (eds) (1992) *Pathways to Industrialisation and Regional Development*, London: Routledge.

Streeck, W. (1992) *Social Institutions and Economic Performance: Studies of Industrial Relations in Advanced Capitalist Economies*, London: Sage.

Streeck, W. (1995) 'From Market Making to State Building? Reflections on the Political Economy of European Social Policy', in S. Leibfried and P. Pierson (eds) *European Social Policy: Between Fragmentation and Integration*, Washington DC: The Brookings Institute.

Subirats Martori, M., Masats Folgueras, M. and Carrasquer Oto, P. (1992) *Enquesta de la Regio Metropolitana de Barcelona 1990*, Vol. 6, Barcelona: Institut d'Estudis de Barcelona.

Swedish Institute (1994) 'Immigrants In Sweden', Fact Sheets on Sweden, Stockholm.

Teekens, R. and Zaidi, A. (1990) 'Relative and Absolute Poverty in the European Community', in R. Teekens and M. S. van Praag (eds) *Analysing Poverty in the EC*, Eurostat News, Special Edition, Luxembourg: Office for Official Publications of the European Communities.

Tezanos, J. F. (1990) 'Classes Sociales' in S. Giner (ed.) *España: Sociedad y Politica*, Madrid: Espasa-Calpe.

Therborn, G. (1991) 'Swedish Social Democracy and the Transition from Industrial to Post-industrial Politics', in F. Fox Piven (ed.) *Labor Parties in Post-industrial Societies,* Cambridge: Polity Press.

Thompson, P. and McHugh, D. (1995) *Work Organisation: A Critical Introduction*, Second Edition, London: Macmillan.

Threlfall, M. (1989) 'Social Policy Towards Women in Spain, Greece and Portugal', in T. Gallagher and A. M. Williams (eds) *Southern European Socialism*, Manchester: Manchester University Press.

Threlfall, M. (1996) 'Feminist Politics as Social Transformation in Spain', in M. Threlfall (ed.), *Mapping the Women's Movement*, London: Verso.
Tobio, C. (1994) 'The Family-employment Relationship in Spain', in M. Letablier and L. Hantrais, *The Family-Employment Relationship*, Cross-National Research Papers, Fourth Series, European Research Centre, Loughborough: Loughborough University.
Tomaney, J. (1994) 'A New Paradigm of Work Organisation and Technology', in A. Amin (ed.) *Post-Fordism: A Reader*, Oxford: Blackwell.
Townsend, P. (1979) *Poverty in the United Kingdom: A Survey of Household Resources and Standards of Living*, Harmondsworth: Penguin Books.
Trehorning, P. (1993) *Measures to Combat Unemployment in Sweden: Labour Market Policies in the Mid-1990s*, Stockholm: The Swedish Institute.
Ungerson, C. (1990) *Gender and Caring: Work and Welfare in Britain and Scandinavia*, Hemel Hempstead: Harvester Wheatsheaf.
Van Ruysseveldt, J. and Visser, J. (eds) *Industrial Relations in Europe: Traditions and Transitions*, London: Sage.
Van Ruysseveldt, J. et al. (1995) *Comparative Industrial and Employment Relations* London: Sage.
Visser, J. (1996) 'Traditions and Transitions in Industrial Relations: a European View' in J. Van Ruysseveldt and J. Visser (eds) *Industrial Relations in Europe: Traditions and Transitions*, London: Sage.
Waddington, J. and Whitson, C. (1995) 'Trade Unions, Growth, Structure and Policy', in P. Edwards (ed.) *Industrial Relations: Theory and Practice in Britain*, Oxford: Blackwell.
Walby, S. (1994) 'Is Citizenship Gendered?' *Sociology*, 28 (2): 379–95.
Walby, S. (1997) *Gender Transformations*, London: Routledge.
Webb, S. (1994) 'Social Insurance and Poverty Alleviation: An Empirical Analysis', in S. Baldwin and J. Falkingham (eds) *Social Security and Social Change: New Challenges to the Beveridge Model*, London: Harvester Wheatsheaf.
Webb, S., Kemp, M. and Millar, J. (1996) 'The Changing Face of Low Pay', *Policy Studies*, 17 (4): 255–70.
Whitehouse, G. (1992) 'Legislation and Labour Market Gender Equality: An Analysis of OECD Countries', *Work, Employment and Society*, 6: 65–86.
Williams, F. (1989) *Social Policy: A Critical Introduction*, Cambridge: Polity Press.
Williams, F. (1993) 'Gender, "Race" and Class in British Welfare Policy', in Cochrane A. and Clarke, J. (eds) *Comparing Welfare States: Britain in International Context*, London: Sage.
Williams, F. (1994) 'Social Relations, Welfare and the Post-Fordism Debate', in R. Burrows and B. Loader (eds) *Towards a Post-Fordist Welfare State?*, London: Routledge.
Williams, F. (1995) 'Race/Ethnicity, Gender and Class in Welfare States: A Framework for Analysis', *Social Politics*, 2 (2): 119–59.
Williams, K. Cutler, T, Williams, R. and Haslam, C. (1987) 'The End of Mass Production?' *Economy and Society*, 16 (3): 405–39.

Wilpert, C. (1993) 'The Ideological and Institutional Foundations of
    Racism in the Federal Republic of Germany', in J. Wrench and
    J. Solomos (eds) *Racism and Migration in Western Europe*, Oxford:
    Berg.
Wilson, M (1993) 'The German Welfare State: A Conservative Regime
    in Crisis', in A. Cochrane and J. Clark (eds) *Comparing Welfare States;
    Britain in International Perspective*, London: Sage.
Yeandle, S. (1997) 'Non-Standard Working: Diversity and Change in
    European Countries', Paper presented to the 15th Annual International
    Labour Process Conference, April, Edinburgh University.

Author Index

Subject Index

paraphilia
  Cannot control the urge
no social boundries none Socialsation
will Supress urges

paraphilia

DR. Mauri zol
  ~~Jackson son brolm~~
  6 - 8 cm

been informed

I have just ~~found~~ out
         to day
that the person ~~suppose~~
            at work
to covering for ~~me~~ on the

        ... is now unable to.

This consiquently means
I will not be able
to atendar ...   birthday

celebration.   which I am

            Most
~~I~~ ~~been~~ ~~sorry~~   disapoint

    dsamt.
My apologies
Caroline